Fas

# TUR

## PHRASE BOOK
### &
## DICTIONARY

**Over 3,000 Words, Phrases and Sentences
for Every Situation**

**English-Turkish / Turkish-English
Dictionary
with over 5,000 Words**

**Turkish Alphabet and Pronunciation Guide**

B. ORHAN DOĞAN

NET
TURİSTİK YAYINLAR
SANAYİ VE TİCARET A.Ş.

**Fast & Easy**
**Turkish Phrase Book & Dictionary**

Copyright © Bekir Orhan Doğan

ISBN : 978-605-124-044-2

Published by:
**NET TURİSTİK YAYINLAR SAN. TİC. A.Ş.**

Şakir Kesebir cad. Gazi Umur Paşa sok.
Balmumcu Plz. 2  No: 32 / 2
Balmumcu / Beşiktaş – İSTANBUL
Tel: 212 275 65 77
Fax: 212 274 65 17

Mithat Paşa cad. No: 643 / B    Köprü - İzmir
Tel: 232 244 86 44
Fax: 232 231 84 18

E-mail: info@netyayin.com.tr
Web: www.netyayin.com.tr

Second edition 2012

Printed in Turkey by:
**ÖMÜR MATBAACILIK A.Ş.**
Beysan Sanayi Sitesi
Birlik Caddesi No: 20
Haramidere / İstanbul
Tel: 0212 422 76 00
Fax: 0212 422 46 00

Sertifika no: 14713

# CONTENTS İÇİNDEKİLER

**İÇİNDEKİLER**

CONTENTS

İÇİNDEKİLER

CONTENTS

İÇİNDEKİLER

CONTENTS

## Turkish Alphabet and Pronunciation Guide

The Turkish alphabet consists of 29 letters - 8 vowels (a, e, ı, i, o, ö, u, ü) and 21 consonants.

Turkish spelling is phonetic. The same letter always indicates the same sound. Each letter has exactly one associated sound which never changes.

| LETTER | NAME | PRONUNCIATION |
|---|---|---|
| A a | ah | as **u** in "run"<br>as **o** in "some"<br>as **a** in "car" |
| B b | beh | as in English |
| C c | jeh | as **g** in "gender"<br>as **j** in "jeep" |
| Ç ç | cheh | as **ch** in "chair" |
| D d | deh | as in English |
| E e | eh | as **e** in "get" |
| F f | feh | as in English |
| G g | geh | as **g** in "get", "go" (\*\*) |
| Ğ ğ | (soft g) | (\*) |
| H h | heh | as **h** in "hello" |
| I ı | ı | as **io** in "nation",<br>"dictionary"<br>as **u** in "measure"<br>as **e** in "kitchen" |
| İ i | ee | as **i** in "bit"<br>as **ee** in "keen" |
| J j | zheh | as **s** in "measure"<br>as **ge** in "garage" |

| K k | keh | as **k** in "**k**itchen" (**\*\***) |
| | | as **c** in "**c**ook" |
| L l | leh | as in English |
| M m | meh | as in English |
| N n | neh | as in English |
| O o | o | as **o** in "b**o**y" |
| Ö ö | ö (ur) | as **u** in "**u**rge" |
| | | as **i** in "g**i**rl" |
| | | as **eu** in French "p**eu**" |
| | | as **ö** in German "**ö**sterreich" |
| P p | peh | as in English |
| R r | reh | as **r** in "**r**ent" |
| S s | seh | as **s** in "**s**end" |
| Ş ş | sheh | as **sh** in "**sh**op", "**sh**ut" |
| T t | teh | as in English |
| U u | oo | as **u** in "p**u**t" |
| | | as **oo** in "b**oo**k" |
| Ü ü | ü (ew) | as **u** in "s**u**per" |
| | | as **ü** in German "**ü**ber" |
| V v | veh | as in English |
| Y y | yeh | as **y** in "**y**es" |
| Z z | zeh | as in English |

## (\*) SOFT G (Yumuşak g : ğ - Ğ )

When it is preceded and followed by **e**, **i**, **ö** or **ü** (front vowels, formed in the front of the mouth), it sounds approximately like English '**y**', as in **lawyer** [as in **değil** (*deh-yeel* - not)].

If it is preceded and followed by **a**, **ı**, **o** or **u** (back vowels, formed in the back of the mouth) or it is word-final, it indicates that the preceding vowel is lengthened, as in **dağ** (da**ah** / da**hw** / da**ahw**: mountain). The '**yumuşak g**' never begins a word.

(\*\*) When the letters **G** and **K** are preceded and followed by a front vowel, they are followed by a **y**-sound as in 'an**g**ular' and '**c**ure'.

☞ Note that **Q**, **W** and **X** do not occur in the Turkish alphabet.

☞ The English Alphabet does not have the following letters which the Turkish Alphabet contains:

| | | | |
|---|---|---|---|
| Ç | ç | I | ı (the undotted i) (\*) |
| Ğ | ğ | Ö | ö |
| Ş | ş | Ü | ü |

(\*) The capital form of ' ı ' is ' I '
    The capital form of ' i ' is ' İ ' (the dotted I).

### Stress

In Turkish words the stress is variable and depends on the position of the word in the sentence. It normally falls on the last syllable except in place-names and adverbs. In compound words the stress falls on the last syllable of the first element.

☞ Note that in this book **the pronunciation of stressed syllables is in bold letters**.

Turkish Alphabet and Pronunciation Guide

## Pronunciation symbols used in the book

| | | |
|---|---|---|
| A a | : | ah , u , a |
| C c | : | j |
| Ç ç | : | ch |
| E e | : | eh , a |
| G g | : | g |
| Ğ ğ | : | hw |
| H h | : | h |
| I ı | : | ı |
| İ i | : | ee , i |
| J j | : | zh |

| | | |
|---|---|---|
| K k | : | k , c |
| O o | : | o , oh |
| Ö ö | : | ö |
| R r | : | r , rr |
| S s | : | s , ss |
| Ş ş | : | sh |
| U u | : | oo |
| Ü ü | : | ew , u |
| Y y | : | y , i |

## The circumflex accent ( ^ )

This accent may stand over the vowels 'a' and 'ı'.

When it stands over the letter 'a' which is preceded by **g**, **k** or **l**, the circumflex accent indicates that the preceding consonant is followed by a short 'y' sound.

- kârlı          k**(y)**ahr-lı          profitable
- kâğıt          k**(y)**ah-ıt          paper
- kâse          k**(y)**aah-seh          bowl
- rüzgâr          rewz-g**(y)**ahr          wind
- dükkân          dewk-k**(y)**ahn          shop

Elsewhere the circumflex indicates that the vowel it stands over is to be prolonged.

- âciz          **aah**-jeez          weak, incapable
- dâhi          **daah**-hee          genius
- millî          mil-**lee**          national

# ESSENTIALS
## TEMEL KONULAR

TEMEL KONULAR

# Some useful statements
## Bazı yararlı deyişler

| Yes. | No. | Please. | Thanks. |
|---|---|---|---|
| Evet. | Hayır. | Lütfen. | Teşekkürler |
| **eh**veht | **hah**-yır | **lewt**fehn | teh-shehk-kewrr-**lehr** |

**Thank you.**
Teşekkür ederim.
teh-shehk-**kewrr** ehdehreem

**Welcome.**
Hoş geldiniz.
**hosh** gehldeeneez

**That's all right / You're welcome.**
Bir şey değil (Rica ederim).
beer shay **deh**-yeel (ree-**jah** ehdehreem)

Hoş geldiniz!

**Here it is.**
Burada.
**boo**rahdah

**Here they are.**
Buradalar.
**boo**rahdahlahr

**There it is.**
Orada.
**o**rahdah

**There they are.**
Oradalar.
**o**rahdahlahr

**There is / are ...**
... var(dır).
... **vahr**(dır)

**Is / Are there ...?**
... var mı?
... **vahr** mı

**There isn't / aren't ...**
... yok(tur).
... **yok**toor

**There isn't / aren't any.**
Hiç yok(tur).
**heech** yok(toor)

**I know.**
Biliyorum.
bee**lee**yoroom

**I don't know.**
Bilmiyorum.
**beel**meeyoroom

ESSENTIALS

**I think so.**
**Öyle sanıyorum.**
**öy**leh sahnıyoroom

**I'm in a hurry.**
**Acelem var.**
ahjeh**lehm** vahr

**Leave me alone!**
**Beni rahat bırakın!**
beh**nee** rah**haht** bırahkın

**This way, please.**
**Bu taraftan, lütfen.**
**boo** tahrahftahn **lewt**fehn

**This way, please.**
**Bu taraftan, lütfen.**
**boo** tahrahftahn **lewt**fehn

**Come in.**
**İçeri gelin.**
eeche**ree** g(y)ehleen

**Just a minute, please.**
**Bir dakika, lütfen.**
**beer** dahkeekah **lewt**fehn

## Questions   Sorular

**What?**
**Ne?**
neh

**What is that?**
**O ne(dir)?**
**neh**(deer)

**Who?**
**Kim?**
k(y)eem

**Who is that?**
**O kim(dir?**
o **k(y)eem**(deer)

**How?**
**Nasıl?**
**nah**sıl

**Where?**
**Nerede?**
**neh**rehdeh

**How much?**
**Ne kadar?**
**neh** kahdahr

**How many?**
**Kaç tane?**
**kahch** taaneh

**When?**
Ne zaman?
neh zahmahn

**Why?**
Niçin? / Neden?
neecheen / nehdehn

**How far?**
Ne kadar uzaklıkta?
neh kahdahr oozahklıktah

**Which?**
Hangi?
hungyee

**How long?**
Ne kadar zaman(dır)?
neh kahdahr zahmahn(dır)

**May I have …?**
… alabilir miyim?
… ahlahbeeleer mee-yeem

**How can I get there?**
Oraya nasıl gidebilirim?
orah-yah nahsıl g(y)eedehbeeleereem

**What must I do?**
Ne yapmam gerek?/Ne yapmalıyım?
neh yahpmahm g(y)ehrehk/neh yahpmahlıyım

**Where can I find …?**
Nerede … bulabilirim?
nehrehdeh … boolahbeeleereem

**Where can I get …?**
Nereden … alabilirim?
nehrehdehn … ahlahbeeleereem

**How are you?**
Nasılsınız?
nahsılsınız

**What's the matter?**
Sorun nedir?
soroon nehdeer

**Fine, thanks. And you?**
İyi(yim), teşekkürler. Ya siz?
ee-**yee**(yeem), teh-shehk-kewrr-**lehr**. yah **seez**

**What would you like?/What do you want?**
Ne istiyorsun(uz)?
neh eesteeyorsoon(ooz)

**Do you have ...?/Have you got ...?**
(Sizde) ... var mı?
(seez**deh**) ... **vahr** mı

**Can you help me?**
Bana yardım edebilir misiniz?
bahnah yahrdım ehdehbee**leer** meesee-neez

**Can I help you?**
Size yardım edebilir miyim?
seezeh yahrdım ehdehbee**leer** mee-yeem

**Can you tell me ...?**
Bana ... söyleyebilir misiniz?
bahnah söyleh-yehbee**leer** meesee-neez

**Can you show me ...?**
Bana ... gösterebilir misiniz?
bahnah ... göstehrehbee**leer** meesee-neez

## Greetings
Selamlaşmalar, Karşılaşmalar

**Hello/Hi !**
Merhaba !
**mehr**hahbah

**Good morning.**
Günaydın.
gewn-ai-**dın**

**Good day / Good afternoon.**
İyi günler.
ee-yee gewn**leh**r

**Good night.**
İyi geceler.
ee-yee g(y)ehjeh**leh**r

**Congratulations.**
Tebrikler.
tehbreek**leh**r

**Good evening.**
İyi akşamlar.
ee-yee ahkshahm**lah**r

**Good luck! / All the best.**
İyi şanslar.
ee-yee shahnss**lah**r

**Best wishes.**
İyi dileklerimle.
ee-yee deelehklehreem**leh**

**Happy birthday.**
Mutlu yıllar.
mootloo yıl**lah**r

**Have a good holiday.**
İyi tatiller.
ee-yee taateel**leh**r

**Have a good journey.**
İyi yolculuklar.
ee-yee yoljoolook**lah**r

**Happy New Year!**
İyi yıllar.
ee-yee yıl**lah**r

**How are you?**
Nasılsınız?
**nah**sılsınız

**Fine, thanks. And you?**
İyi, teşekkürler. Ya siz?
ee-**yee**, teh-shehk-kewrr-**leh**r. yah **seez**

**How is your wife?**
Eşiniz (Karınız) nasıl?
ehshee**neez** (kahrı**nız**) **nah**sıl

**How is your husband?**
Eşiniz (Kocanız) nasıl?
ehsheeneez (kojahnız) nahsıl

**How is your 'son/daughter'?**
'Oğlunuz/Kızınız' nasıl?
'ohw-loonooz/kızınız' nahsıl

**See you 'later/tomorrow'.**
'Sonra / Yarın' görüşürüz.
'sonrah/yahrın' görewshewrewz

**My regards to …**
…'(y)a/(y)e selamlar.
…'(y)ah/(y)eh sehl(y)amlahr

**Goodbye.**
Allahaısmarladık(\*) / Hoşça kalın(\*) / Güle güle (\*\*).
ahlahsmaahlahdık/hohsh-chah kahlın/gewleh gewleh

**Excuse me.**
Affedersiniz.
ahfehdehrseeneez

**Sorry.**
Özür dilerim.
özewr deelehreem

**Thank you (very much).**
(Çok) Teşekkür ederim.
(choke) teh-shehk-kewrr ehdehreem

**That's all right /You're welcome /Don't mention it.**
Bir şey değil.
beer shay deh-yeel

| (\*) | : | said by the person who leaves |
|---|---|---|
| (\*\*) | : | said by the person who remains |

**I beg your pardon.**
Pardon/Affedersiniz/Efendim? (Duyamadım!)
pahrdon / ahfehdehrseeneez / ehfehndeem
(dooyahmahdım)

**Thank you for your help.**
Yardımınız için teşekkür ederim.
yahrdımınız eecheen teh-shehk-kewrr ehdehreem

# Language problems Dil sorunları

**I don't speak Turkish.**
Türkçe bilmiyorum.
tewrk-che beelmeeyoroom

**Do you understand?**
Anlıyor musunuz?
ahnlıyor moosoonooz

**I understand.**
Anlıyorum.
ahnlıyoroom

**I don't understand.**
Anlamıyorum.
ahnlahmıyoroom

**Please speak (more) slowly.**
Lütfen (daha) yavaş konuşun.
lewtfehn (dahhah) yahvash konooshoon

**Would you say that again, please?**
Tekrar söyler misiniz, lütfen?
tehkrahr söylehr meesee-neez lewtfehn

**Could you spell it?**
Heceler misiniz, lütfen?
hehjehlehr meesee-neez lewtfehn

**Please would you write it down?**
Lütfen onu yazar mısınız?
lewtfehn ohnoo yah**zahr** mısınız

**What does that mean in Turkish?**
O, Türkçe'de ne anlama gelir?
o, tewrk-chedeh **neh** ahnlahmah g(y)ehleer

**What do you call this in Turkish?**
Türkçe'de buna ne denir?
tewrk-chedeh boonah **neh** dehneer

**How do you say that in Turkish?**
Türkçe'de o nasıl söylenir?
tewrk-chedeh o **nah**sıl söylehneer

**I'll see if I can find it in the book.**
Bakayım, onu kitapta bulabilir miyim.
bahkah-yım ohnoo keetahptah boolahbee**leer** mee-yeem

**Could you point to the 'word / phrase / sentence' in the book?**
'Sözcüğü / Deyimi / Tümceyi' kitapta gösterir misiniz, lütfen?
'sözjewyew / deh-yeemee / tewmjeh-yee' keetahptah gösteh**reer** meesee-neez **lewt**fehn

**Can you translate this for me?**
Bunu bana tercüme edebilir misiniz?
boo**noo** bahnah tehrjewmeh ehdehbee**leer** meesee-neez

**Does anybody here speak English?**
Burada birisi İngilizce biliyor mu?
boorahdah beereesee eeng(y)eeleezjeh bee**lee**yor moo

# Wanting Bir şey isteme

**I'd like …**
… istiyorum / rica ediyorum.
eesteeyoroom / ree-**jah** ehdeeyoroom

**We'd like …**
… istiyoruz / rica ediyoruz.
eesteeyorooz / ree-**jah** ehdeeyorooz

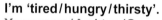

**I'm 'tired / hungry / thirsty'.**
Yorgunum / Acıktım / Susadım.
yor**goo**noom / ahjık**tım** / soosah**dım**

**'I'm / We're' looking for …**
… arıyorum / arıyoruz.
… ahrıyoroom / ahrıyorooz

**Please 'give / bring / show' me …**
Lütfen bana … 'verin(iz) / getirin(iz) / gösterin(iz)'.
**lewt**fehn bahnah …. '**veh**reen(eez) /
g(y)eh**tee**reen(eez) / gös**teh**reen(eez)'

**'I'm / We're' lost.**
Kayboldum / Kaybolduk.
**k**ai-boldoom / **k**ai-boldook

**It's 'urgent / important'.**
Acildir / Önemlidir.
aa**jeel**deer /
önehm**lee**deer

## Introductions Tanışma

**My name is ...**
**Benim adım ...**
behneem ahdım ...

**What's your name?**
**Adınız ne(dir)?**
ahdınız neh(deer)

**May I introduce ...?**
**(Size) ...'yi tanıştırabilir miyim?**
seezeh ...'yee tahnıshtırahbeeleer mee-yeem

**This is my 'wife/husband/partner'.**
**Bu benim 'karım/kocam/eşim'.**
boo behneem 'kahrım/kojahm/ehsheem'

**This is my 'girlfriend/boyfriend'.**
**Bu benim 'kız arkadaşım/erkek arkadaşım'.**
boo behneem 'kız ahrkahdahshım/ehrk(y)ehk
ahrkahdahshım'

**Nice to meet you./How do you do?**
**Tanıştığımıza sevindim (Memnun oldum).**
tahnıshtıımızah sehveendeem/mehmnoon ohldoom

## Talking about yourself and your family
*Kendiniz ve aileniz hakkında konuşma*

**What nationality are you?**
**Milliyetiniz nedir?**
meelleeyehteeneez nehdeer

| I'm ... | Ben ... (y)ım/im/um/üm. | |
|---------|------------------------|---|
| | behn .... (y)ım/eem/oom/ewm | |
| American | Amerikalı | ahmehreekahlı |
| British | İngiliz | eeng(y)eeleez |
| Canadian | Kanadalı | kahnahdahlı |
| French | Fransız | frahnsız |
| German | Alman | ahlmahn |
| Greek | Yunanlı | yoonahnlı |
| Italian | İtalyan | eetahlyahn |
| Russian | Rus | roos |
| Spanish | İspanyol | eespahnyol |
| Turkish | Türk | tewrk |

### 'He/She' is American.
**'O (erkek)/O (kadın)' Amerikalı(dır).**
'o [ehrk(y)ehk]/o (kahdın)' ahmehreekahlı(dır)

### Where do you come from? / Where are you from?
**Nerelisiniz?**
nehrehleeseeneez

### I come from Switzerland./I'm from Switzerland.
**İsviçreliyim.**
eess-veechrehlee-yeem

### Where does 'he/she' come from?
**'O (erkek)/O (kadın)' nereli?**
'o [ehrk(y)ehk]/o (kahdın)' nehrehlee

### 'He/She' comes from Scotland.
**'O (erkek)/O (kadın)' İskoçyalı.**
'o [ehrk(y)ehk]/o (kahdın)' eeskoch-yahlı

**How long have you been here?**
Ne kadar zamandır buradasınız?
neh kahdahr zahmahndır boorahdahsınız

**I've been here for three 'days/weeks'.**
Üç 'gündür/haftadır' buradayım.
ewch 'gewndewr/hahftahdır' boorahdah-yım

**Are you on your own?**
Yalnız mısınız?
yahlnız mısınız

**I'm with ...**                    ... ile birlikteyim.
                              ... eeleh beerleekteh-yeem

| my children | Çocuklarım | chojooklahrım |
| my daughter | Kızım | kızım |
| my family | Ailem | aaeelehm |
| my friend | Arkadaşım | ahrkahdahshım |
| my husband | Kocam | kojahm |
| my partner | Eşim | ehsheem |
| my son | Oğlum | ohw-loom |
| my wife | Karım | kahrım |

**Are you 'single/married'?**
Bekar mısınız?/Evli misiniz?
behk(y)ahr mısınız/ehvlee meesee-neez

**I'm 'single/married'.**
Bekarım/Evliyim.
behk(y)ahrım/ehv-lee-yeem

**Do you have any children?**
Hiç çocuğunuz var mı?
heech chojoohwoonooz vahr mı

**I have three children.**
Üç çocuğum var.
**ewch** chojoohwoom vahr

**I have one son.**
Bir (tane) oğlum var.
**beer** taaneh ohw-**loom** vahr

**I have two daughters.**
İki kızım var.
eek(y)ee kızım vahr

**How old is your 'son/daughter'?**
'Oğlunuz/Kızınız' kaç yaşında?
'ohw-loonooz/kızınız' **kahch** yahshındah

**My 'son/daughter' is three years old.**
'Oğlum/Kızım' üç yaşında.
'ohw-loom/kızım' **ewch** yahshındah

**Do you have any brothers or sisters?**
Erkek kardeşiniz ya da kız kardeşiniz var mı?
ehr**k(y)ehk** kahrdehsheeneez yah dah **kız**
kahrdehsheeneez **vahr** mı

**I have two 'brothers/sisters'.**
İki 'erkek kardeşim/kız kardeşim' var.
eek**(y)ee** 'ehrk(y)ehk kahrdehsheem/kız
kahrdehsheem' vahr

**Where are you staying?**
Nerede kalıyorsunuz?
**neh**rehdeh kahlıyorsoonooz

**I'm staying in a hotel.**
Bir otelde kalıyorum.
beer otehl**deh** kahlıyoroom

**Are you on holiday?**
Tatilde misiniz?
taadeel**deh** meesee-neez

**I'm on holiday.**
Tatildeyim.
taadeel**deh**-yeem

**I'm here on a business trip.**
Burada bir iş gezisindeyim.
**boo**rahdah beer **eesh** g(y)ehzeeseendeh-yeem

**Is this your first visit?**
Bu ilk gelişiniz mi?
boo **eelk** g(y)ehleesheeneez mee

**This is my first visit.**
Bu ilk gelişim.
boo **eelk** g(y)ehleesheem

**This is the 'second/third' time I've been here.**
Bu buraya 'ikinci/üçüncü' gelişim.
boo **boo**rah-yah 'eek(y)een**jee** / ewchewn**jew**'
g(y)ehleesheem

**Where do you live?**
Nerede yaşıyorsunuz?
**neh**rehdeh yahshıyorsoonooz

**I live in London.**
Londra'da yaşıyorum.
**lon**drahdah yahshıyoroom

**What are your hobbies?**
Hobileriniz nelerdir?
**ho**beelehreeneez neh**lehr**deer

**My hobbies are 'music/sports/cinema'.**
Hobilerim 'müzik/spor/sinema' ...
**ho**beelehreem 'mew**zeek**/s**por**/seeneh**mah**'

**Do you like ...?**
**...den/dan hoşlanır mısınız?**
...dehn/dahn hoshlah**nır** mısınız

**I like ...**   **...den/dan hoşlanırım.**
...dehn/dahn hoshlah**nır**ım

| dancing | Dans etme | dahn**ss** ehtmeh |
| reading | Okuma | ohkoo**mah** |
| swimming | Yüzme | yewz**meh** |
| travelling | Yolculuk etme | yoljoo**look** ehtmeh |

## Jobs   Meslekler

**What's your job?**
**Mesleğiniz nedir?**
mehsleh-yee**neez** nehdeer

**I'm a 'teacher/student'.**
**Ben bir 'öğretmenim/**
**öğrenciyim'.**
behn beer 'öö'reht**meh**neem/
öö'rehn-**jee**-yeem'

**I'm a 'businessman / businesswoman'.**
**Ben bir 'iş adamıyım / iş kadınıyım'.**
behn beer '**eesh** ahdahmıyım/**eesh** kahdınıyım'

**What is 'his/her' job?**
Onun mesleği nedir?
onoon mehsleh-**yee** nehdeer

**'He/She' is a journalist.**
O bir gazeteci.
o beer gah**zeh**tehjee

| accountant | muhasebeci | moohahsehbeh**jee** |
| actor | aktör, erkek oyuncu | |
| | ahk**tör**, ehr**k(y)ek** oyoon**joo** | |
| actress | aktris, kadın oyuncu | |
| | ahk-**treess**, (kah**dın**) oyoon**joo** | |
| advertiser | reklamcı | rehk**l(y)ahm**jı |
| announcer | spiker | spee**k(y)ehr** |
| archaeologist | arkeolog | ahr**k(y)eho**log |
| architect | mimar | mee**mahr** |
| artist | sanatçı | sahnaht**chı** |
| artist, painter | ressam | rehs-**sahm** |
| author, writer | yazar | yah**zahr** |
| baker | fırıncı | fırın**jı** |
| bank official | banka memuru | bahn**kah** mehmooroo |
| barber | berber | behr**behr** |
| barman | barmen | bahr**mehn** |
| businessman | iş adamı | **eesh** ahdahmı |
| businesswoman | iş kadını | **eesh** kahdını |
| butcher | kasap | kah**sahp** |
| cameraman | kameraman | kahmehrah**mahn** |
| captain | kaptan | kahp**tahn** |
| carpenter | marangoz | mahrahn**goz** |
| cashier | kasiyer | kah-see-**yehr** |
| chemist | eczacı | ehj**zaa**jı |
| civil servant | memur | meh**moor** |
| cook | aşçı | ahsh**chı** |
| customs officer | gümrük görevlisi | |
| | gewm**rewk** görehvleesee | |

| dancer | dansçı, dansör (man), dansöz (woman) |
|---|---|
| | dahnss-**chı**, dahn**sör**, dahn**söz** |
| decorator | dekoratör — dehkorah**tör** |
| dentist | diş hekimi — **deesh** hehk(y)eemee |
| doctor | doktor — dohk**tohr** |
| doorkeeper | kapıcı — kahpı**jı** |
| driver | şoför — sho**för** |
| economist | ekonomist — ehkono**meest** |
| electrician | elektrikçi — ehlehktreek**chee** |
| engineer | mühendis — mewhehn**deess** |
| farmer | çiftçi — cheeft**chee** |
| fashion designer | modacı — **mo**dahjı |
| fireman | itfaiyeci — eetfaheeyeh**jee** |
| fisherman | balıkçı — bahlık**chı** |
| fishmonger | balık satıcısı — **bahlık** sahtıjısı |
| florist | çiçekçi — cheechek-**chee** |
| footballer | futbolcu — footbol**joo** |
| furniture-maker | mobilyacı — mo**beel**yahjı |
| gardener | bahçıvan — bahhchı**vahn** |
| glazier | camcı — jahmjı |
| graphic designer | grafiker — grahfeek**(y)ehr** |
| greengrocer | manav — mah**nahv** |
| grocer | bakkal — bahk**kahl** |
| guide | rehber — rehh**behr** |
| hairdresser | kuaför — kooah**för** |
| hostess | hostes — hos**tess** |
| housewife | ev hanımı — **ehv** hahnımı |
| industrialist | sanayici — sahnaa-yee**jee** |
| inspector | müfettiş — mewfeht**teesh** |
| insurer | sigortacı — see**gor**tahjı |
| jeweller | kuyumcu — kooyoom**joo** |
| jockey | jokey — **zho**-kaye |
| journalist | gazeteci — gah**zeh**tehjee |
| judge | hakim — haak**(y)eem** |
| lawyer | avukat — ahvoo**kaht** |
| librarian | kütüphane görevlisi |
| | ku-tewp-haa**neh** görehvleesee |
| locksmith | çilingir — cheeleeng**(y)eer** |

| | | |
|---|---|---|
| mechanic | tamirci | taameerjee |
| merchant | tüccar | tuj-**jahr** |
| miner | madenci | maadehnjee |
| model | manken | mahnk(y)ehn |
| musician | müzisyen | mewzeesyehn |
| newsagent | gazete bayii | gahzehteh bah-yeeee |
| notary | noter | notehr |
| nurse | hemşire | hehmsheereh |
| officer | subay, memur | soo-**bai**, mehmoor |
| photographer | fotoğrafçı | fotohwrahfchı |
| pilot | pilot | peelot |
| plumber | su tesisatçısı | soo tehseesahtchısı |
| poet | şair | shaheer |
| policeman, policewoman | polis | police |
| politician | politikacı | poleeteekahjı |
| porter | hamal | hahmahl |
| postman | postacı | postahjı |
| priest | papaz | pahpahz |
| printer | matbaacı | mahtbahahjı |
| programmer | programcı | programhjı |
| prosecutor | savcı | sahvjı |
| psychologist | psikolog | pseekolog |
| publisher | yayımcı/yayıncı | yah-yımjı/yah-yınjı |
| real-estate agent | emlakçı | ehml(y)ahkchı |
| receptionist | resepsiyon görevlisi | |
| | | rehsehpseeyon görehvleesee |
| referee | hakem | hahk(y)ehm |
| reporter | muhabir | moohaabeer |
| retired | emekli | ehmehklee |
| sailor | denizci | dehneezjee |
| scientist | bilim adamı | beeleem ahdahmı |
| sculptor | heykeltıraş | heyk(y)ehltırash |
| secretary | sekreter | sehkrehtehr |
| servant | hizmetçi | heezmehtchee |
| shop assistant | tezgâhtar | tehzgahhtahr |
| singer | şarkıcı | shahrkıjı |
| soldier | asker | ahsk(y)ehr |
| sportsman, sportswoman | sporcu | sporjoo |

| surgeon | cerrah | jehrrahh |
| tailor | terzi | tehrzee |
| teacher | öğretmen | öörehtmehn |
| technician | teknisyen | tehkneesyehn |
| trade unionist | sendikacı | segndeekahjı |
| translator | çevirmen | cheveermehn |
| treasurer | veznedar | vehznehdahr |
| veterinarian | veteriner | vehtehreenehr |
| waiter, waitress | garson | gahrson |
| watch repairer | saat tamircisi | sah-aht tahmeerjeesee |
| watchmaker | saatçi | sah-aht-chee |
| worker | işçi | eeshchee |

## The weather  Hava

**What 'lovely/awful' weather.**
**Ne 'güzel/kötü' (bir) hava!**
neh 'gewzehl/kö-tu' (beer) hahvah

**It's 'hot/cold' today, isn't it?**
**Bugün 'sıcak/soğuk', değil mi?**
boo-gewn 'sıjahk / sohwook', deh-yeel mee

**Is it usually as warm as this?**
**Her zaman bu kadar sıcak olur mu?**
hehr zahmahn **boo** kahdahr sıjahk ohloorr moo

**What's the weather forecast?**
**Hava raporu nasıl?**
hahvah rahporoo **nah**sıl

**Will it be sunny tomorrow?**
**Yarın güneşli olur mu ?**
yahrın gewnehshlee ohloorr moo

**I think it's going to be a nice day tomorrow.**
Sanırım yarın güzel bir gün olacak.
sahnırım **yah**rın gew**zehl** beer gewn ohlah**jahk**

| cloud | bulut | boo**loot** |
|-------|-------|-------------|
| fog | sis | seess |
| frost | don | don |
| ice | buz | booz |
| lightning | şimşek | sheem**shehk** |
| moon | ay | ai |
| rain | yağmur | yahw**moor** |
| sky | gök | gök |
| snow | kar | khar |
| star | yıldız | yıl**dız** |
| sun | güneş | gew**nehsh** |
| thunder | gök gürültüsü | **gök** gewrewl-tu-sew |
| thunderstorm | fırtına | fırtınah |
| wind | rüzgâr | rewz**g(y)ahr** |

## Emergency & Lost
Acil durum & Kayıp

**Help !**
İmdat !
eem**daht**

**Look out !**
Dikkat !
deek**kaht**

**Danger !**
Tehlike !
tehhlee**k(y)eh**

**Call the police !**
Polis çağırın !
po**lice** chahwırın

**Fire !**
Yangın !
yahn**gın**

**Poison!**
Zehir!
zeh**heer**

**Get a doctor !**
Doktor çağırın !
dohk**tohr** chahwırın

**I'm ill !**
Hastayım !
hahs**tah**-yım

**Gas !**
Gaz !
gahz

TEMEL KONULAR

**Stop thief!**
Hırsızı durdurun!
hırsızı door**dooroon**

**Get help quickly!**
Çabuk yardım getirin !
chah**book** yahr**dım** g(y)ehteereen

**Stop that 'man/woman'!**
Şu 'adamı/kadını' durdurun!
**shoo** 'ahdah**mı**/kah**dını**' door**dooroon**

**Leave me alone!**
Beni rahat bırakın!
beh**nee** rah**haht** bırah**kın**

**I'm lost.**
Kayboldum.
**kai**-boldoom

**Embassy**
Büyükelçilik
bew**yewk**ehlcheeleek

**Consulate**
Konsolosluk
konsolos**look**

**Where's the 'police station/lost property office'?**
'Polis karakolu/Kayıp eşya bürosu' nerededir?
'po**lice** kahrahkoloo/kah-**yıp** ehsh-**yah** bewrosoo'
**neh**rehdehdeer

**'My 'money/wallet/handbag' has been stolen.**
'Param/Cüzdanım/El çantam' çalındı.
'pah**rahm**/jewzdah**nım**/**ehl** chahntahm' chahlındı'

| | | |
|---|---|---|
| **POLICE RESCUE** | : | 155 |
| **TRAFFIC POLICE** | : | 154 |
| **GENDARME (in rural areas)** | : | 156 |
| **FIRE** | : | 110 |
| **AMBULANCE** | : | 112 |
| **DOCTOR** | : | 113 |

ESSENTIALS

# Telling the time Zamanı söylemek

**What time is it?**
Saat kaç?
sah-**aht** kahch

**It's five o'clock.**
Saat beş.
sah**aht behsh**

**It's ten past six.**
Altıyı on geçiyor.
ahl**tıyı ohn** g(y)ehcheeyor

**It's five to seven.**
Yediye beş var.
yehdee-**yeh behsh** vahr

**It's half past nine.**
Dokuz buçuk.
do**kooz** boochook

**It's a quarter to two.**
İkiye çeyrek var.
eek(y)ee-**yeh** chay-**rehk** vahr

**It's a quarter past ten.**
Onu çeyrek geçiyor.
oh**noo** chay-**rehk** g(y)ehcheeyor

# Some useful words
Bazı yararlı sözcükler

| about | hakkında | hahkkın**dah** |
| above | üstünde | ewstewn**deh** |
| after | ...den sonra | ...**dehn** sonrah |
| along | boyunca | boyoon**jah** |
| among | arasında | ahrahsın**dah** |
| and | ve | veh |
| around | çevresinde | chev-reh-seen**deh** |
| at | -da / -de | dah / deh |
| before | önce | **ön**jeh |
| behind | arka(sın)da | ahrkahsın**dah** |
| below / under | altında | ahltın**dah** |
| between | arasında | ahrahsın**dah** |
| down | aşağıda | ahshahwı**dah** |
| downstairs | aşağı katta | ahshahwı katta |

| during | sırasında, esnasında | |
|---|---|---|
| | sırahsındah, ehsnahsındah | |
| for | için | eecheen |
| from | -den/-dan | dehn/dahn |
| in | içinde | eecheendeh |
| inside | içeride | eechereedeh |
| near | yakın | yahkın |
| never | hiç | heech |
| next to | yanında, bitişik | yahnındah, beeteesheek |
| none | hiç biri(si) | **heech** beeree(see) |
| not | değil | **deh**-yeel |
| nothing | hiçbir şey | heech**beer** shay |
| now | şimdi | **sheem**dee |
| on | üstünde | ewstewn**deh** |
| only | yalnızca, sadece | **yahl**nızjah, **sah**dehjeh |
| or | veya, ya da | **veh**-yah, **yah** dah |
| outside | dışarıda | dısahrı**dah** |
| perhaps | belki | **behl**k(y)ee |
| since | beri | behree |
| soon | yakında, çok geçmeden | |
| | yahkın**dah**, choke **g(y)ech**mehdehn | |
| then | sonra | **son**rah |
| through | içinden | eecheen**dehn** |
| to | -e/-a/-ye/-ya | -eh/-ah/yeh/yah |
| too (also) | de/da , bir de , ayrıca | |
| | deh/dah, beer deh, ai-rıjah | |
| towards | -e doğru | -eh dohwroo |
| until | -e kadar | -eh kahdahr |
| up | yukarıda | yookahrı**dah** |
| upstairs | yukarı katta | yookahrı kahttah |
| very | çok | choke |
| with | ile | eeleh |
| without | -sız/-siz | -sız/-seez |
| yet | henüz | **heh**newz |

# **Some opposites** Bazı karşıtlar

| | |
|---|---|
| beautiful/ugly | güzel/çirkin |
| | gewzehl/cheerk(y)een |
| before/after | önce/sonra |
| | önjeh/sonrah |
| better/worse | daha iyi/daha kötü |
| | dahhah ee-yee/dahhah kö-tu |
| cheap/expensive | ucuz/pahalı |
| | oojooz/pahhahlı |
| cold/hot | soğuk/sıcak |
| | sohwook/sıjahk |
| early/late | erken/geç |
| | ehrk(y)ehn/g(y)ehch |
| easy/difficult | kolay/zor |
| | ko-lai/zor |
| empty/full | boş/dolu |
| | bosh/doloo |
| free (vacant)/occupied | serbest/meşgul |
| | sehrbehst/mehshgool |
| good/bad | iyi/kötü |
| | ee-yee/kö-tu |
| here/there | burada/orada |
| | boorahdah/ohrahdah |
| inside/outside | içeride/dışarıda |
| | eechereedeh/dıshahrıdah |
| light/heavy | hafif/ağır |
| | hahfeef/ahwır |
| near/far | yakın/uzak |
| | yahkın/oozahk |
| new/old | yeni/eski |
| | yehnee/ehsk(y)ee |
| next/last | gelecek/son |
| | g(y)ehlehjehk/son |

**TEMEL KONULAR**

| open/shut | açık/kapalı |
|---|---|
| | ahchık/kahpahlı |
| right/wrong | doğru/yanlış |
| | dohwroo/yahnlısh |
| slow/quick | yavaş/çabuk |
| | yahvahsh/chabook |
| small/big | küçük/büyük |
| | k(y)ewchewk/bewyewk |
| young/old | genç/yaşlı |
| | g(y)ehnch/yahshlı |

## Quantities  Miktarlar

| a little/a lot | biraz/çok | beerahz/choke |
|---|---|---|
| few/a few | az/birkaç | ahz/beerkahch |
| how much? | ne kadar ? | neh kahdahr |
| how many? | kaç tane? | kahch tahneh |
| much/too much | çok/pek çok | choke/pehk choke |
| many/too many | çok/pek çok | choke/pehk choke |
| enough/too | yeter/daha | yehtehr/dahhah |
| some/any | biraz/hiç | beerahz/heech |
| more/less | daha çok/daha az | |
| | dahhah choke/dahhah ahz | |

| a bowl of soup | bir tas çorba |
|---|---|
| | beer tahss chore-bah |
| a bunch of roses | bir demet (deste) gül |
| | beer dehmeht (dehsteh) gewl |
| a can of fruit juice | bir kutu meyve suyu |
| | beer kootoo mayveh sooyoo |
| a cup of tea | bir fincan çay |
| | beer feenjahn chai |
| a glass of water | bir bardak su |
| | beer bahrdahk soo |
| a jar of jam | bir kavanoz reçel |
| | beer kahvahnoz rehchel |

**ESSENTIALS**

**a packet of chocolate**  bir paket çikolata
                          **beer** pahk(y)eht cheekolahtah

**three slices of bread**  üç dilim ekmek
                          **ewch** deeleem ehkmehk

## Signs and Notices
## Levhalar ve Uyarılar

| | | |
|---|---|---|
| **Acil çıkışı** | ahjeel chıkıshı | Emergency Exit |
| **Açık** | ahchık | Open |
| **Ana hatlar** (train, etc.) ahnah hahtlahr | | Main lines |
| **Asansör** | ahshansör | Lift , Elevator |
| **Banliyö hatları** | bahnleeyö hahtlahrı | Suburban lines |
| **Bayanlar** | bah-yahnlahr | Ladies, Women |
| **Baylar** | bai-lahr | Gentlemen, Men |
| **Bekleme odası** | behklehmeh ohdahsı | Waiting Room |
| **Bekleyiniz** | behkleh-yeeneez | Wait |
| **Bisiklet Yolu** | beeseekleht yoloo | Cycle Path |
| **Boş** | bosh | Vacant |
| **Boş yer yok(tur)** | bosh yehr yok)toor) | No Vacancy |
| **Çekiniz** | chek(y)eeneez | Pull |
| **Çıkış** | chıkısh | Exit |
| **Danışma** | dahnıshmah | Information |
| **Dikkat** | deekkaht | Caution |
| **Dokunmayınız** | dokoonmah-yınız | Do not touch |
| **Geliş, Varış** | g(y)ehleesh, vahrısh | Arrival |

| | | |
|---|---|---|
| **Gidiş, Hareket** | g(y)ee**dee**sh, hahreh**k(y)eht** | Departure |
| **Girilmez** | g(y)eeree**lmehz** | No entrance |
| **Giriş** | g(y)ee**ree**sh | Entrance |
| **Giriş serbest** | g(y)ee**ree**sh sehr**behst** | Admission free |
| **İçilmez (su)** | eechee**lmehz** (soo) | Not for drinking |
| **İçme suyu** | **eech**meh sooyoo | Drinking water |
| **İtiniz** | **ee**teneez | Push |
| **Kapalı** | kah**pah**lı | Closed |
| **Kasa** | **kah**sah | Cash desk |
| **Kayıp eşya** | kah-**yıp** ehsh-**yah** | Lost property |
| **Kiralık** | k(y)ee**rah**lık | For rent, to hire |
| **Köpek var** | kö**pehk** vahr | Beware of the dog |
| **Lütfen zili çalınız** | **lewt**fehn zeelee chah**lı**nız | Please ring |
| **Meşgul** | mehsh**gool** | Occupied / Engaged |
| **Metro** | **meht**ro | Underground |
| **Otobüs** | oto**bewss** | Bus |
| **Otobüs durağı** | oto**bewss** doorahwı | Bus stop |
| **Ölüm tehlikesi** | ölewm tehh**lee**kehsee | Danger of death |
| **Özel** | ö**zehl** | Private |
| **Rezerve** | rehzehr**veh** | Reserved |
| **Satılık** | **sah**tılık | For sale |
| **Sigara içilmez** | seegahrah echee**lmehz** | No smoking |
| **Tehlike** | tehh**lee**k(y)eh | Danger |
| **Tek yönlü yol** | **tehk** yönlew yol | One-way street |
| **... yasak(tır)** | ... yah**sahk**(tır) | ... forbidden |

**Yetkili olmayan giremez**      No unauthorized access
yehtk(y)ee**lee** **ol**mah-yahn g(y)eeree**mehz**

# MONEY
## PARA

PARA

## Changing money Para bozdurma

**Where is the nearest 'bank/currency exchange office/bureau de change'?**
En yakın 'banka/döviz bürosu' nerede(dir)?
**ehn** yahkın 'bahnkah/döveez bewrosoo'
**neh**rehdehdeer

**I'd like to change some 'dollars/pounds'.**
'Dolar/Sterlin' bozdurmak istiyorum.
'do**lahr**/stehr**leen**' bozdoormahk eesteeyoroom

**I'd like to change some traveller's cheques.**
Seyahat çeki bozdurmak istiyorum.
seh-yah-**haht** chek(y)ee bozdoormahk eesteeyoroom

**Where can I change some 'dollars/pounds'?**
Nerede biraz 'dolar/sterlin' bozdurabilirim?
**neh**rehdeh beerahz 'do**lahr**/stehr**leen**'
bozdoorahbeeleereem

**What's the rate for the 'dollar/pound' today?**
Bugünkü 'dolar/sterlin' kuru nedir?
boo-gewnk(y)ew 'do**lahr**/stehr**leen**' kooroo **neh**deer

**What commission do you charge?**
Ne kadar komisyon alıyorsunuz?
**neh** kahdahr komeesyon ahlıyorsoonooz

**Please give me some smaller notes.**
Daha küçük kâğıt para verin, lütfen.
dah**hah** k(y)ewchewk k(y)ahıt pahrah vehreen **lewt**fehn

MONEY

## **At the bank**  Bankada

**I'd like to open an account.**
**Bir hesap açtırmak istiyorum.**
beer heh**sahp** ahch-tırmahk eesteeyoroom

**How much do I have in my account?**
**Hesabımda ne kadar param var?**
hehsahbımdah **neh** kahdahr pahrahm vahr

**I'd like to pay some money into my account.**
**Hesabıma biraz para yatırmak istiyorum.**
hehsahbımah beerahz pah**rah** yahtırmahk eesteeyoroom

**I'd like to pay this into my account.**
**Bunu hesabıma yatırmak istiyorum.**
boo**noo** hehsahbı**mah** yahtırmahk eesteeyoroom

**I'd like to withdraw some money.**
**Biraz para çekmek istiyorum.**
beerahz pah**rah** chekmehk eesteeyoroom

**I'm expecting some money from London. Has it arrived?**
**Londra'dan para bekliyorum. Geldi mi (acaba)?**
**lon**drahdahn pah**rah** behkleeyoroom. g(y)ehl**dee** mee (ahjahbah)

**Give me … notes (bills), please.**
**…lık banknotlar verin, lütfen.**
…lık bahnknot**lahr** vehreen **lewt**fehn

**Do you have any identification?**
**Bir kimliğiniz var mı?**
beer k(y)eemleeeeneez **vahr** mı

**Sign here, please.**
**Burayı imzalayın, lütfen.**
**boo**rah-yı eemzahlah-yın **lewt**fehn

**Go to the cashier, please.**
**Veznedara gidin, lütfen.**
vehznehdah**rah** g(y)eedeen **lewt**fehn

## Business terms İş terimleri

| **My name is …** | **Here's my card.** |
|---|---|
| **Adım … (dir).** | **Buyurun, kartım.** |
| ahdım …(deer) | boo**yoo**roon, kahr**tım** |

**I have an appointment with …**
**… ile bir randevum var.**
… eeleh beer rahndeh**voom** vahr

| balance | bilanço | bee**lahn**cho |
|---|---|---|
| bond | senet | seh**neht** |
| capital | sermaye | sehrmaa-**yeh** |
| cheque | çek | chek |
| company | şirket | sheer**k(y)eht** |
| consumption | tüketim | tu-k(y)eh**teem** |
| contract | sözleşme | sözlehsh**meh** |
| cost | maliyet | maalee**yeht** |
| cost | bedel | beh**dehl** |
| demand | talep | tah**lehp** |
| discount | indirim (ıskonto) | eendee**reem** (ıskonto) |
| economy | ekonomi | ehkono**mee** |
| expenses | masraflar | mahsrahf**lahr** |
| export | ihracat (dış satım) | eehraa**jaht** (**dısh** sahtım) |

PARA

| goods | mallar | mahllahr |
|---|---|---|
| import | ithalat (dış alım) | eethaal(y)aht (dısh ahlım) |
| inflation | enflasyon | ehnflahsyon |
| interest | faiz | faaeez |
| investment | yatırım | yahtırım |
| invoice | fatura | fahtoorah |
| labour | emek, iş gücü | ehmehk, eesh gewjew |
| loss | kayıp (zarar) | kah-yıp (zahrahr) |
| market | pazar | pahzahr |
| mortgage | ipotek | eepotehk |
| packing | ambalajlama | ahmbahlahzhlahmah |
| payment | ödeme | ödehmeh |
| percentage | yüzde | yewzdeh |
| price | fiyat | feeyaht |
| product | ürün | ewrewn |
| production | üretim | ewrehteem |
| productivity | verimlilik | vehreemleeleek |
| profit | kâr | k(y)ar |
| purchase | satın alma | sahtın ahlmah |
| quality | kalite | kahleeteh |
| quantity | miktar | meektahr |
| rate | oran | orahn |
| resource | kaynak | kai-nahk |
| sale | satış | sahtısh |
| sample | örnek | örnehk |
| savings | tasarruf, birikim | tahsahrroof [beereek(y)eem] |
| services | hizmetler | heezmehtlehr |
| share | hisse senedi | heess-seh sehnehdee |
| stock exchange | borsa | borsah |
| supply | arz | ahrz |
| value | değer | deh-yehr |

MONEY

# TRAVEL
## YOLCULUK

## On arrival Varışta

**Your passport, please.**
Pasaportunuz, lütfen.
pahsahportoo**nooz lewt**fehn

**Here's my passport.**
İşte pasaportum.
eeshteh pahsahpor**toom**

**How long will you be staying here?**
Burada ne kadar kalacaksınız?
**boo**rahdah **neh** kahdahr kahlahjahksınız

**I'll be staying 'a few days/a week/a month'.**
'Birkaç gün/Bir hafta/Bir ay' kalacağım.
'beer**kahch** gewn/**beer** hahftah/**beer** ai' kahlah**jahw**ım

**Are you together?**
Birlikte misiniz?
beerleek**teh** meesee-neez

**I'm travelling alone.**
Yalnız yolculuk ediyorum.
yahl**nız** yoljoolook ehdeeyoroom

**I'm travelling with a friend.**
Bir arkadaşımla yolculuk ediyorum.
beer ahrkahdah**shım**lah yoljoolook ehdeeyoroom

YOLCULUK

**How much money have you got?**
**(Yanınızda) Ne kadar paranız var?**
(yahnınızdah) **neh** kahdahr pahrahnız vahr

**I have …'dollars/pounds'.**
**… 'dolarım/sterlinim' var.**
…. 'dolahrım/stehrleeneem' vahr

**I'm here on 'business / holiday'.**
**'İş / Tatil' için buradayım.**
'**eesh** / taa**teel**' eecheen boorahdah-yım

**I'm just passing through.**
**Yalnızca transit geçiyorum.**
**yahl**nızjah trahn**seet** g(y)ehcheeyoroom

**Do you have anything to declare?**
**Deklare edecek (Bildirecek) bir şeyiniz var mı?**
dehklah**reh** ehdehjehk (beeldeereh**jehk**) beer sheh-
yeeneez **vahr** mı

**Please open this bag.**
**Lütfen bu çantayı açın.**
**lewt**fehn boo chahntah-yı **ah**-chın

**Do you have any other luggage?**
**Başka bagajınız var mı?**
bahsh**kah** bahgahzhınız **vahr** mı

**I have …**
**Yanımda … var.**
yahnımdah … vahr

**It's for my personal use.**
**O, özel kullanımım için.**
o, ö**zehl** koollahnımım eecheen

TRAVEL

**You'll have to pay duty on this.**
**Bunun için gümrük vergisi ödemeniz gerekiyor.**
boo**noon** eecheen gewm**rewk** vehrg(y)eesee
ödehmeh**neez** g(y)ehrehk(y)eeyor

| **Where is the …?** | **… nerede(dir)?** |
| --- | --- |
| | … **neh**rehdeh(deer) |

| | | |
| --- | --- | --- |
| booking office | Bilet gişesi | bee**leht** g(y)eeshehsee |
| bus stop | Otobüs durağı | oto**bewss** doorahwı |
| information office | Danışma bürosu | |
| | | dahnısh**mah** bewrosoo |
| newsstand | Gazete bayii | gah**zeh**teh **baa**-yeeee |
| platform four | Peron dört | peh**ron** dört |
| restaurant | Restoran | reh**sto**rahn |
| station | İstasyon | eestahss**yon** |

**Where can I get a taxi?**
**Nerede bir taksi bulabilirim?**
**neh**rehdeh beer tahksee boolahbee**lee**reem

**How can I get to the town centre?**
**Şehir merkezine nasıl gidebilirim?**
sheh-heer mehrk(y)ehzeeneh **nah**sıl
g(y)eedehbee**lee**reem

**Is there a bus into town?**
**Şehir merkezine bir otobüs var mı?**
sheh-heer mehrk(y)ehzeeneh beer oto**bewss** **vahr** mı

**How long does it take to get there?**
**Oraya gitmek ne kadar zaman alır?**
**o**rah-yah g(y)eetmehk **neh** kahdahr zahmahn ah**lır**

**How many kilometres?**
**Kaç kilometre?**
**kahch** k(y)eelomehtreh

YOLCULUK

## Baggage Bagaj

**Where are the luggage trolleys?**
Bagaj arabaları nerede(dir)?
bahgahzh ahrahbahlahrı **neh**rehdeh(deer)

**Porter!**
Hamal!/Bakar mısınız?
hah**mahl**/bah**kahr** mısınız

**Please take these.**
Lütfen bunları alın.
**lewt**fehn boonlahrı **ah**lın

**Please take this luggage to 'the taxi/the bus'**
Şu bagajı 'taksiye/otobüse' götürün, lütfen.
shoo bahgahzhı '**tahk**see-yeh/otobew**seh**' gö-tu-rewn
**lewt**fehn

**I'd like to register my luggage.**
Bagajımı teslim etmek istiyorum.
bahgahzhı**mı** tehsleem ehtmehk eesteeyoroom

## Buying a ticket Bilet alma

**Where's the booking office?**
Bilet gişesi nerededir?
bee**leht** g(y)eeshehsee **neh**rehdehdeer

**Where's the nearest travel agent's?**
En yakın seyahat ajansı nerededir?
**ehn** yahkın seh-yah-**haht** ah-zhahn-sı **neh**rehdehdeer

**I'd like a ticket to …**
…'ya bir bilet rica ediyorum.
…'yah beer bee**leht** ree-**jah** ehdeeyoroom

TRAVEL

**I'd like to reserve a seat.**
**Bir yer ayırtmak istiyorum.**
beer **yehr** ah-yırtmahk eesteeyoroom

**Do you have a timetable, please?**
**Bir tarife var mı acaba?**
beer tahreefeh **vahr** mı ahjahbah

**Is there a special rate for children?**
**Çocuklar için özel bir fiyat var mı?**
chojook**lahr** eecheen özehl beer feeyaht **vahr** mı

**How long is this ticket valid for?**
**Bu bilet ne kadar süre geçerli?**
boo beeleht **neh** kahdahr sewreh g(y)eh-cherr-lee

| | |
|---|---|
| **single(one-way)** | **gidiş** |
| | g(y)ee**deesh** |
| **return (roundtrip)** | **gidiş-dönüş** |
| | g(y)ee**deesh**-dö**newsh** |
| **first/second class** | **birinci/ikinci mevki** |
| | beereen**jee**/eek(y)een**jee** mehvk(y)ee |

# Bus, Coach, Tram
## Otobüs, Uzun yol Otobüsü, Tramvay

  Many tourists prefer travelling by bus in Turkey, because Turkey has an excellent bus service to virtually any single corner of the country. It is cheap, reliable, on time and exceptionally comfortable, unlike many European and US bus carriers.

YOLCULUK

TRAVEL

All bus companies operate new and luxurious buses. Hosts and hostesses serve soft drinks such as coffee, water, cola, juice and tea, which are complimentary. Also long-distance tickets usually include breakfast. Many buses are equipped with a video system, and recent movies are shown during the journeys on selected routes.

All major cities are also connected by rail, but bus service is superior to the rail service.

### How often do the 'buses/trams' run?
**'Otobüsler/Tramvaylar' ne sıklıkta çalışıyor?**
'otobewsslehr/trahm-why-lahr' **neh** sıklıktah chahlıshıyor

### The 'buses/trams' run every ten minutes.
**'Otobüsler/Tramvaylar'on dakikada bir kalkar.**
'otobewsslehr/trahmv-why-lahr' **on** dahk(y)eekahdah beer kahlkahr

### How long does the journey take?
**Yolculuk ne kadar sürüyor?**
yoljoolook **neh** kahdahr sewrewyor

### Which bus do I take to …?
**…'ye gitmek için hangi otobüse binmeliyim?**
…'yeh g(y)eet**mehk** eecheen **hun**gyee otobewseh beenmeh-lee-yeem

### You should take a number …
**… numaralı otobüse binmelisiniz.**
… noomahrahlı otobewseh beenmehleeseeneez

### Where is the ticket office?
**Bilet gişesi nerede?**
bee**leht** g(y)eeshehsee **neh**rehdeh

**When is the 'first/last/next' bus to …?**
**…'ya 'ilk/son/bir sonraki' otobüs ne zaman?**
…'yah '**eelk** / **son** / **beer** sonrahk(y)ee' otobewss **neh** zahmahn

**What's the fare to …?**
**…'e yolculuk ücreti nedir?**
…'eh yoljoolook ewjrehtee **neh**deer

**Does the coach stop in …?**
**Otobüs …'da duruyor mu?**
otobewss …'dah doo**roo**yor moo

**When does the coach leave?**
**Otobüs ne zaman kalkıyor?**
otobewss **neh** zahmahn kahlkıyor

**What time does the coach arrive in …?**
**Otobüs …'ya ne zaman varıyor?**
otobewss …'yah **neh** zahmahn vahrıyor

**I want to get off at …**
**…'de inmek istiyorum.**
…'deh een**mehk** eesteeyoroom

**Can we stop, please?**
**Durabilir miyiz, lütfen?**
doorahbee**leer** mee-yeez, **lewt**fehn

**Can you tell me when to get off?**
**Ne zaman ineceğimi söyler misiniz?**
**neh** zahmahn eenehjeh-yeemee söy**lehr** meesee-neez

**You get off at the next stop.**
**Bir sonraki durakta inin.**
**beer** sonrahk(y)ee doorahk**tah** eeneen

# Train and Underground
Tren ve Metro

## *Reservations and Inquiries*
*Yer ayırtma ve Bilgi alma*

**Where is the 'railway station/ticket office'?**
**'Tren istasyonu/Bilet gişesi' nerede(dir)?**
'trehn eestahsyonoo/beeleht g(y)eeshehsee'
**neh**rehdeh(deer)

**There is a train to … at nine.**
**…'a saat dokuzda bir tren var.**
…'ah sah-aht dokooz**dah** beer trehn vahr

**Is there 'an earlier/a later' train?**
**'Daha önce/Daha sonra' bir tren var mı?**
'dah**hah** önjeh/dah**hah** sonrah' beer trehn **vahr** mı

**Is this the train to Istanbul?**
**Bu İstanbul treni midir?**
boo ees**tahn**bool trehnee meedeer

**How long does it take to get there?**
**Oraya gitmek ne kadar zaman alır?**
orah-yah g(y)eetmehk **neh** kahdahr zahmahn ahlır

**Where's platform six?**
**Altı numaralı peron nerededir?**
ah**ltı** noomahrahlı pehron **neh**rehdehdeer

**On the right/On the left/Over there'.**
**Sağda/Solda/Orada.**
sahw**dah**/sol**dah**/**o**rahdah

**Is there a sleeping car on the train?**
**Trende yataklı vagon var mı?**
trehndeh yahtahk**lı** vahgon **vahr** mı

## *Changing*   *Aktarma*

**Is this a through train?**
**Bu tren ekspres midir?**
boo trehn ex**press** meedeer

**Do I have to change trains?**
**Tren değiştirmem gerekiyor mu?**
trehn deh-yeeshteermehm g(y)ehreh**k(y)ee**yor moo

**Where do I change?**
**Nerede aktarma yapacağım?**
**neh**rehdeh ahktahr**mah** yahpahjahwım

**You have to change at …**
**…'de aktarma yapmanız gerekiyor.**
…'deh ahktahr**mah** yahpmahnız g(y)ehrehk(y)eeyor

## *Departure*   *Kalkış*

**What time does the train to … leave?**
**… treni ne zaman kalkıyor?**
… trehnee **neh** zahmahn kahlkıyor

**Which platform does the train to … leave from?**
**… treni hangi perondan kalkıyor?**
… trehnee **hun**gyee pehrondahn kahlkıyor

**Your train will leave from platform five.**
**Treniniz beş numaralı perondan kalkacak.**
trehneeneez **behsh** noomahrahlı pehron**dahn**
kahlkahjahk

## *Arrival* Varış

**What time does it arrive in …?**
**…'a ne zaman varıyor?**
…'ah **neh** zahmahn vahrıyor

**Does the train stop at …?**
**Tren …'de/da durur mu?**
trehn …'deh/dah doo**roor** moo

**Which platform does the train from … arrive at?**
**… treni hangi perona geliyor?**
… trehnee **hun**gyee pehronah g(y)ehleeyor

## *On the train* Trende

**Is this seat free?**
**Bu yer boş mu?**
boo yehr **bosh** moo

**I think this is my seat.**
**Sanırım burası benim yerim.**
sah**nı**rım **boo**rahsı behn**eem** yehreem

**Where is the sleeping car?**
**Yataklı vagon nerede(dir)?**
yahtahklı vahgon **neh**rehdeh(deer)

**When do we get to …?**
**…'a ne zaman varırız?**
…'ah **neh** zahmahn vahrırız

**Would you let me know before we get to …?**
**…'a varmadan önce, bana bildirir misiniz?**
…'ah **vahr**mahdahn önjeh, bahnah beeldee**reer**
meesee-neez

**How long does the train stop here for?**
**Tren burada ne kadar duruyor?**
trehn boorahdah **neh** kahdahr doorooyor

# Boat and Hydrofoil service
## Vapur ve Deniz otobüsü servisi

If you would like to travel between the European and Asian sides in İstanbul, in addition to crossing the bridges, there are boats, ferries and hydrofoils that depart from certain locations (European side: Eminönü, Karaköy, Beşiktaş, Bakırköy, Aksaray. Asian side: Kadıköy, Üsküdar, Kartal, Haydarpaşa) on both sides.

The ships which depart from İstanbul travel along the coasts of the Aegean and Mediterranean Sea.

There are a number of private ferry boats running between the Greek Islands of Rhodes, Cos, Samos, Chios and the Turkish ports of İzmir, Çeşme, Ayvalık, Bodrum, Marmaris and Kuşadası.

**Where's the embarkation point?**
İskele nerede(dir)?
eesk(y)ehleh nehrehdeh(deer)

**Is there a 'boat/(car) ferry' from here to ...?**
Buradan ...'a bir 'vapur/araba vapuru' var mı?
boorahdahn ...ah beer 'vahpoor/ahrah**bah** vahpooroo'
**vahr** mı

**How often do the boats leave?**
Vapurlar ne sıklıkta kalkıyor?
vahpoorlahr **neh** sıklıktah kahlkıyor

**When does the next boat leave?**
Bir sonraki vapur ne zaman kalkıyor?
**beer** sonrahk(y)ee vahpoor **neh** zahmahn kahlkıyor

**I'd like a boat 'token/ticket' to ...**
...'a bir vapur 'jetonu/bileti' rica ediyorum.
...'ah beer vah**poor** 'zhehtonoo/beelehtee' ree-**jah**
ehdeeyoroom

**How many berths are there in the cabin?**
Kamarada kaç ranza (yatak) var?
kahmahrahdah **kahch** rahnzah (yahtahk) vahr

**How long does it take to get there?**
Oraya varmak ne kadar zaman alır?
orah-yah vahrmahk **neh** kahdahr zahmahn ahlır

**How long does the crossing take?**
Karşıya geçiş ne kadar zaman alır?
kahrshı-**yah** g(y)ehcheesh **neh** kahdahr zahmahn ahlır

**How long do we stay in port?**
Limanda ne kadar süre kalıyoruz?
leemahndah **neh** kahdahr sewreh kahlıyorooz

| | | |
|---|---|---|
| boat | **vapur** | vah**poor** |
| cabin | **kamara** | kah**mah**rah |
| deck | **güverte** | gew**vehr**teh |
| double | **çift yataklı** | **cheeft** yahtahklı |
| ferry | **araba vapuru** | ahrah**bah** vahpooroo |
| hydrofoil | **deniz otobüsü** | deh**neez** otobewsew |
| lifebelt | **can simidi / emniyet kemeri** | |
| | **jahn** seemeedee / ehmnee**yeht** k(y)ehmehree | |
| lifeboat | **cankurtaran sandalı** | |
| | jahnkoortah**rahn** sahndahlı | |
| lifejacket | **can yeleği** | **jahn** yehleh-yee |
| port | **liman** | lee**mahn** |
| ship | **gemi** | g(y)eh**mee** |

## Plane  Uçak

Turkish Airlines provide an extensive network of service to many Turkish cities, including Adana, Ankara, Antalya, Bodrum, Bursa, Dalaman, Denizli, Diyarbakir, Erzurum, Gaziantep, Izmir, Kayseri, Konya, Malatya, Samsun, Trabzon and Van from Istanbul. Many other Anatolian destinations have direct flights from Ankara.

In addition to Turkish Airlines, other private companies provide service on these domestic routes.

**Where's the airline office?**
**Havayolları bürosu nerede(dir)?**
hah**vah**-yollahrı bewrosoo **neh**rehdeh(deer)

YOLCULUK

### Is there a flight to …?
**…'a uçuş var mı?**
…'ah oochoosh **vahr** mı

### Is it a direct flight?
**Direkt bir uçuş mu?**
dee**rehkt** beer oochoosh moo

### When is the next flight to …?
**…'a bir sonraki uçuş ne zaman?**
…'ah **beer** sonrahk(y)ee oochoosh **neh** zahmahn

### I'd like a ticket to …
**…'a bir bilet rica ediyorum.**
…'ah beer bee**leht** ree-**jah** ehdeeyoroom

### I'd like to book two seats on the plane to …
**… uçağında iki kişilik yer ayırtmak istiyorum.**
… oochahwındah **ee**k(y)ee k(y)eesheeleek **yehr** ah-yırtmahk eesteeyoroom

| | | |
|---|---|---|
| **first class** | birinci mevki | beereen**jee** mehvk(y)ee |
| **single** | gidiş | g(y)ee**deesh** |
| **return (roundtrip)** | gidiş-dönüş | |
| | | g(y)ee**deesh**-dönewsh |
| **economy** | turist mevki | too**reest** mehvk(y)ee |
| **departure** | kalkış | kahl**kısh** |
| **arrival** | varış | vah**rısh** |

### How can I get to the airport?
**Havaalanına nasıl gidebilirim?**
hahvahahlahnınah **nah**sıl g(y)eedehbeeleereem

### Is there a bus to the airport?
**Havaalanına bir otobüs var mı?**
hahvahahlahnınah beer otobewss **vahr** mı

TRAVEL

**What's the flight number?**
**Uçuş numarası nedir?**
oo**choosh** noomahrahsı nehdeer

**What time do we take off?**
**Ne zaman kalkıyoruz?**
**neh** zahmahn kahlkıyorooz

**What time do we arrive?**
**Ne zaman varıyoruz?**
**neh** zahmahn vahrıyorooz

**What time do I have to check in?**
**Bagajların kaydını saat kaçta yaptırmalıyım?**
bahgahzhlahrın kai-dını sah-aht **kahch**tah
yahptırmahlıyım

**I'd like to change my reservation.**
**Rezervasyonumu değiştirmek istiyorum.**
rehzehrvahsyonoomoo deh-yeeshteer**mehk**
eesteeyoroom

## Taxi   Taksi

**Please call me a taxi.**
**Bana bir taksi çağırın, lütfen.**
bahnah beer **tahks**ee chahwırın **lewt**fehn

**Where can I find a taxi?**
**Nerede bir taksi bulabilirim?**
**neh**rehdeh beer **tahks**ee boolahbeeleereem

**How far is it to …?**
**Orası …'ye/ya ne kadar uzaklıkta(dır)?**
**o**rahsı …'yeh/yah **neh** kahdahr oozahklıktah(dır)

**Are you free?**
**Boş musunuz?**
**bosh** moosoonooz

**Take me to ...**   Beni ... (n)e/(n)a götürün.
           behnee ...(n)eh/(n)ah gö-tu-rewn

| | | |
|---|---|---|
| **this address** | **bu adres** | boo ahdrehs |
| **the ... Hotel** | **... oteli** | ... otehlee |
| **the airport** | **havaalanı** | hah**vah**ahlahnı |
| **the railway station** | **tren istasyonu** | |
| | | t**r**ehn eestahsyonah |
| **the town centre** | **şehir merkezi** | |
| | | sheh-**heer** mehrk(y)ehzee |

**Go straight ahead.**
**Doğru gidin.**
**dohw**roo g(y)eedeen

**Can you hurry? I'm late.**
**Acele edebilir misiniz?**
**Geciktim.**
ahjehleh ehdehbee**leer** meesee-neez g(y)ehjeek**teem**

**Could you drive more slowly?**
**Daha yavaş kullanabilir miydiniz?**
dah**hah** yahvahsh koollahnahbee**leer** meeydeeneez

**Turn 'left/right' at the next corner.**
**Bir sonraki köşeden 'sola/sağa' dönün.**
**beer** sonrahk(y)ee kösheh**dehn** 'so**lah**/sah-ah'
dönewn

**Please stop here.**
**Burada durun, lütfen.**
**boo**rahdah **doo**roon **lewt**fehn

**Could you wait for me?**
**Beni bekler misiniz, lütfen?**
behnee behk**lehr** meesee-neez **lewt**fehn

## Dolmuş (Shared Taxi)

A Turkish **dolmuş** (dol**moosh** – *literally 'filled'*) is a shared taxi or minibus running a predetermined route, with each passenger paying only a portion of the normal fare.

Dolmushes operate within cities, and between cities and nearby towns and villages. Every small city and country town has a **dolmuş** terminal as well as a bus terminal. In city centers there may be legally designated **dolmuş** stops, usually marked by blue signs bearing a big white 'D'.

The car or minibus waits at the beginning of its route until most or all of its seats are filled.

When you want to get out, say 'İnecek var!' (eeneh**jehk** vahr – *'Someone wants to get off!'*)

Fares are usually under $ 2.00 within a city. City-to-village routes, which tend to be longer, may have higher fares but are still far less than a private taxi.

**Where can I get a 'dolmuş' to ...**
**...'e giden bir dolmuş nerede bulabilirim?**
...'eh g(y)eedehn beer dolmoosh **neh**rehdeh boolahbeeleereem

**Where is the 'dolmuş' stop?**
**Dolmuş durağı nerededir?**
dol**moosh** doorahı **neh**rehdehdeer

YOLCULUK

**Is this the 'dolmuş' to …?**
**Bu … dolmuşu mu?**
boo … dolmooshoo moo

**Is … on the 'dolmuş' route?**
**… dolmuş yolu üzerinde midir?**
… dol**moosh** yoloo ewzehreendeh meedeer

**How much is it to Taksim?**
**Taksim ne kadar?**
tahkseem **neh** kahdahr

**I want to get off at …**
**…'de inmek istiyorum.**
…'deh een**mehk** eesteeyoroom

# Asking the way & Directions
Yol sorma & Tarifler

## *Asking the way* *Yol sorma*

**How far is it to … from here?**
**… buradan ne kadar uzaklıktadır?**
… **boo**rahdahn **neh** kahdahr oozahklıktahdır

**Can you tell me the way to …?**
**Bana … yolunu tarif edebilir misiniz?**
bahnah … yoloonoo tahreef ehdehbee**leer** meesee-neez

**How do I get to …?**
**…'a nasıl giderim?**
…'ah **nah**sıl g(y)eedehreem

TRAVEL

**In which direction is ...?**
**... hangi yöndedir?**
… **hun**gyee yöndehdeer

**Where does this road lead to?**
**Bu yol nereye çıkıyor?**
boo yol **neh**reh-yeh chıkıyor

**Are we on the right road for ...?**
**... için doğru yolda mıyız?**
… eecheen dohw**roo** yoldah mıyız

**How long does it take to get there?**
**Oraya varmak ne kadar zaman alır?**
orah-yah vahrmahk **neh** kahdahr zahmahn ahlır

**Where can I find this address?**
**Bu adresi nasıl (nerede) bulabilirim?**
**boo** ahdrehsee **nah**sıl (**neh**rehdeh) boolahbeeleereem

**Can I get there on foot?**
**Oraya yürüyerek gidebilir miyim?**
orah-yah yewrewyehrehk g(y)eedehbee**leer** mee-yeem

**Can you show me on the map where it is?**
**Onun nerede olduğunu haritada gösterebilir misiniz?**
ohnoon **neh**rehdeh oldoohwoonoo hahreetahdah göstehrehbee**leer** meesee-neez

**Can you tell me where ... is?**
**Bana, ...'nin nerede olduğunu söyleyebilir misiniz?**
bahnah, …'neen **neh**rehdeh oldoohwoonoo söyleh-yeh-bee**leer** meesee-neez

## *Directions* Tarifler

**You're on the wrong road.**
**Yanlış yoldasınız.**
yahn**lish** yoldahsınız

**Go straight ahead.**
**Doğru gidin.**
**dohw**roo g(y)eedeen

**Follow the signs for ...**
**... işaretlerini izleyin.**
... eeshahrehtlehree**nee** eezleh-yeen

**It's there on the 'left/right'.**
**Orada 'solda/sağda'.**
**o**rahdah 'sol**dah**/sahw**dah**'

**Take the ... road**
**... yolundan gidin.**
... yoloon**dahn** g(y)eedeen

**Straight ahead.**
**Doğru ileride.**
**dohw**roo eelehreedeh

**You have to go back to ...**
**...'a geri dönmeniz gerekiyor.**
...'ah g(y)eh**ree** dönmehneez g(y)ehrehk(y)eeyor

**It's about fifteen minutes from here.**
**Buradan yaklaşık olarak on beş dakika (tutar).**
**boo**rahdahn  yahklah**shık**  olahrahk  **ohn**  behsh
dahk(y)eekah (tootahr)

**'Opposite/next to/behind' ...**
**...nin 'karşısında/yanında/arkasında'.**
...**neen** 'kahrshısın**dah**/yahnın**dah**/ahrkahsın**dah**'

**Turn 'right / left' at the traffic lights.**
**Trafik ışıklarından 'sağa / sola' dönün.**
trah**feek** ıshıklahrındahn 'sahw-**ah** / so**lah**' dönewn

**Take the 'first / second / third' turning on the right.**
**Sağdaki 'birinci/ikinci/üçüncü' yola sapın.**
sahwdah**k(y)ee** 'beereen**jee**/eek(y)een**jee**/
ewchewn**jew**' yolah sahpın

## Travelling by car
Arabayla yolculuk etme

**TEM** (Trans Europe Motorway) connects all European cities to Istanbul, and from there an extensive network of Turkish interstates and highways connects Istanbul to all Turkish cities.

### *General* Genel

**Where's the (nearest) 'car park/garage'?**
**(En yakın) 'Otopark/Garaj' nerededir?**
(**ehn** yahkın) 'otopahrk/gahrahzh' **neh**rehdehdeer

**What's the charge per hour?**
**Saat ücreti ne kadar?**
sah-**aht** ewjrehtee **neh** kahdahr

**May I park here?**
**Buraya park edebilir miyim?**
**boo**rah-yah pahrk ehdehbee**leer** mee-yeem

**How far to the next filling station?**
**Gelecek (Bir sonraki) benzin istasyonu ne kadar uzakta?**
gehleh**jehk** (**beer** sonrahkee) behnzeen eestahsyonoo **neh** kahdahr oozahktah

YOLCULUK

**Fill it up, please.**
Doldurun, lütfen.
dol**doo**roon **lewt**fehn

**Could you give me … 'gallons / litres' of petrol (gasoline)?**
… 'galon / litre' benzin verir misiniz?
… 'gahlon / leetreh' behnzeen veh**reer** meesee-neez

| diesel | motorin | moto**reen** |
|--------|---------|--------------|
| regular | normal | ñor**mahl** |
| super | süper | **sew**pehr |

**Please clean the windscreen.**
Ön camı silin, lütfen.
ön jahmı **see**leen **lewt**fehn

**Please check the …      … kontrol edin, lütfen.**
                          …. kon**trol** ehdeen **lewt**fehn

| brake fluid | Fren hidrolik yağını | |
| | | **frehn** heedroleek yahwını |
| water | Suyu | soo**yoo** |
| oil | Yağı | yahwı |
| spare tyre | Yedek lastiği | yeh**dehk** lahstee(y)ee |

**The oil needs changing.**
Yağın değişmesi gerekiyor.
yahwın deh-yeeshmeh**see** g(y)ehrehk(y)eeyor

**Please wash the car.**
Arabayı yıkayın, lütfen.
ahrahbah-yı yı**kah**-yın **lewt**fehn

**Can you change the …?**
… değiştirebilir misiniz?
… deh-yeeshteerehbee**leer** meesee-neez

TRAVEL

| **fan-belt** | Vantilatör kayışını | vahnteelah**tör** kah-yıshını |
| **spark plugs** | Bujileri | boozheeleh**ree** |
| **tyre** | Lastiği | lahstee**(y)ee** |
| **wipers** | Cam sileceğini | **jahm** seelehjeh-yeenee |

### Check the tyre pressures, please.
Lastiklerin havasını kontrol edin, lütfen.
l(y)ahsteeklehreen hahvahsını kon**trol** ehdeen
**lewt**fehn

### Can you fix this flat tyre?
Bu patlak lastiği tamir edebilir misiniz?
boo paht**lahk** l(y)ahstee(y)ee taameer ehdehbee**leer**
meesee-neez

## *Breakdown*  *Arıza*

### May I use your telephone?
Telefonunuzu kullanabilir miyim?
tehlehfonoonoozoo koollahnahbee**leer** mee-yeem

### Where's the nearest garage?
En yakın garaj nerededir?
**ehn** yahkın gahrahzh **neh**rehdehdeer

### My car has broken down.
Arabam bozuldu.
ahrah**bahm** bozooldoo

### Please send a 'tow truck / mechanic'.
Lütfen bir 'çekme aracı / tamirci' gönderin.
**lewt**fehn beer 'chek**meh** ahrahjı / tahmeer**jee**'
göndehreen

### The radiator is leaking.
Radyatör su sızdırıyor.
rahdyah**tör** **soo** sızdırıyor

YOLCULUK

**The battery needs charging.**
Akünün şarj edilmesi gerekiyor.
ahk(y)ewnewn **shahrzh** ehdeelmehsee g(y)ehrehk(y)eeyor

**The engine is overheating.**
Motor aşırı ısınıyor.
mo**tor** ahshırı ısınıyor

**There's a 'petrol/oil' leak.**
Bir 'benzin/yağ' sızıntısı var.
beer 'beh**nzeen**/**yahw**' sızıntısı vahr

**My car won't start.**
Arabam çalışmıyor.
ahrahbahm chah**lısh**mıyor

**There is something wrong with the ...**
...(n)de/da bir problem var.
...(**n**)**deh/dah** beer prob**lehm** vahr

| brakes | frenler | frehnlehr |
|---|---|---|
| carburettor | karbüratör | kahrbewrahtör |
| engine | motor | motor |
| fan-belt | vantilatör kayışı | vahnteelah**tör** kah-yıshı |
| gearbox | vites kutusu | vee**tehs** kootoosoo |
| radiator | radyatör | rahdyahtör |
| wheel | tekerlek | tehk(y)ehrlehk |

**How long will it take to repair?**
Tamir etmek ne kadar sürer?
taa**meer** ehtmehk **neh** kahdahr sewrehr

TRAVEL

## Road signs Yol işaretleri

| | |
|---|---|
| ASGARİ HIZ | MINIMUM SPEED |
| AZAMİ HIZ | MAXIMUM SPEED |
| BOZUK YOL | POOR SURFACE |
| ÇIKIŞ | EXIT |
| DARALAN YOL | ROAD NARROWS |
| DİKKAT | CAUTION |
| DÖNEL KAVŞAK | ROUNDABOUT |
| DUR | STOP |
| DURULMAZ | NO STOPPING |
| DÜŞÜK BANKET | LOW VERGE |
| FARLARI YAKINIZ | HEADLIGHTS ON |
| GEÇMEK YASAKTIR | NO PASSING |
| GİRİLMEZ | NO ENTRY |
| GÜVENLİK ŞERİDİ | HARD SHOULDER |
| KAVŞAK | JUNCTION |
| KAYA DÜŞEBİLİR | FALLING ROCK |
| KAYGAN YOL | SLIPPERY ROAD |
| OKUL | SCHOOL |
| PARK YAPILMAZ | NO PARKING |
| TEHLİKE | DANGER |
| TEHLİKELİ VİRAJ | DANGEROUS BEND |
| TEK YÖNLÜ YOL | ONE-WAY STREET |
| TRAFİK IŞIKLARI | TRAFFIC SIGNALS |
| VİRAJ / DÖNEMEÇ | BEND |
| YAVAŞ | SLOW DOWN |
| YAYA | PEDESTRIANS |
| YOL ÇALIŞMASI | ROAD WORKS |

YOLCULUK

## Car hire Araba kiralama

**I'd like to rent (hire) a car.**
Bir araba kiralamak istiyorum.
beer ahrah**bah** k(y)eerahlahmahk eesteeyoroom

**A 'small/big/automatic' car.**
'Küçük/Büyük/Otomatik' bir araba.
'k(y)ew**chewk**/bew**yewk**/otomah**teek**' beer ahrahbah

**I'd like it for a 'day/week'.**
Bir 'günlüğüne/haftalığına' istiyorum.
**beer** 'gewnlewewneh/hahftahlıınah' eesteeyoroom

**How much does it cost per 'day/week'?**
'Günlüğü/Haftalığı' ne kadar?
'gewnlew**ew**/hahftahlıı' **neh** kahdahr

**I want to leave the car in Istanbul.**
Arabayı İstanbul'da bırakmak istiyorum.
ahrahbah-yı ees**tahn**booldah bırahkmahk eesteeyoroom

**How much is the deposit?**
Depozito ne kadar?
dehpo**zee**to **neh** kahdahr

**May I see your driving licence?**
Ehliyetinizi görebilir miyim?
ehhleeyehteeneezee görehbee**leer** mee-yeem

**Here is my driving licence.**
Buyurun, ehliyetim.
booyooroon, ehhleeyeh**teem**

TRAVEL

# ACCOMMODATION
## KONAKLAMA

## HOTELS, MOTELS, GUEST HOUSES, HOLIDAY VILLAGES

OTELLER, MOTELLER, PANSİYONLAR, TATİL KÖYLERİ

At the majority of five-star and four-star hotels, all rooms and suites have private bathrooms, central heating, air-conditioning, direct dial telephones, music, satellite TVs, minibars and baby sitting, dry-cleaning and room service.

At the majority of motels, all rooms have private baths. Some motels include air-conditioning and a fridge.

Bathrooms and toilets are usually communal at guest houses. At the majority of guest houses, there may be a kitchen where you can cook and share a fridge.

At the majority of holiday villages, there is a swimming pool. Shopping facilities are provided.

## Booking a room & Checking in

Oda ayırtma & Kaydolma (Giriş yapma)

| My name is … | I have a reservation. |
|---|---|
| **Adım ... (dır)** | **Rezervasyonum var.** |
| ahdım …(dır) | rehzehrvahsyo**noom** vahr |

**I've reserved two rooms.**
**İki oda rezerve ettirdim.**
ee**k(y)ee** odah rehzehr**veh** ehtteerdeem

**Do you have any vacancies?**
**Hiç boş odanız var mı?**
heech **bosh** odahnız **vahr** mı

**We don't have any vacancies.**
Hiç boş yerimiz yok.
**heech** bosh yehreemeez **yok**

**Do you know another good hotel?**
Başka iyi bir otel biliyor musunuz?
bahshkah ee-**yee** beer otehl bee**lee**yor moosoonooz

**How long will you be staying?**
Ne kadar kalacaksınız?
**neh** kahdahr kahlahjahksınız

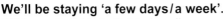

**We'll be staying overnight only.**
Yalnızca bir gece kalacağız.
**yahl**nızjah **beer** g(y)ehjeh kahlah**jahw**ız

**We'll be staying 'a few days / a week'.**
'Birkaç gün / Bir hafta' kalacağız.
'beer**kahch** gewn / **beer** hahftah' kahlah**jahw**ız

**What floor is the room on?**
Oda kaçıncı katta?
odah kahchınjı kahttah

**The room is on the 'second / third' floor.**
Oda 'ikinci / üçüncü' katta.
odah 'eek(y)een**jee** / ewchewn**jew**' kahttah

**Do you have another room?**
Başka bir odanız var mı?
bahsh**kah** beer odahnız **vahr** mı

**This is the only room vacant.**
Tek boş oda bu.
**tehk** bosh odah boo

KONAKLAMA

## I'd like a 'single/double' room.
**'Tek yataklı/Çift yataklı' bir oda rica ediyorum.**
'**tehk** yahtahklı / **cheeft** yahtahklı' beer odah ree-**jah** ehdeeyoroom

| ROOMS TO LET/VACANCIES | KİRALIK ODALAR |
|---|---|
| NO VACANCIES | BOŞ ODA YOK |

## Do you have a room ...?   ... bir odanız var mı?
... beer odahnız **vahr** mı

| | | |
|---|---|---|
| at the back | Arka tarafta | ahr**kah** tahrahftah |
| at the front | Ön tarafta | ön tahrahftah |
| overlooking the sea | Denize bakan | dehnee**zeh** bahkahn |
| with a balcony | Balkonlu | bahlkon**loo** |
| with a bathroom | Banyolu | **bahn**yoloo |
| with a double bed | Çift kişilik (duble) yataklı | |
| | cheeft k(y)eesheeleek (**doob**leh) yahtahklı | |
| with a shower | Duşlu | doosh**loo** |
| with a telephone | Telefonlu | tehlehfon**loo** |
| with a television | Televizyonlu | tehlehveezyon**loo** |
| with a toilet | Tuvaletli | toovahleht**lee** |
| with a view | Manzaralı | **mahn**zahrahlı |
| with heating | Isıtmalı | ısıtmahlı |
| with hot water | Sıcak sulu | sı**jahk** sooloo |
| with running water | Lavabolu | l(y)ahvahboloo |
| with twin beds | İki yataklı | eek(y)ee yahtahklı |

## Is there air conditioning?
**Soğuk hava tertibatı var mı?**
soh**wook** hahvah tehrteebahtı **vahr** mı

## I'd like a quiet room.
**Sessiz bir oda rica ediyorum.**
sehss-**seez** beer odah ree-**jah** ehdeeyoroom

ACCOMMODATION

**Could you put a cot in the room?**
**Odaya bir çocuk karyolası koyabilir misiniz?**
odah-yah beer cho**jook** kahryolahsı koyahbee**leer** meesee-neez

**Is there 'a laundry service/room service'?**
**'Çamaşır servisi/Oda servisi' var mı?**
'chahmah**shır** sehrveesee/o**dah** sehrveessee' **vahr** mı

**Is there a 'telephone/radio/television' in the room?**
**Odada 'telefon/radyo/televizyon' var mı?**
odahdah 'tehleh**phone**/**rahd**yo/tehleh**veez**yon' **vahr** mı

**May we see the room?**
**Odayı görebilir miyiz?**
odah-yı göreh**bee**leer mee-yeez

**I don't like this room.**
**Bu odayı beğenmedim.**
boo odah-yı beh-**yehn**mehdeem

**Fine. I'll take this room.**
**İyi. Bu odayı tutuyorum.**
ee-**yee**. boo odah-yı too**too**yoroom

| It's too ... | Çok ... | choke ... |
|---|---|---|
| cold | soğuk | sohwook |
| dark | karanlık | kahrahnlık |
| hot | sıcak | sıjahk |
| noisy | gürültülü | gewrewl-tu-lew |
| small | küçük | k(y)ewchewk |

**Could we have another room?**
**Başka bir oda alabilir miyiz?**
bahsh**kah** beer odah ahlahbee**leer** mee-yeez

**How much is the room per 'night/week'?**
**Odanın 'gecelik/haftalık' fiyatı ne kadar?**
odahnın 'g(y)ehjeh**leek**/hahftahlık' feeyahtı **neh** kahdahr

**Is 'service/breakfast' included?**
**'Servis/Kahvaltı' dahil mi?**
'sehrveess/kahhvahltı' dah**heel** mee

**Does that include V.A.T.(value added tax)?**
**K.D.V.(katma değer vergisi) dahil mi?**
kah.deh.veh (kaht**mah** deh-**yehr** vehrg(y)eesee) dah**heel** mee

**What's the price for bed and breakfast?**
**Yatak ve kahvaltı fiyatı ne kadar?**
yahtahk veh kahhvahltı feeyahtı **neh** kahdahr

**What's the price for 'full board/half board'?**
**'Tam pansiyon / Yarım pansiyon' fiyatı ne kadar?**
'**tahm** pahnseeyon/yah**rım** pahnseeyon' feeyahtı **neh** kahdahr

**That's too expensive.**
**Çok pahalı.**
**choke** pahhahlı

**What do we pay for the children?**
**Çocuklar için ne kadar ödüyoruz?**
chojook**lahr** eecheen **neh** kahdahr ödewyorooz

**Do you charge for the baby?**
Bebek için ücret alıyor musunuz?
beh**behk** eecheen ewjreht ahlıyor moosoonooz

**What's the room number?**
Oda numarası kaç?
o**dah** noomahrahsı **kahch**

**Where can I park my car?**
Arabamı nereye park edebilirim?
ahrahbahmı **neh**reh-yeh pahrk ehdehbeeleereem

**May I see your passport, please?**
Pasaportunuzu görebilir miyim, lütfen?
pahsahportoonoozoo görehbee**leer** mee-yeem
**lewt**fehn

**Would you mind filling in this registration form?**
Bu kayıt formunu doldurur musunuz?
boo kah-yıt formoonoo doldoo**roor** moosoonooz

**Please sign here.**
Burayı imzalayın, lütfen.
**boo**rah-yı eemzahlah-yın
**lewt**fehn

**Will you have our luggage
sent up?**
Bagajımızı yukarı
gönderir misiniz?
bahgahzhımızı yookahrı
göndeh**reer** meesee-neez

KONAKLAMA

ACCOMMODATION

## Registration form Kayıt formu

| | |
|---|---|
| **Soyadı - Adı** | **Last name - First name** |
| soyahdı – ahdı | |
| **Pasaport Numarası** | **Passport number** |
| pahsah**port** noomah**rah**sı | |
| **Adres** ahd**rehs** | **Address** |
| **Semt/ Mahalle** sehmt/mahhah**lleh** | **Home town** |
| **Sokak/Cadde** so**kahk**/jahdd**deh** | **Street** |
| **Numara** noomah**rah** | **Number** |
| **Şehir - Ülke** sheh-**heer**-ewl**k(y)eh** | **City - Country** |
| **Uyruk (Tabiiyet)** ooy**rook** (taab**ee**yeht) | **Nationality** |
| **Meslek** mehs**lehk** | **Occupation** |
| **Doğum yeri** dohw**oom** yehree | **Place of birth** |
| **Doğum tarihi** dohw**oom** tahreehee | **Date of birth** |
| **Tarih** taa**reeh** | **Date** |
| **İmza** eem**zah** | **Signature** |

## General requirements
## Genel gereksinimler

**Where's the dining room?**
**Yemek salonu nerededir?**
yehmehk sahlonoo **neh**rehdehdeer

**Where are the toilets?**
**Tuvaletler nerededir?**
toovahleht**lehr neh**rehdehdeer

**When is breakfast?**
**Kahvaltı ne zaman?**
kahhvahlt**ı neh** zahmahn

**Do you have a buffet?**
**Büfe(niz) var mı?**
**bew**feh(neez) **vahr** mı

**Any messages for me?**
Benim için mesaj var mı ?/Beni arayan var mı?
behneem eecheen mehsahzh **vahr** mı/
behnee ahrah-yahn **vahr** mı

**Can I leave this in your safe?**
Bunu kasanıza bırakabilir miyim?
boo**noo** kahsahnızah bırahkahbee**leer** mee-yeem

**Please order a taxi.**
Bir taksi çağırın, lütfen.
beer **tahk**see chahwırın **lewt**fehn

**Where's the lift (elevator)?**
Asansör nerede?
ahsahn**sör neh**rehdeh

**The key to room ..., please.**
... (numaralı) odanın anahtarı, lütfen.
... (noomahrahlı) odahnın ahnahhtahrı **lewt**fehn

**Would you wake me at ..., please?**
Beni (saat) ...'de uyandırır mısınız, lütfen?
behnee (sah-aht) ...'deh ooyahndırır mısınız **lewt**fehn

**May I have some more hangers, please?**
Biraz daha askı alabilir miyim, lütfen?
**bee**rahz dahhah ahskı ahlahbee**leer** mee-yeem **lewt**fehn

**May I have another sheet?**
Başka bir çarşaf alabilir miyim?
bahsh**kah** beer chahrshahf ahlahbee**leer** mee-yeem

**May I have a blanket?**
Bir battaniye alabilir miyim?
beer baht-taanee-yeh ahlahbee**leer** mee-yeem

**KONAKLAMA**

**There's no 'ashtray/soap' in my room.**
**Odamda hiç 'kül tablası/sabun' yok.**
odahmdah **heech** 'k(y)ewl tahblahsı/sahboon' **yok**

**There's no '(hot) water/towels' in my room.**
**Odamda hiç '(sıcak) su/havlu' yok.**
odahmdah **heech** '(sıjahk) soo/hahvloo' **yok**

**Our room hasn't been prepared.**
**Odamız hazırlanmamış.**
odahmız hahzır**lahn**mahmısh

**The tap (faucet) is dripping.**
**Musluk damlıyor.**
moos**look** dahmlıyor

**The washbasin is blocked.**
**Lavabo tıkalı.**
l(y)ah**vah**bo tıkahllı

**There's no toilet paper in the lavatory.**
**Tuvalette hiç tuvalet kâğıdı yok.**
toovahlehtteh **heech** toovahleht k(y)aaıdı **yok**

**The ... doesn't work.**   ... çalışmıyor.
                           ... chah**lısh**mıyor

| | | |
|---|---|---|
| **air conditioning** | Klima | **klee**mah |
| **fan** | Vantilatör | vahnteel(y)ah**tör** |
| **heating** | Isıtma | ısıt**mah** |
| **light** | Işık | ıshık |
| **switch** | Elektrik düğmesi | ehlehk**treek** dewmehsee |
| **television** | Televizyon | tehlehveez**yon** |

**The bulb is burned out.**
**Ampul yanmış.**
ahm**pool** yahnmısh

ACCOMMODATION

**KONAKLAMA**

**The 'plug/shutter/blind' is broken.**
'Elektrik fişi/Panjur/Kepenk' bozuk.
'ehlehk**treek** feeshee/pahn**zhoor**/k(y)eh**pehnk**'
bo**zook**

# Hotel staff Otel personeli

| | | |
|---|---|---|
| bellboy | komi | **ko**mee |
| hall porter | kapıcı | kah**pı**jı |
| maid | oda temizlikçisi | o**dah** tehmeezleekcheesee |
| manager | müdür | mew**dewr** |
| porter | hamal | hah**mahl** |
| receptionist | resepsiyonist | rehsehpseeyo**neest** |
| switchboard operator | santral memuru | |
| | | sahn**trahl** mehmooroo |
| waiter | garson | gahr**son** |
| waitress | bayan garson | bah-**yahn** gahrson |

# Checking out Ayrılış

**I'm leaving early in the morning.**
Sabah erkenden ayrılıyorum.
sahbahh **ehr**k(y)ehndehn ai-rılıyoroom

**We'll be checking out around noon.**
Öğleye doğru ayrılacağız.
ööleh-**yeh** dohw**roo** ai-rılah**jahw**ız

**I'll pay 'cash/by credit card'.**
'Nakit/Kredi kartı ile' ödeyeceğim.
'nah**k(y)eet**/kreh**dee** kahrtı eeleh' ödeh-yeh-jeh-yeem

**May I have my bill, please?**
Hesabımı alabilir miyim, lütfen?
hehsahbımı ahlahbee**leer** mee-yeem **lewt**fehn

ACCOMMODATION

KONAKLAMA

**I think there's a mistake in the bill.**
Sanırım hesapta bir yanlışlık var.
sahnırım hehsahptah beer yahnlıshlık vahr

**Please order a taxi for me.**
Bana bir taksi çağırır mısınız, lütfen?
bahnah beer **tahk**see chahwırır mısınız **lewt**fehn

**Could you have my luggage brought down?**
Bagajımı aşağı getirtir misiniz, lütfen?
bahgahzhımı ahshahwı g(y)ehteer**teer** meesee-neez **lewt**fehn

**It's been a very enjoyable stay.**
Burada kalmak çok güzeldi.
**boo**rahdah kahlmahk **choke** gewzehldee

## Camping Kamp yapma

Campsites are open from April to October. They offer showers, toilets, laundry facilities, kitchen, electricity and a shop.

**Can we camp here?**
Burada kamp yapabilir miyiz?
**boo**rahdah kahmp yahpahbee**leer** mee-yeez

**Is there a camping site near here?**
Yakınlarda bir kamping yeri var mı?
yahkınlahrdah beer kahm**peeng** yehree **vahr** mı

**Do you have room for a 'tent/caravan'?**
'Çadır/Karavan' için boş yer var mı?
'chah**dır**/kahrah**vahn**' eecheen **bosh** yehr **vahr** mı

ACCOMMODATION

**KONAKLAMA**

### What's the charge for a 'car/tent/caravan'?
**Bir 'araba/çadır/karavan' için ücret ne kadar?**
beer 'ahrah**bah**/chah**dır**/kahrah**vahn**' eecheen
ewjreht **neh** kahdahr

### What's the charge …?
**… ücret ne kadar?**
… ewjreht **neh** kahdahr

| | | |
|---|---|---|
| **per day** | Günlük | gewn**lewk** |
| **per person** | Kişi başına | k(y)ee**shee** bahshınah |
| **per week** | Haftalık | hahftah**lık** |

### Can we park our caravan here?
**Karavanımızı burada park edebilir miyiz?**
kahrahvahnımızı boorahdah pahrk ehdehbee**leer** mee-
yeez

### Where are the 'toilets/showers'?
**'Tuvaletler/Duşlar' nerede?**
'toovahleht**lehr**/doosh**lahr**' **neh**rehdeh

### Are there shopping facilities?
**Alışveriş olanakları var mı?**
ahlıshveh**reesh** ohlahnahklahrı **vahr** mı

### Is there drinking water?
**İçme suyu var mı?**
eech**meh** sooyoo **vahr** mı

### Is there electricity?
**Elektrik var mı?**
ehlehktreek **vahr** mı

### Is there a 'playground/restaurant'?
**'Oyun alanı/Restoran' var mı?**
'o**yoon** ahlahnı/rehstorahn' **vahr** mı

### May we light a fire?
**Ateş yakabilir miyiz?**
ah**tehsh** yahkahbee**leer**
mee-yeez

**ACCOMMODATION**

# RESTAURANT
## RESTORAN

RESTORAN

### *Turkish Cuisine*   *Türk Mutfağı*

An absolutely wonderful surprise, when you visit Turkey, is the food! It is fresh, tasty and filling. Whether you eat in restaurants, at stand-up food booths, outside at the seashore, literally on the sidewalk in town, or at a friend's home, the eating experience is wonderful.

When you first visit Turkey and see the customary fully garnished table, you might easily imagine yourself at a Sultan's banquet. The everyday table is arrayed with a fantastic variety of dishes: soups like 'Kırmızı Mercimek Çorbası' (red lentil soup), 'meze' (hors d'oeuvres), aubergine purée, white cheese, 'Pilaki' (cold beans in sauce), deep-fried shellfish, börek (dumpling), melons, delicious seasonal fruits and the 'Zeytinyağlılar' (dishes cooked with olive oil).

## Going to a restaurant & Reservation
## Restorana gidiş & Yer ayırtma

**I'm hungry/I'm thirsty.**
**Acıktım/Susadım.**
ahjık**tım**/soosahd**ım**

**Can you suggest a 'good/cheap' restaurant?**
**'İyi/Ucuz' bir restoran önerebilir misiniz?**
'ee-**yee**/oo**jooz**' beer rehstorahn önehrehbee**leer** meesee-neez

RESTAURANT

### I'd like to reserve a table for four.
**Dört kişilik bir masa ayırtmak istiyorum.**
dört k(y)eesheeleek beer **mah-sah** ah-yırtmahk
eesteeyoroom

### Do you have a table for four?
**Dört kişilik bir masanız var mı?**
dört k(y)eesheeleek beer mah-sahnız **vahr** mı

### Is there a table …? … bir masa var mı?
… beer mah-sah **vahr** mı

| | | |
|---|---|---|
| **by the window** | Pencere kenarında | |
| | pehnjeh**reh** k(y)ehnahrındah | |
| **in a corner** | Köşede | kösheh**deh** |
| **on the terrace** | Terasta | tehrahs**tah** |
| **outside** | Dışarıda | dıshahrı**dah** |
| **in a non-smoking area** | Sigara içilmeyen bir yerde | |
| seegahrah eecheelmeh-**yehn** beer yehrdeh | | |

### I'd like to reserve a table for dinner.
**Akşam yemeği için bir masa ayırtmak istiyorum.**
ahks**hahm** yehmeh-yee eecheen beer **mah-**sah ah-
yırtmahk eesteeyoroom

### We'll come at eight.
**Saat sekizde geliriz.**
sah-**aht** sehk(y)eezdeh g(y)ehl**ee**reez

### My name is …
**(Benim) adım …**
(behneem) ahdım …

### I've reserved a table for four.
**Dört kişilik bir masa ayırtmıştım.**
dört k(y)eesheeleek beer **mah-**sah ah-yırtmıshtım

## Ordering Sipariş

**Waiter / Waitress!**
**Garson!**
gahrson

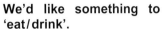

**We'd like something to 'eat / drink'.**
**'Yemek / İçmek' için bir şey istiyoruz.**
'yeh**mehk** / eech**mehk**' eecheen beer **shay** eesteeyorooz

**May I see the menu, please?**
**Mönüye bakabilir miyim, lütfen?**
mönew-yeh bahkahbee**leer** mee-yeem, **lewt**fehn

**Do you have any local dishes?**
**Yerli yemekleriniz var mı?**
yehr**lee** yehmehklehreeneez **vahr** mı

**What do you recommend?**
**Ne tavsiye edersiniz?**
**neh** tahvsee-yeh ehdehrseeneez

**Could I have a … please?**
**Bir … alabilir miyim, lütfen?**
beer … ahlahbee**leer** mee-yeem **lewt**fehn

| fork | çatal | chah**tahl** |
| glass | bardak | bahr**dahk** |
| knife | bıçak | bı**chahk** |
| napkin | peçete | peh-**che**-teh |
| plate | tabak | tah**bahk** |
| spoon | kaşık | kah**shık** |

RESTORAN

**May I have some ...?**
**Biraz ... alabilir miyim?**
beerahz ... ahlahbee**leer** mee-yeem

| bread | ekmek | ehk**mehk** |
| lemon | limon | lee**mon** |
| salt | tuz | tooz |
| sugar | şeker | sheh**k(y)ehr** |
| vinegar | sirke | seer**k(y)eh** |

**Without 'sauce / oil', please.**
**'Sossuz (Salçasız) / Yağsız' (olsun), lütfen.**
'**sos**-sooz (sahl**chah**sız) / **yahw**sız' (olsoon) **lewt**fehn

**I'd like some more.**
**Biraz daha rica ediyorum.**
beerahz dah**hah** ree-**jah** ehdeeyoroom

**Nothing more, thanks.**
**Bu kadar yeter, teşekkür ederim.**
**boo** kahdahr yeh**tehr**, teh-shehk-**kewrr** ehdehreem

**I'm on a special diet.**
**Özel bir rejimdeyim.**
ö**zehl** beer reh**zheem**deh-yeem

**I mustn't eat food containing ...**
**... içeren yemekler yememeliyim.**
... eecherehn yehmehklehr **yeh**mehmeh-lee-yeem

| fat | yağ | yahw |
| flour | un | oon |
| salt | tuz | tooz |
| sugar | şeker | sheh**k(y)ehr** |

**Do you have any vegetarian dishes?**
**Vejetaryen yemekleriniz var mı?**
veh-zhehtahr**yehn** yehmehklehreeneez **vahr** mı

RESTAURANT

**Do you have … for diabetics?**
**Şeker hastaları için ... var mı?**
sheh**k(y)ehr** hahstahlahrı eecheen … **vahr** mı

| **a special menu** | **özel bir mönü** | **özehl** beer mönew |
| **cakes** | **pasta** | pahstah |
| **fruit juice** | **meyve suyu** | may**veh** sooyoo |

**Can I have artificial sweetener?**
**Yapay tatlandırıcı (Sakarin) alabilir miyim?**
yah-**pai** tahtlahndırıjı (sahkahreen) ahlahbee**leer** mee-yeem

**Where are the toilets?**
**Tuvaletler nerede?**
toovahleht**lehr neh**rehdeh

**What would you like?**
**Ne arzu edersiniz?**
**neh** ahrzoo ehdehrseeneez

**Would you like …?**
**... ister misiniz?**
… ees**tehr** meesee-neez

**What would you like to drink ?**
**Ne içersiniz?**
**neh** eecherr-seeneez

**I recommend this.**
**Bunu tavsiye ederim.**
boo**noo** tahvsee-yeh ehdehreem

**Would you like to try …?**
**... denemek (tatmak) ister miydiniz?**
… dehnehmehk (tahtmahk) ees**tehr** meeydeeneez

## Breakfast and Tea
### Kahvaltı ve Çay

**I'd like breakfast, please.**
**Kahvaltı istiyorum, lütfen.**
kahhvahltı eesteeyoroom **lewt**fehn

**I'll have (a/an/some) ...**
**(Bir/Biraz) ... alırım.**
(beer/beerahz) ... ahlırım

| | | |
|---|---|---|
| eggs | yumurta | yoomoor**tah** |
| soft-boiled egg | rafadan yumurta | |
| | rahfah**dahn** yoomoortah | |
| hard-boiled egg | katı yumurta | kahtı yoomoortah |
| fruit juice | meyve suyu | may**veh** sooyoo |
| grapefruit | greyfurt (suyu) | gray**foort** (sooyo) |
| ham and eggs | jambon ve yumurta | |
| | zhahm-**bon** veh yoomoor**tah** | |
| jam | reçel | reh**chel** |
| marmalade | marmelat | mahrmeh**laht** |
| orange | portakal suyu | portah**kahl** sooyoo |
| toast | kızarmış ekmek | kızahr**mish** ehkmehk |
| yoghurt | yoğurt | yohw**oort** |

**May I have some ...?** **... alabilir miyim?**
... ahlahbee**leer** mee-yeem

| | | |
|---|---|---|
| bread | ekmek | ehk**mehk** |
| butter | tereyağı | teh**reh**-yahwı |
| cheese | peynir | pay**neer** |
| coffee | kahve | kahh**veh** |
| black | koyu | ko**yoo** |
| decaffeinated | kafeinsiz | kahfeheen**seez** |
| with milk | sütlü | sewt**lew** |
| honey | bal | bahl |
| hot chocolate | sütlü kakao | sewt**lew** kahkaho |

| milk | **süt** | sewt |
|------|---------|------|
| cold | **soğuk** | sohwook |
| hot | **sıcak** | sıjahk |
| olives | **zeytin** | zayteen |
| pepper | **karabiber** | kahrahbeebehr |
| rolls | **küçük ekmek(ler)** | |
| | k(y)ewchewk | ehkmehk(lehr) |
| salt | **tuz** | tooz |
| sugar | **şeker** | shehk(y)ehr |
| tea | **çay** | chai |
| with lemon | **limonlu** | leemonloo |
| with milk | **sütlü** | sewtlew |

## Drinks İçkiler

**What will you have to drink?**
İçecek ne alırsınız?
eechejehk **neh** ahlırsınız

**I'd like a glass of 'vodka / gin and tonic'.**
Bir bardak 'votka / cin-tonik' rica ediyorum.
beer bahrdahk '**vot**kah / jeen-to**neek**' ree-**jah**
ehdeeyoroom

**A (double) whisky, please.**
Bir (duble) viski, lütfen.
beer (doobleh) **vees**k(y)ee **lewt**fehn

| a bottle | bir şişe | **beer** sheesheh |
|----------|----------|-------------------|
| a double | bir duble | **beer** doobleh |
| a glass | bir bardak | **beer** bahrdahk |
| double | duble | **doob**leh |
| half a bottle | yarım şişe | **yah**rım sheesheh |
| neat (straight) | sek | sehk |
| on the rocks | buzlu | **booz**loo |
| single | tek | tehk |

RESTORAN

| with fruit juice | meyve suyuyla | mayveh sooyooylah |
| with soda | sodayla | so-dai-lah |
| with water | suyla | sooylah |

| Cheers! | Şerefe! | shehrehfeh |
| Your health! | Sağlığınıza! | sahwlıınızah |

## I'd like a bottle of (local) wine, please.
**Bir şişe (yöresel / yerli) şarap rica ediyorum.**
**beer** sheesheh (yöreh**sehl** / yehr**lee**) shah**rahp** ree-**jah** ehdeeyoroom

## What's this wine called?
**Bu şarabın adı nedir?**
**boo** shahrahbın ahdı **neh**deer

| white wine | beyaz şarap | beh-**yahz** shahrahp |
| red wine | kırmızı şarap | kırmızı shahrahp |
| half a bottle | yarım şişe | yah**rım** sheesheh |
| a glass | bir bardak | **beer** bahrdahk |
| a carafe | bir sürahi | **beer** sewrahhee |
| light | hafif | hah**feef** |
| dry | sek | sehk |
| sweet | tatlı | tahtlı |
| sparkling | köpüklü | köpewk**lew** |
| at room temperature | oda ısısında | odah ısısındah |
| chilled | soğutulmuş | sohwootool**moosh** |

## Please bring me another ...
**Bir ... daha getirir misiniz, lütfen?**
**beer** ... dah**hah** g(y)ehtee**reer** meesee-neez **lewt**fehn

## Please bring me some champagne.
**Şampanya getirir misiniz, lütfen?**
shahm**pahn**-yah g(y)ehtee**reer** meesee-neez **lewt**fehn

RESTAURANT

**I'd like a glass of water, please.**
**Bir bardak su rica ediyorum.**
**beer** bahrdahk **soo** ree-**jah** ehdeeyoroom

**I'd like a 'mineral water/fruit juice', please.**
**Bir 'maden suyu/meyve suyu' rica ediyorum.**
beer 'mah**dehn** sooyoo / may**veh** sooyoo' ree-**jah** ehdeeyoroom

**A cup of 'tea/coffee', please.**
**Bir fincan 'çay/kahve', lütfen.**
**beer** feenjahn '**chai**/kahh**veh**', **lewt**fehn

## Complaints  Şikâyetler

**There's a 'glass/plate' missing.**
**Bir 'bardak/tabak' eksik.**
beer 'bahr**dahk**/tah**bahk**' ehkseek

**This isn't what I ordered.**
**Bu ısmarladığım şey değil.**
**boo** ısmahrlahdıim shay deh-**yeel**

**I don't have a 'spoon/fork/ knife'.**
**'Kaşığım / Çatalım / Bıçağım' yok.**
'kahshıım/chahtahlım/bıchahwım' yok

**I don't like this.**
**Bunu beğenmedim.**
boo**noo** beh-**yehn**mehdeem

**This is too 'salty/sour/spicy'.**
**Bu çok 'tuzlu/ekşi/baharatlı'.**
boo **choke** 'toozloo/ehkshee/bahhahrahtlı'

| The meat is ... | Et ... | eht ... |
|---|---|---|
| overdone | çok pişmiş | **choke** peeshmeesh |
| too rare | çok çiğ | **choke** chee(y) |
| tough | sert | sehrt |
| underdone | az pişmiş | **ahz** peeshmeesh |

**The food is cold.**
Yemek soğuk.
yehmehk sohw**ook**

**This is stale.**
Bu bayat.
boo bah-**yaht**

**This 'plate/knife/spoon/glass' isn't clean.**
Bu 'tabak/bıçak/kaşık/bardak' temiz değil.
boo 'tah**bahk**/bıc**hahk**/kah**shık**/bahr**dahk**' tehmeez
deh-**yeel**

## Paying   Hesap ödeme

**The bill, please!**
Hesap, lütfen !
heh**sahp** lewt**fehn**

**I'd like to pay.**
Hesabı ödemek istiyorum.
heh**sahbı** ödeh**mehk** eesteeyoroom

**May we have separate bills?**
Ayrı hesaplar alabilir miyiz?
ai-**rı** hehsahp**lahr** ahlahbee**leer**
mee-yeez

**Does it include service?**
Servisi içeriyor mu?/Servis dahil mi?
sehr**veesee** eeche**ree**yor moo/sehr**veess** daa**heel**
mee

**RESTORAN**

**I think there's a mistake in this bill.**
Sanırım bu hesapta bir yanlışlık var.
sahnırım **boo** hehsahptah beer yahnlıshlık vahr

**I didn't have 'soup/chicken'.**
'Çorba/Tavuk' almadım.
'chore-bah/tahvook' **ahl**mahdım

**Can I pay by credit card?**
Kredi kartı ile ödeyebilir miyim?
kreh**dee** kahrtı eeleh ödeh-yehbee**leer** mee-yeem

**Keep the change.**
Üstü kalsın.
ews-tu kahl**sın**

**That was delicious.**
Çok güzeldi.
**choke** gewzehldee

**We enjoyed it. Thank you.**
Beğendik. Teşekkür ederiz.
beh-yehn**deek**. teh-shehk-**kewrr** ehdehreez

# Restaurant Vocabulary
## Restoran Sözlüğü

| az pişmiş | **ahz** peeshmeesh | rare |
|---|---|---|
| az şekerli | **ahz** shehk(y)ehrlee | slightly sweet |
| baharat | bahhah**raht** | seasoning (spice) |
| bahşiş | bahh**sheesh** | tip |
| bardak | bahr**dahk** | glass |
| bıçak | bı**chahk** | knife |
| biber | bee**behr** | pepper |
| çatal | chah**tahl** | fork |
| ekmek | ehk**mehk** | bread |
| fincan | feen**jahn** | cup |
| fincan tabağı | feen**jahn** tahbahwı | saucer |
| garson | gahr**son** | waiter, waitress |
| hardal | hahr**dahl** | mustard |

**RESTAURANT**

RESTORAN

| | | |
|---|---|---|
| **kaşık** | kah**shık** | spoon |
| **kül tablası** | **k(y)ewl** tahblahsı | ashtray |
| **kürdan** | k(y)ewr**dahn** | toothpick |
| **limon** | lee**mon** | lemon |
| **masa** | **mah**-sah | table |
| **masa örtüsü** | mah-**sah** ör-tu-sew | tablecloth |
| **peçete** | peh-**che**-teh | napkin |
| **sirke** | seer**k(y)eh** | vinegar |
| **sos** | sos | sauce |
| **sulu yemek** | soo**loo** yehmehk | home cooking |
| **şef garson** | **shehf** gahrson | headwaiter |
| **şeker** | sheh**k(y)ehr** | sugar |
| **tabak** | tah**bahk** | plate |
| **tas, kâse** | tahss, k(y)aa**seh** | bowl |
| **tereyağı** | teh**reh**-yahwı | butter |
| **tuz** | tooz | salt |
| **vestiyer** | vehstee**yehr** | cloakroom |
| **yağ** | yahw | oil |
| **zeytinyağı** | zay**teen**-yahwı | olive oil |

## The menu Mönü

## *Mezeler* *Starters (Appetizers)*

'Meze' is the general category of successive small dishes that begin the Turkish meal. These are eaten, along with wine or raki, until the main course is served. Meze specialties exalt the originality and skill of a restaurant.

RESTAURANT

RESTORAN

A typical meze menu includes dried and marinated mackerel; fresh salad greens in thick yogurt sauce with garlic; plates of cold vegetable dishes, cooked or fried in olive oil; savory deep-fried mussels and calamari; tomato and cucumber salad; fish eggs; marinated stuffed aubergine; red lentil balls; and peppers with spices and nuts.

| | | |
|---|---|---|
| **ançüez** | ahnchew-**ehz** | anchovies |
| **beyaz peynir** | beh-**yahz** payneer | |
| | **medium soft-brined cheese** | |
| **beyin salatası** | beh-**yeen** sahlahtahsı | brain salad |
| **böbrek** | böb**rehk** | kidneys |
| **cacık** | jahjık | |
| | **whipped yogurt with garlic, oil and cucumber** | |
| **ciğer** | jee**(y)ehr** | liver |
| **çerkez peyniri** | cherr-**k(y)ehz** payneeree | |
| | **buffalo cheese** | |
| **deniz ürünleri kokteyli** | dehneez ewrewnlehree koktay**lee** | |
| | **seafood cocktail** | |
| **dil** | deel | tongue |
| **domuz pastırması** | domooz pahss-tırmahsı | bacon |
| **enginar** | ehng(y)ee**nahr** | artichoke |
| **havyar** | hahv**yahr** | caviar |
| **ıstakoz** | ıstah**koz** | lobster |
| **istiridye** | eestee**reed**yeh | oysters |
| **jambon** | zhahm-**bon** | ham |
| **kalamar** | kahlah**mahr** | calamary |
| **(taze / eski) kaşar peyniri** | | |
| (taa**zeh** / ehs**k(y)ee**) kah**shahr** payneeree | | |
| **(fresh / mature) firm yellowish cheese** | | |
| **kavun** | kah**voon** | melon |
| **kılıç balığı füme** | kılıch bahlıı **few**meh | |
| | **smoked swordfish** | |
| **köfte** | köf**teh** | rissole |
| **midye** | **meed**yeh | mussels |

RESTAURANT

RESTORAN

| pastırma | **pahss-tırmah** | pastrami |
|---|---|---|
| patlıcan salatası | pahtlıjahn sahlahtahsı | |
| | **aubergine salad, aubergine purée** | |
| pavurya | pahvooryah | **crab** |
| peynir | payneer | **cheese** |
| piyaz | peeyahz | **haricot bean salad** |
| salyangoz | sahlyahngoz | **snails** |
| sardalya | sahrdahlyah | **sardines** |
| som balığı füme | som bahllı fewmeh | **smoked salmon** |
| sosis | sosees | **sausage** |
| ton balığı | ton bahllı | **tuna fish** |
| tulum peyniri | tooloom payneeree | |
| | **dry, salty goat's milk cheese** | |
| turşu | toorshoo | **pickle** |
| yeşil zeytin | yehsheel zayteen | **green olives** |
| yılan balığı füme | yılahn bahllı fewmeh | **smoked eel** |
| yoğurt | yohwoort | **yoghurt** |
| zeytin | zayteen | **olives** |

## *Soups* Çorbalar

| bezelye çorbası | behzehl-yeh chore-bahsı **pea soup** |
|---|---|
| domates çorbası | domahtehss chore-bahsı **tomato soup** |
| et suyuna çorba | eht sooyoonah chore-**bah** **broth** |
| fasulye çorbası | fahsool-yeh chore-bahsı **bean soup** |
| havuç çorbası | hahvooch chore-bahsı **carrot soup** |
| irmik çorbası | eermeek chore-bahsı **semolina soup** |
| kereviz çorbası | k(y)ehrehveez chore-bahsı **celery soup** |
| mercimek çorbası | mehrjeemehk chore-bahsı **lentil soup** |

RESTAURANT

| | | |
|---|---|---|
| **pirinç çorbası** | peereench chore-bahsı **rice soup** | |
| **sebze çorbası** | sehbzeh chore-bahsı **vegetable soup** | |
| **tavuk çorbası** | tahvook chore-bahsı **chicken soup** | |
| **tavuk suyu** | tahvook sooyoo **chicken consommé** | |
| **un çorbası** | oon chore-bahsı **flour soup** | |

## *Meat* Et

| | | |
|---|---|---|
| **biftek** | beeftehk | **steak** |
| **bonfile** | bonfeeleh | **beefsteak** |
| **böbrek** | böbrehk | **kidney** |
| **ciğer** | jee(y)ehr | **liver** |
| **dana eti** | dahnah ehtee | **veal** |
| **dana pirzola** | dahnah peerzolah | **veal cutlet(s)** |
| **fileto** | feelehto | **fillet** |
| **göğüs** | göews | **breast** |
| **kıyma** | kıymah | **mince** |
| **koyun eti** | koyoon ehtee | **mutton** |
| **köfte** | köfteh | **rissole** |
| **kuzu (eti)** | koozoo (ehtee) | **lamb** |
| **pirzola** | peerzolah | **chop** |
| **sığır eti** | sıır ehtee | **beef** |

| | | |
|---|---|---|
| **haşlama** | hahshlahmah | **stew** |
| **koyun haşlama** | koyoon hahshlahmah | **mutton stew** |
| **koyun rosto** | koyoon rosto | **roast mutton** |
| **kuzu rosto** | koozoo rosto | **roast lamb** |
| **tas kebap** | tahss k(y)ehbahp | **goulash** |

## *Fish and Seafood*
*Balık ve Deniz ürünleri*

Turkey offers a large variety of freshly caught seafood. Seafood is delicious, but it's also expensive.

| | | |
|---|---|---|
| **alabalık** | ah**lah**bahlık | trout |
| **barbunya** | bahr**boon**-yah | red mullet |
| **dil balığı** | **deel** bahlıı | sole |
| **gümüş balığı** | gew**mewsh** bahlıı | sand smelt |
| **hamsi** | hahm**see** | anchovies |
| **ıstakoz** | ıstah**koz** | lobster |
| **istavrit** | eestah**vreet** | horse macker |
| **istiridye** | eestee**reed**yeh | oysters |
| **kalkan** | kahl**kahn** | turbot |
| **karagöz** | kahrah**göz** | black bream |
| **karides** | kah**ree**dehs | shrimp, prawns |
| **kefal, tekir** | k(y)eh**fahl**, tehk**(y)eer** | mullet |
| **kılıç balığı** | kı**lıch** bahlıı | swordfish |
| **kırlangıç balığı** | kırlahn**gıch** bahlıı | gurnard |
| **lakerda** | lahk**(y)ehr**dah | salted tuna |
| **levrek** | lehv**rehk** | sea bass |
| **lüfer** | lew**fehr** | blue fish |
| **mercan** | mehr**jahn** | red sea bream |
| **mezgit** | mehzg**(y)eet** | whiting, haddock |
| **midye** | **meed**yeh | mussels |
| **morina** | mor**ee**nah | cod |
| **pavurya** | pah**voor**yah | crab |
| **pisi balığı** | pee**see** bahlıı | plaice, halibut |
| **ringa balığı** | **reen**gah bahlıı | herring |

| | | |
|---|---|---|
| **sardalye** | sahr**dahl**yeh | sardines |
| **sazan** | sah**zahn** | carp |
| **som balığı (somon)** | som bahlıı (somon) | salmon |
| **tekir** | tehk(y)eer | striped mullet |
| **ton balığı** | **ton** bahlıı | tuna fish |
| **turna** | **toor**nah | pike |
| **uskumru** | oos**koom**roo | mackerel |
| **yılan balığı** | yı**lahn** bahlıı | eel |
| **zargana** | **zahr**gahnah | garfish |

## *Egg dishes* *Yumurtalı yemekler*

**haşlanmış yumurta** hahshlahn**mış** yoomoortah
**boiled eggs**

| **katı** | **kah**tı | hard |
| **rafadan** | rahfah**dahn** | soft |

**çılbır** chılbır **poached eggs with yoghurt**

**omlet** om**leht** **omelette**
  **peynirli omlet** payneer**lee** ohmleht
  **omelette with cheese**

  **yeşillikli omlet** yehsheelleek**lee** ohmleht
  **omelette with herbs**

  **ıspanaklı omlet** ıspahnahklı ohmleht **spinach omelette**

  **mantarlı omlet** mahntahrlı ohmleht
  **omelette with mushrooms**

**yağda (sahanda) yumurta** fried eggs
yahw**dah** (sah-hahn**dah**) yoomoortah

## *Vegetables-Salads* *Sebzeler-Salatalar*

| | | |
|---|---|---|
| **bakla** | bahk**lah** | broad beans |
| **bamya** | **bah**myah | okra |
| **bezelye** | beh**zehl**yeh | peas |

RESTORAN

| biber | bee**behr** | **peppers** |
|---|---|---|
| **çalı fasulyesi** | chah**lı** fah**sool**yehsee | **string beans** |
| **çoban salatası** | cho**bahn** sah**lah**tahsı | |
| | **tomato, cucumber and onion salad** | |
| domates | do**mah**tehs | **tomatoes** |
| **domates salatası** | do**mah**tehss sah**lah**tahsı | |
| | **tomato salad** | |
| enginar | ehng(y)ee**nahr** | **artichoke** |
| fasulye | fah**sool**yeh | **beans** |
| havuç | hah**vooch** | **carrots** |
| **havuç salatası** | hah**vooch** sah**lah**tahsı | **carrot salad** |
| ıspanak | ıspah**nahk** | **spinach** |
| kabak | kah**bahk** | **pumpkin** |
| **kapuska, lahana** | kah**poos**kah, l(y)ah**hah**nah | **cabbage** |
| **karışık salata** | kah**rı**shık sah**lah**tah | **mixed salad** |
| karnabahar | kah**rnah**bah**hahr** | **cauliflower** |
| **karnabahar salatası** | kah**rnah**bah**hahr** sah**lah**tası | |
| | **cauliflower salad** | |
| kereviz | k(y)ehreh**veez** | **celery** |
| **kereviz salatası** | k(y)ehreh**veez** sah**lah**tahsı | |
| | **celery salad** | |
| kestane | k(y)ehstaa**neh** | **chestnuts** |
| kuşkonmaz | kooshkon**mahz** | **asparagus** |
| mantar | mahn**tahr** | **mushrooms** |
| marul | mah**rool** | **lettuce** |
| **marul salatası** | mah**rool** sah**lah**tahsı | **lettuce salad** |
| mercimek | mehrjee**mehk** | **lentils** |
| **mevsim salatası** | mehv**seem** sah**lah**tahsı | |
| | **salad of the season** | |
| mısır | mı**sır** | **sweet corn** |
| pancar | pahn**jahr** | **beetroot** |
| **pancar salatası** | pahn**jahr** sah**lah**tahsı | **beetroot salad** |
| patates | pah**tah**tehs | **potatoes** |
| **patates salatası** | pah**tah**tehss sah**lah**tahsı | **potato salad** |
| patlıcan | pah**tlı**jahn | **eggplant (aubergine)** |
| **patlıcan salatası** | pah**tlı**jahn sah**lah**tahsı | |
| | **aubergine(eggplant) salad** | |
| pırasa | pı**rah**sah | **leeks** |

RESTAURANT

| | | |
|---|---|---|
| **pirinç** | peereench | rice |
| **piyaz** | peeyahz | haricot bean salad |
| **rus salatası** | roos sahlahtahsı | diced vegetable salad |
| **sakız kabağı** | sahkız kahbahwı | marrow |
| **salatalık (hıyar)** | sahlahtahlık (hıyahr) | cucumber |
| **sarımsak** | sahrımsahk | garlic |
| **semizotu** | sehmeezotoo | purslane |
| **semizotu salatası** | sehmeezotoo sahlahtahsı | |
| | purslane salad | |
| **soğan** | sohwahn | onions |
| **şalgam** | shahlgahm | turnip |
| **tatlı biber** | tahtlı beebehr | sweet peppers |
| **taze fasulye** | tahzeh fahsoolyeh | green beans |
| **taze soğan** | tahzeh sohwahn | spring onions |
| **turp** | toorp | radish |
| **turp salatası** | toorp sahlahtahsı | radish salad |
| **yeşil salata** | yehsheel sahlahtah | green salad |

## *Game and Poultry*
*Av ve kümes hayvanları*

| | | |
|---|---|---|
| **bıldırcın** | bıldırjın | quail |
| **hindi** | heendee | turkey |
| **keklik** | k(y)ehkleek | partridge |
| **sülün** | sewlewn | pheasant |
| **tavuk** | tahvook | chicken |
| **yaban domuzu** | yahbahn domoozoo | wild boar |
| **yaban kazı** | yahbahn kahzı | wild goose |
| **yaban ördeği** | yahbahn ördeh-yee | wild duck |
| **yaban tavşanı** | yahbahn tahvshahnı | hare |

## *Pastry* *Hamurişi*

| | | |
|---|---|---|
| **börek** | börehk | dumpling |
| **etli / meyveli börek** | ehtlee / mayvehlee börehk | pie |
| **kıymalı börek** | kıymahlı börehk | minced meat pie |
| **otlu börek** | otloo börehk | herb dumplings |
| **patatesli börek** | pahtahtehslee börehk | potato dumplings |

| makarna | mahkahrnah | macaroni |
| mantı | mahntı | ravioli |

## *Desserts and Cakes*
*Tatlılar ve Pastalar*

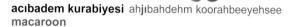

**acıbadem kurabiyesi** ahjıbahdehm koorahbeeyehsee
**macaroon**

**aşure** ahshooreh
**a pudding** made from cereals, dried and fresh fruits, nuts, sugar and spices

| komposto | komposto | **stewed fruit** |
| baklava | bahklahvah | |

**a Turkish dessert** made of paper-thin layers of pastry, chopped nuts and honey. One of the most well-known sweets associated with Turkish cuisine

**bülbül yuvası** bewlbewl yoovahsı
**(nightingale's nest) pastry** filled with a pistachio and walnut purée

| dondurma | dondoormah | ice cream |
| karışık | kahrıshık | assorted |
| sade | saadeh | ice cream |
| meyveli | mayvehlee | sorbet (sherbet) |
| elmalı pasta | ehlmahlı pahstah | apple cake |
| fındıklı pasta | fındıklı pahstah | nut cake |
| gözleme | gözlehmeh | pancake |
| güllaç | gewllahch | rose-flavoured pudding |
| helva | hehlvah | |

**a sweetmeat** dessert made by pan-sautéing flour, semolina and pine nuts in butter, sugar and water

**kabak tatlısı** kahbahk tahtlısı
**a dessert** made by cooking pieces of pumpkin in syrup

**kadayıf** kahdah-yıf
**finely-shredded pastry** baked in syrup

**kadın göbeği tatlısı** kahdın göbeh-yee tahtlısı **doughnut**
**krem karamel** krehm kahrahmehl **creme caramel**

**kazan dibi** kah**zahn** deebee **caramelized milk puding**
**keşkül** kehsh**kewl**
a milk pudding made from coconuts

**krem şokola** krehm sho**ko**lah **chocolate pudding**
**lokum** lo**koom**
a Turkish delight made from sugar, cornstarch, gelatin and grape juice

| | | |
|---|---|---|
| **meyveli pasta** | mayveh**lee** pahstah | **fruit cake** |
| **meyve salatası** | may**veh** sahlahtahsı | **fruit salad** |
| **muhallebi, puding** | moohahlleh**bee**, **poo**deeng | **pudding** |
| **peynir pastası** | pay**neer** pahstahsı | **cheesecake** |
| **revani** | reh**vaa**nee | (a soft) **semolina cake** |
| **sufle** | soof**leh** | **soufflé** |
| **şekerpare** | shehk(y)ehrpaa**reh** | |

baked biscuits with sugary syrup

**tahin** taa**heen**
a thick paste made of ground sesame seeds

**tavuk göğsü** tah**vook** göösew
**chicken breast pudding**

| | | |
|---|---|---|
| **turta, pasta** | toor**tah** | **tart** |
| **yoğurt** | yohw**oort** | **yoghurt** |

## *Fruit* Meyve ve Yemiş

| | | |
|---|---|---|
| **ahududu** | ahh**oo**doodoo | **raspberries** |
| **ananas** | ahnah**nahss** | **pineapple** |
| **armut** | ahr**moot** | **pear** |
| **ayva** | ai-**vah** | **quince** |
| **badem** | bah**dehm** | **almond** |
| **bektaşi üzümü** | behktah**shee** ewzewmew | **gooseberries** |
| **böğürtlen** | böewrt**lehn** | **blackberries** |
| **ceviz** | jeh**veez** | **walnuts** |
| **çilek** | chee**lehk** | **strawberries** |
| **dut** | doot | **mulberries** |
| **elma** | ehl**mah** | **apple** |
| **erik** | eh**reek** | **plums** |
| **fındık** | fındık | **hazelnuts** |

RESTORAN

| frenk üzümü | frehnk ewzewmew | blackcurrants |
|---|---|---|
| incir | eenjeer | figs |
| karpuz | kahrpooz | watermelon |
| hindistan cevizi | heendeestahn jehveezee | coconut |
| hurma | hoormah | dates |
| kavun | kahvoon | melon |
| kayısı | kah-yısı | apricot |
| kiraz | k(y)eerahz | cherries |
| mandalina | mahndahleenah | tangerine, mandarin |
| muz | mooz | banana |
| nar | nahr | pomegranate |
| portakal | portahkahl | orange |
| şeftali | shehftahlee | peach |
| üzüm | ewzewm | grapes |

## *Spices and Herbs*
*Baharatlar ve Otlar*

| hardal | hahrdahl | mustard |
|---|---|---|
| karabiber | kahrahbeebehr | black pepper |
| kekik | k(y)ehk(y)eek | thyme |
| kırmızı biber | kırmızı beebehr | red pepper (chilli) |
| kimyon | k(y)eemyon | cumin |
| maydanoz | mydahnoz | parsley |
| nane | nahneh | mint |
| sarımsak | sahrımsahk | garlic |
| tuz | tooz | salt |

## *Drinks* İçkiler

| ayran | ai-rahn | |
|---|---|---|

a Turkish drink made from beaten yogurt, cold water and salt

| bira | beerah | beer |
|---|---|---|
| buzlu çay | boozloo chai | iced tea |
| cin-tonik | jeen-toneek | gin and tonic |
| çay | chai | tea |
| sütlü çay | sewtlew chai | tea with milk |

RESTAURANT

| | | |
|---|---|---|
| **elma suyu** | ehl**mah** sooyoo | apple juice |
| **elma şarabı** | ehl**mah** shahrahbı | cider |
| **İspanyol şarabı** | eespahn**yol** shahrahbı | sherry |
| **kahve** | kahh**veh** | coffee |
| **konyak** | kohn**yahk** | brandy |
| **likör** | lee**kör** | liqueur |
| **limonata** | leemo**nah**tah | lemonade |
| **maden suyu** | mah**dehn** sooyoo | mineral water |
| **meyve suyu** | may**veh** sooyoo | fruit juice |
| **portakal suyu** | portah**kahl** sooyoo | orangeade |
| **porto** | **por**to | port |
| **rakı** | rah**kı** | |

the anise-flavoured, stirred, national Turkish drink. Sometimes referred to as 'lion's milk' because of its intense flavour

| | | |
|---|---|---|
| **rom** | rom | rum |
| **salep** | sah**lehp** | |

a popular drink made from powdered iris root

| | | |
|---|---|---|
| **soda** | **so**dah | soda water |
| **su** | soo | water |
| **süt** | sewt | milk |
| **şarap** | shah**rahp** | wine |
| **açık, bardakla** | ah-**chık**, bahr**dahk**lah | open, by glass |
| **beyaz** | beh-**yahz** | white |
| **kırmızı** | kırmızı | red |
| **sek** | sehk | dry |
| **tatlı** | tahtlı | sweet |
| **vermut** | vehr**moot** | vermouth |
| **viski** | **vees**k(y)ee | whisky (whiskey) |
| **votka** | **vot**kah | vodka |

RESTORAN

## *Some cooking methods*
*Bazı yemek yapma yöntemleri*

| buğulama | boohwoolah**mah** | steamed |
|---|---|---|
| dolma | dol**mah** | stuffed |
| fırında | fırın**dah** | baked |
| haşlama | hahshlah**mah** | poached |
| ızgara | ızgah**rah** | grilled |
| kızarmış | kızahr**mış** | roasted |
| yağda kızarmış | yah**wdah** kızahrmış | fried |

**tandır** tahn**dır**   **a beehive-shaped oven** used to bake 'pide' and other Turkish breads

**tava** tah**vah**   **a Turkish term** referring to a frying pan, or food that has been breaded and fried

**sarma** sahr**mah**  **a generic Turkish term** that refers to any dish of wrapped grape or cabbage leaves. Fillings are either minced meat or rice.

## Some Traditional Turkish Meals
Bazı Geleneksel Türk yemekleri

### Dolma   dol**mah**
The generic term for stuffed vegetables; a derivative of the Turkish verb 'doldurmak' meaning 'to fill' or 'to stuff'. The most commonly used vegetables are zucchini, aubergine, tomatoes, cabbage and vine leaves.

RESTAURANT

**Biber dolması**     bee**behr** dolmahsı
Stuffed peppers

**Domates dolması**     do**mah**tehss dolmahsı
Stuffed tomatoes

**Kabak dolması**     kah**bahk** dolmahsı
Stuffed vegetable marrow

**Midye dolması**     meed-**yeh** dolmahsı
Minced mussels with rice and onions

**Fırında arpa şehriyesi**
fırındah ahr**pah** shehhreeyehsee
Baked oat noodles

**İmam Bayıldı**   eemahm bah-yıl**dı**
Eggplant cooked in olive oil

**Kavurma**   kahvoor**mah**
Small cubes of braised, browned lamb. Served in stews.

**Kebap**   k(y)eh**bahp**
Marinated and spiced small pieces of poultry, fish, ground meat or vegetables, skewered and grilled in a tandir

**Adana kebap**     ahdah**nah** k(y)ehbahp
Spicy skewered ground meat, named after the southern city where it originated.

**Döner Kebap**   dö**nehr** k(y)ehbahp
A Turkish kebab made by stacking alternating layers of ground meat and sliced leg of lamb on a large upright skewer, then slowly rotating them in front of vertical grills. As the outer layer of the meat is roasted, thin slices are shaved and served.

**Şiş Kebap**   sheesh k(y)ehbahp
Grilled cubes of skewered meat.

**Kıymalı su böreği**   kıymahlı **soo** böreh-yee
Minced meat pie

**Kuzu güveç** koo**zoo** gewvehch
Lamb stew with garlic, onions, tomatoes, potatoes, dill and bay leaves

**Mantı** mah**ntı**
Small pasta dumplings of dough, filled with minced meat. Similar to ravioli, manti is traditionally complemented with generous servings of garlic yogurt, a dash of melted butter and paprika.

**Menemen** mehneh**mehn**
Eggs with tomato and pepper

**Pide** **pee**deh   Turkish-style pizza

**Pilaki** peel(y)a**kee**
A Turkish dish consisting of beans, onions and olive oil. Served with lemon.

**Pilav** peel**ahv**   A steamed rice dish often made with meat, shellfish or vegetables in a seasoned broth. Along with bread, pilav is another staple in Turkish cuisine. The most common versions are cracked-wheat and rice. The Turkish pilaff is distinguished by its smooth, soft buttery morsels of rice.

**Bulgur pilavı** bool**goor** peelah**vı**
Cracked wheat pilaw

**İç pilav** eech peel**ahv**
Fried chicken pilaw

**Kuzu pilav** koo**zoo** peel**ahv**
Lamb pilaw with raisins, pine nuts and onions

**Piyaz** pee**yahz**
A dried bean, egg and vegetable salad.

**Sucuk** soo**jook**
A Turkish cooked meat made from lamb and beef. Similar to pepperoni.

**Türlü** tur-**lew**   mixed vegetables

# SIGHTSEEING
## TURİSTİK GEZİ

## What are the main places of interest?
**Görülmeye değer (ilgi çekici) yerler nelerdir?**
görewl-meh-yeh deh-**yehr** [eel**g(y)ee** chek(y)eejee]
yehrlehr nehlehrdeer

## We are here for a 'day/week'.
**Bir 'günlüğüne/haftalığına' buradayız.**
**beer** 'gewnlewewneh/hahftahlıınah' **boo**rahdah-yız

## Is there 'a Turkish/an English'-speaking guide?
**'Türkçe/İngilizce' bilen bir rehber var mı?**
'**tewrk**-che / eeng(y)ee**leez**jeh' beelehn beer rehhbehr
**vahr** mı

## Can you recommend a sightseeing tour?
**Bir turistik tur önerebilir misiniz?**
beer tooreese**teek** toor önehrehbee**leer** meesee-neez

## What time does the tour start?
**Tur saat kaçta başlıyor?**
toor sah-aht kahch**tah** bahshlıyor

## Where do we leave from?
**Nereden hareket edeceğiz?**
**neh**rehdehn hahrehk(y)eht ehdehjeh-yeez

## Can the bus pick us up at the hotel?
**Otobüs bizi otelden alabilir mi?**
otobewss beezee otehldehn
ahlahbee**leer** mee

## What time do we get back?
**Ne zaman geri dönüyoruz?**
**neh** zahmahn g(y)ehree
dönewyorooz

**Where is/are the …?** ... nerededir?

... **neh**rehdehdeer

| | | |
|---|---|---|
| art gallery | Sanat galerisi | sah**naht** gahlehreesee |
| bazaar | Çarşı | chahr**shı** |
| castle | Şato | **shah**to |
| cathedral | Katedral | kahtehd**rahl** |
| cave | Mağara | mah-**ah**rah |
| church | Kilise | k(y)ee**lee**seh |
| city centre/downtown area | Şehir merkezi | |
| | | sheh-**heer** mehrk(y)eh**zee** |
| city walls | Surlar | soor**lahr** |
| concert hall | Konser salonu | kon**sehr** sahlonoo |
| exhibition | Sergi | sehr**g(y)ee** |
| factory | Fabrika | fahb**ree**kah |
| fair | Fuar | foo**ahr** |
| flea market | Bit pazarı | **beet** pahzahrı |
| fortress | Kale | kah**leh** |
| fountain | Çeşme | chesh-**meh** |
| harbour | Liman | lee**mahn** |
| lake | Göl | göl |
| library | Kütüphane | k(y)ewtewp-haa**neh** |
| market | Pazar | pah**zahr** |
| memorial | Anıt | **ah**nıt |
| monastery/convent | Manastır | mah**nahs**tır |
| monument | Abide | aabee**deh** |
| mosque | Cami | jaa**mee** |
| museum | Müze | **mew**zeh |
| old town | Eski şehir | ehs**k(y)ee** sheh-heer |
| opera house | Opera binası | o**peh**rah beenahsı |
| palace | Saray | sah-**rye** |
| park | Park | pahrk |
| parliament building | Parlamento binası | |
| | | pahrlah**mehn**to beenahsı |
| ruins | Harabeler | hahrahbeh**lehr** |
| shopping area | Alışveriş bölgesi | |
| | | ahlıshveh**reesh** bölg(y)ehsee |
| square | Meydan | may**dahn** |

TURISTIK GEZI

| | | |
|---|---|---|
| stadium | Stadyum | stahd**yoom** |
| statue | Heykel | heyk(y)ehl |
| stock exchange | Borsa | **bor**sah |
| temple | Tapınak | tahpınahk |
| theatre | Tiyatro | tee**yaht**ro |
| tower | Kule | **koo**leh |
| university | Üniversite | ewnee**vehr**seeteh |
| zoo | **Hayvanat bahçesi** | hai-vah**naht** bahh-chesee |

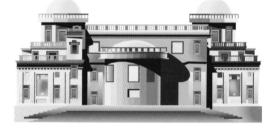

## Opening times   Açılış saatleri

**When is the museum open?**
**Müze ne zaman açıktır?**
mewzeh **neh** zahmahn ah-chıktır

**What time does the palace open?**
**Saray saat kaçta açılıyor?**
sah-rye sah-aht kahch**tah** ah-chılıyor

**Can we have a look?**
**Bir bakabilir miyiz?**
beer bahkahbee**leer** mee-yeez

**When does it close?**
**Saat kaçta kapanıyor?**
sah-aht kahch**tah** kahpahnıyor

SIGHTSEEING

**It's 'open/closed' today.**
**Bugün 'açıktır/kapalıdır'.**
boo-gewn 'ah**chık**tır/kahpah**lı**dır'

## Visiting places
Yerleri ziyaret etme

**Where is the ticket office?**
**Bilet gişesi nerededir?**
bee**leht** g(y)ee**sheh**see **neh**rehdehdeer

**How much is the entrance fee?**
**Giriş ücreti ne kadar?**
g(y)ee**reesh** ewjrehtee **neh** kahdahr

**Is there a reduction for …?**
**… için bir indirim var mı?**
… eecheen beer eendeereem **vahr** mı

| | | |
|---|---|---|
| **children** | **çocuklar** | chojook**lahr** |
| **groups** | **gruplar** | groop**lahr** |
| **pensioners** | **emekliler** | ehmehklee**lehr** |
| **students** | **öğrenciler** | öörehnjee**lehr** |
| **the disabled** | **özürlüler** | özewrlew**lehr** |

**Will there be a guide?**
**Rehber olacak mı?**
rehhbehr ohlah**jahk** mı

**Two adults and one child.**
**İki yetişkin ve bir çocuk.**
ee**k(y)ee** yehteeshk(y)een veh **beer** chojook

**Where can I get a catalogue?**
**Nereden bir katalog alabilirim?**
**neh**rehdehn beer kahtahlog ahlahbeeleereem

**Can we take photos?**
**Fotoğraf çekebilir miyiz?**
fotohw-rahf chek(y)ehbee**leer** mee-yeez

**Follow the guide, please.**
**Rehberi izleyin, lütfen.**
rehhbeh**ree** eezleh-yeen **lewt**fehn

| **What's that building?** | **When was it built?** |
|---|---|
| **Şu bina nedir?** | **Bu ne zaman yapıldı?** |
| shoo beenah **neh**deer | boo **neh** zahmahn yahpıldı |

| amazing | şaşırtıcı | shahshırtıjı |
|---|---|---|
| beautiful | güzel | gew**zehl** |
| gloomy | karanlık (kasvetli) | kahrahnlık (kahsveht**lee**) |
| impressive | etkileyici | ehtk(y)eeleh-yee**jee** |
| interesting | ilginç | eelg(y)eench |
| magnificent | görkemli | görk(y)ehm**lee** |
| pretty | sevimli | sehveem**lee** |
| strange | tuhaf | too**hahf** |
| tremendous | müthiş | mewt**heesh** |

**Who was the 'painter / sculptor / architect'?**
**'Ressam / Heykeltıraş / Mimar' kimdi?**
'rehss-**sahm** / heyk(y)ehltı**rahsh** / mee**mahr**'
k(y)eemdee

**When did 'he / she' live?**
**Ne zaman yaşadı?**
**neh** zahmahn yahshahdı

**Where's the house where**
**... lived?**
**...'nin yaşamış olduğu ev**
**nerededir?**
...'neen yahshah**mısh** oldoohwoo ehv **neh**rehdehdeer

I'm interested in …
**… ile ilgileniyorum.**
… eeleh eelg(y)eelehneeyoroom

| | | |
|---|---|---|
| antiques | Antika eşya | ahn**tee**kah ehs-yah |
| archaeology | Arkeoloji | ahrk(y)eholo**zhee** |
| art | Sanat | sah**naht** |
| botany | Botanik (Bitkibilim) | |
| | botah**neek** (beet**k(y)ee**beeleem) | |
| coins | Madeni paralar | mahdeh**nee** pahrahlahr |
| economics | Ekonomi | ehkono**mee** |
| fine arts | Güzel sanatlar | gew**zehl** sahnahtlahr |
| geology | Jeoloji | zheholo**zhee** |
| handicrafts | El sanatları | **ehl** sahnahtlahrı |
| history | Tarih | taa**reeh** |
| medicine | Tıp | tıp |
| music | Müzik | mew**zeek** |
| painting | Resim | reh**seem** |
| pottery | Çömlekçilik | chömlehkchee**leek** |
| religion | Din | **deen** |
| sculpture | Heykeltıraşlık | heyk(y)ehltırahsh**lık** |

Is it possible to buy a 'postcard / souvenir' here?
**Burada 'posta kartı / hatıralık eşya' almak olanaklı mı (mümkün mü) ?**
**boo**rahdah 'pos**tah** kahrtı / hahtırah**lık** ehs-yah' ahlmahk ohlahnahklı mı (mewm**k(y)ewn** mew)

# Countryside Kırsal Bölge

Is there a scenic route to …?
**…'ye izlenecek manzaralı bir yol var mı?**
…'yeh eezlehnehjehk **mahn**zahrahlı beer yol **vahr** mı

Can we get there on foot?
**Oraya yürüyerek gidebilir miyiz?**
**o**rah-yah yewrew**yeh**rehk g(y)eedehbee**leer** mee-yeez

TURİSTİK GEZİ

### How high is that mountain?
**Şu dağın yüksekliği ne kadardır?**
**shoo** dahwın yewksehklee(y)ee
**neh** kahdahrdır

### How far is it to …?
**… ne kadar uzaklıktadır?**
… **neh** kahdahr oozahklıktahdır

### What kind of 'animal/bird/flower/tree' is that?
**Bu ne tür bir 'hayvan/kuş/çiçek/ağaç?**
boo **neh** tewr beer 'hai-**vahn** / koosh / chee**chek** / ahw-**ahch**

| cliff | uçurum, yar | oochoo**room**, yahr |
|---|---|---|
| farm | çiftlik | cheeft**leek** |
| field | tarla | **tahr**lah |
| footpath | keçi yolu, patika | |
| | | k(y)eh**chee** yoloo, pah**tee**kah |
| forest | orman | or**mahn** |
| garden | bahçe | bahh-**cheh** |
| hill | tepe | teh**peh** |
| house | ev | ehv |
| lake | göl | göl |
| meadow | çayır, otlak | chah-**yır**, oht**lahk** |
| mountain | dağ | dahw |
| mountain pass | geçit | g(y)eh**cheet** |
| path | patika | pah**tee**kah |
| pond | gölcük, gölek | göl**jewk**, gö**lehk** |
| river | nehir, ırmak | neh**heer**, ır**mahk** |
| road | yol | yol |
| sea | deniz | deh**neez** |
| spring | kaynak | kai-**nahk** |
| village | köy | köy |
| vineyard | bağ | bahw |
| waterfall | çağlayan | chahw-lah-**yahn** |

SIGHTSEEING

# MAKING FRIENDS
## ARKADAŞ EDİNME

## Invitations Davetler

**There is a party. Are you coming?**
**Bir parti var. (Siz de) geliyor musunuz?**
beer pahr**tee** vahr. (seez **deh**) g(y)ehlee**yor** moosoonooz

**May I invite you to 'lunch / dinner?**
**Sizi 'öğle yemeğine / akşam yemeğine' davet edebilir miyim?**
seezee 'öö**leh** yehmeh-yeeneh / ahk**shahm** yehmeh-yeeneh daaveht ehdehbee**leer** mee-yeem

**That's very kind of you.**
**Çok naziksiniz.**
**choke** naazeekseeneez

**Great, I'd love to come.**
**Harika. Büyük bir zevkle gelirim.**
hahree**kah**. bew**yewk** beer zehvkleh g(y)ehleereem

**Next time you must come and visit us.**
**Gelecek sefere, sizi bize bekliyoruz.**
gehlehj**jehk** sehfehreh, see**zee** bee**zeh** behkleeyorooz

## Dating & Going out
Randevulaşma & Çıkma

**May I join you?**
**Size katılabilir miyim?**
seezeh kahtılahbee**leer** mee-yeem

**Why don't you join us?**
**Bize katılsanıza.**
beezeh kahtıl**sahn**ızah

**Are you waiting for someone?**
Birisini mi bekliyorsunuz?
beereesee**nee** mee behkleeyorsoonooz

**Do you mind if I sit here?**
Buraya oturmam sizi rahatsız eder mi?
**boo**rah-yah o-toor**mahm** seezee rahhahtsız eh**dehr**
mee

**May I get you a drink?**
Size bir içki getirebilir miyim?
seezeh beer eechk(y)ee g(y)ehteerehbee**leer** mee-
yeem

**Do you have a light, please?**
Ateşiniz var mı acaba?
ahtehsheeneez **vahr** mı ahjahbah

**Would you like a cigarette?**
Bir sigara ister misiniz?
beer seegahrah ees**tehr**
meesee-neez

**Do you smoke?**
Sigara içiyor musunuz?
seegahrah ee**chee**yor moosoonooz

**No, I don't, thanks. I've given it up.**
Hayır, içmiyorum, teşekkürler. Bıraktım.
**hah**-yır, **eech**meeyoroom, teh-shehk-kewrr-**lehr**.
bırahk**tım**

**Do you mind if I smoke?**
Sigara içersem rahatsız olur musunuz?
seegahrah eecherr-**sehm** rahhahtsız ohl**oor**
moosoonooz

### Why are you laughing?
**Neden gülüyorsunuz?**
neh**dehn** gewlewyorsoonooz

### Is my Turkish that bad?
**Türkçem o kadar kötü mü?**
tewrk-chehm o kahdahr kö**tew** mew

### Are you doing anything tonight?
**Bu akşam bir şey yapıyor musunuz?**
**boo** ahkshahm beer shay yah**pı**yor moosoonooz

### Would you like to go out with me tonight?
**Bu akşam benimle çıkmak ister misiniz?**
**boo** ahkshahm behneemleh chıkmahk ees**tehr**
meesee-neez

### Are you free this evening?
**Bu akşam serbest misiniz (boş musunuz) ?**
**boo** ahkshahm sehr**behst** meesee-neez (**bosh**
moosoonooz)

### Would you like to go dancing with me tonight?
**Bu akşam benimle dansa gitmek ister misiniz?**
**boo** ahkshahm behneemleh dahn**sah** g(y)eetmehk
ees**tehr** meesee-neez

### I know a good discotheque.
**İyi bir diskotek biliyorum.**
ee-**yee** beer deesko**tehk**
beeleeyoroom

### Shall we go to the cinema?
**Sinemaya gidelim mi?**
seenehmah-yah g(y)eedeh**leem**
mee

**Would you like to go for a drive?**
**Arabayla gezmek ister misiniz?**
ahrah-**bye**-lah g(y)ehzmehk ees**tehr** meesee-neez

**I'd love to. Thank you.**
**Çok iyi olur. Teşekkür ederim.**
**choke** ee-yee ohloor. teh-shehk-**kewrr** ehdehreem

**Thank you, but I'm busy.**
**Teşekkür ederim, ama meşgulüm.**
teh-shehk-**kewrr** ehdehreem, ahmah mehsh**gool**ewm

**Leave me alone, please.**
**Beni rahat bırakın, lütfen.**
behnee rah**haht** bırahkın, **lewt**fehn

**Where shall we meet?**
**Nerede buluşalım?**
**neh**rehdeh boolooshahlım

**I'll call you at …**
**Sizi saat …'de ararım.**
seezee sah-aht …'deh ahrahrım

**What's your phone number?**
**Telefon numaranız nedir?**
tele**phone** noomahrahnız **neh**deer

**I'll pick you up at your hotel.**
**Sizi otelinizden alırım.**
seezee otehleeneez**dehn** ahlırım

**I'll pick you up at nine.**
**Sizi (saat) dokuzda alırım.**
seezee (sah-aht) dokooz**dah** ahlırım

**What time shall I come?**
**Ne zaman geleyim?**
neh zahmahn g(y)ehleh-yeem

**What time do you have to be back?**
**Ne zaman geri dönmeniz gerekiyor?**
neh zahmahn g(y)ehree dönmehneez
g(y)ehrehk(y)eeyor

**I'll take you home.**
**Sizi evinize götüreyim.**
seezee ehveeneezeh gö-
tu-reh-yeem

**Do you live alone?**
**Yalnız mı**
**yaşıyorsunuz?**
yahlnız mı yahshıyorsoonooz

**Thank you. It's been a wonderful evening.**
**Teşekkür ederim. Nefis (Harika) bir akşam oldu.**
teh-shehk-kewrr ehdehreem. nehfeess (haareekah)
beer ahkshahm oldoo

**Can I see you again?**
**Sizi tekrar görebilir miyim?**
seezee tehkrahr görehbeeleer mee-yeem

**Hope to see you again soon.**
**Yakında sizi yine göreceğimi umarım.**
yahkındah seezee yeeneh görehjeh-yeemee
oomahrım

**See you 'soon/tomorrow'.**
**'Yakında/Yarın' görüşmek üzere.**
'yahkındah/yahrın' görewshmehk ewzehreh

# SHOPPING & SERVICES
# ALIŞVERİŞ & HİZMETLER

ALIŞVERIŞ & HİZMETLER

## Shops, Stores and Services
### Dükkânlar, Mağazalar ve Hizmetler

**Where's the 'best / nearest' ...?**
**'En iyi / En yakın ... nerededir?**
'**ehn** ee-yee / **ehn** yahkın' ... **neh**rehdehdeer

| | | |
|---|---|---|
| **antique shop** | **antikacı dükkânı** | |
| | ahn**tee**kahjı dewkk(y)ahnı | |
| **art gallery** | **sanat galerisi** | sah**naht** gahlehreesee |
| **baker's** | **fırın** | **fı**rın |
| **bank** | **banka** | **bahn**kah |
| **bookshop** | **kitapçı** | k(y)eetahp**chı** |
| **butcher's** | **kasap** | kah**sahp** |
| **cake shop/pastry shop/tearoom** | **pastane** | |
| | | pahstaa**neh** |
| **camera shop** | **fotoğrafçı dükkânı** | |
| foto**hw**-rahf**chı** dewkk(y)ahnı | | |
| **carpet seller's** | **halıcı** | hah**lı**jı |
| **computer store** | **bilgisayar mağazası** | |
| | beelg(y)eesah-**yahr** mahw-ahzahsı | |
| **delicatessen** | **şarküteri** | shahrk(y)ewteh**ree** |
| **drugstore/chemist's/pharmacy** | **eczane** | ehjzaa**neh** |
| **dry-cleaner's** | **kuru temizleyici** | |
| | koo**roo** tehmeezleh-yeejee | |
| **fishmonger's** | **balıkçı dükkânı** | bahlık**chı** dewkk(y)ahnı |
| **florist's** | **çiçekçi dükkânı** | |
| | cheechek**chee** dewkk(y)ahnı | |
| **furrier's** | **kürk mağazası** | k(y)ewrk mahw-ahzahsı |
| **gift shop** | **hediye dükkânı** | hehdee-**yeh** dewkk(y)ahnı |
| **green grocer's** | **manav** | mah**nahv** |
| **grocer's** | **bakkal dükkânı** | bahk**kahl** dewkk(y)ahnı |
| **hairdresser's** | **kuaför** | kooah**för** |
| **hardware store/ironmonger's** | **nalbur** | nahl**boor** |
| **hospital** | **hastane** | hahstaa**neh** |
| **ironmonger's** | **hırdavatçı dükkânı** | |
| | hırdahvaht**chı** dewkk(y)ahnı | |

SHOPPING & SERVICES

| jeweller's | **kuyumcu dükkânı** | |
| | kooyoom**joo** dewkk(y)ahnı | |
| **laundry** | **çamaşırhane** | chahmahshırhaa**neh** |
| **library** | **kütüphane** | ku-tewp-haa**neh** |
| **newsagent's** | **gazete bayii** | gah**zeh**teh bah-yeeee |
| **optician** | **gözlükçü** | gözlewk**chew** |
| **petrol/gas station** | **benzin istasyonu** | |
| | beh**nzeen** eestahsyonoo | |
| **post office** | **postane** | postaa**neh** |
| **second-hand shop** | **eskici dükkânı** | |
| | ehsk(y)ee**jee** dewkk(y)ahnı | |
| **shoe shop** | **ayakkabı mağazası** | |
| | ah-**yahk**kahbı mahw-ahzahsı | |
| **sports shop** | **spor mağazası** | **spor** mahw-ahzahsı |
| **stationer's** | **kırtasiyeci** | kırtahseeyeh**jee** |
| **toy shop** | **oyuncakçı dükkânı** | |
| | oyoonjahk**chı** dewkk(y)ahnı | |
| **travel agency** | **seyahat acentesi** | |
| | seh-yah**haht** ahjehntehsee | |
| **watchmaker's** | **saatçi** | sah-aht-**chee** |

# General phrases  Genel deyişler

### Where's there a good …?
**Nerede iyi bir ... vardır?**
**neh**rehdeh ee-**yee** beer ... vahrdır

### Where can I buy a …?
**Nerede bir ... satın alabilirim?**
**neh**rehdeh beer ... sahtın ahlahbeeleereem

### How do I get there?
**Oraya nasıl giderim?**
**o**rah-yah **nah**sıl g(y)eedehreem

### Is it far from here?
**Buraya uzak mı(dır)?**
**boo**rah-yah oo**zahk** mı(dır)

ALIŞVERIŞ & HIZMETLER

## *In the shop* *Dükkânda, Mağazada*

**Can you help me?**
**Bana yardımcı olabilir misiniz?**
bahnah yahrdımjı ohlahbee**leer** meesee-neez

**Excuse me, do you have any …?**
**Afedersiniz, (sizde) … var mı?**
ahf**ehdehrseeneez**, (seezdeh) … **vahr** mı

**Where's the … department?**
**… bölümü nerede(dir)?**
… bölewmew **neh**rehdeh(deer)

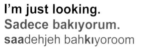

**Where's the lift (elevator)?**
**Asansör nerede(dir)?**
ahsahn**sör** **neh**rehdeh(deer)

**I'm just looking.**
**Sadece bakıyorum.**
**saa**dehjeh bah**kı**yoroom

**Do you sell …?**
**… satıyor musunuz?**
… **sah**tıyor moosoonooz

**I'd like to buy …**
**… satın almak istiyorum.**
… **sah**tın ahlmahk eesteeyoroom

**Can you show me 'this/that'?**
**Bana 'bunu/şunu' gösterir misiniz ?**
bahnah 'boo**noo**/shoo**noo**' gösteh**reer** meesee-neez

**Will I have any difficulty with Customs?**
**Gümrükte bir zorlukla karşılaşır mıyım?**
gewmrewkteh beer zor**look**lah kahrshılah**shır** mıyım

**Would you wrap it up for me, please?**
**Onu benim için sarar mısınız, lütfen?**
onoo behneem eecheen sah**rahr** mısınız, **lewt**fehn

SHOPPING & SERVICES

**Can I help you?**
Size yardımcı olabilir miyim?
seezeh yahrdımjı ohlahbee**leer** mee-yeem

**You'll find them in that corner.**
Onları şu köşede bulursunuz.
onlahrı **shoo** köshehdeh booloorsoonooz

**Will you take it with you?/Shall we send it?**
Yanınızda mı götüreceksiniz?/Gönderelim mi?
yahnınız**dah** mı gö-tu-rehjehkseeneez/göndehreh**leem**
mee

## *Choosing*   *Seçme*

**No, I don't like it.**
Hayır, onu beğenmedim.
hah-yır, oh**noo** beh-**yehn**mehdeem

**I like the one in the window.**
Vitrindekini beğendim.
veetreendehk(y)ee**nee** beh-yehndeem

**Can you show me a 'dark/light' one.**
'Koyu renk/Açık renk' bir tane gösterebilir
misiniz?
'ko**yoo** rehnk/ah-**chık** rehnk' beer tahneh
göstehrehbee**leer** meesee-neez

**I'd like something in 'blue/leather'.**
'Mavi/Deri' bir şey rica ediyorum.
'maa**vee**/deh**ree**' beer shay ree-**jah** ehdeeyoroom

**Do you have anything 'better/cheaper'?**
'Daha iyi/Daha ucuz' bir şeyiniz var mı?
'dah**hah** ee-yee / dah**hah** oojooz' beer sheh-yeeneez
**vahr** mı

**I'll take it.**
Bunu alıyorum.
boo**noo** ahlıyoroom

**How much is it?**
Ne kadar?
**neh** kahdahr

## *Defining the article* Eşyayı tanımlama

**I'd like a ... one.**
... bir tane istiyorum.
... beer tahneh eesteeyoroom

| big | Büyük | bew**yewk** |
|-----|-------|-------------|
| cheap | Ucuz | oo**jooz** |
| dark | Koyu renk | ko**yoo** rehnk |
| good | İyi | ee-**yee** |
| heavy | Ağır | ahwır |
| large | Büyük | bew**yewk** |
| light | Hafif | hah**feef** |
| oval | Oval | o**vahl** |
| rectangular | Dikdörtgen | deekdörtg(y)ehn |
| round | Yuvarlak | yoovahr**lahk** |
| small | Küçük | k(y)ew**chewk** |
| square | Kare | **kah**reh |
| sturdy | Sağlam | sahw**lahm** |

## *Colours* Renkler

**I don't like the colour.**
Bu rengi beğenmedim.
**boo** rehng(y)ee beh-**yehn**mehdeem

**Something to match this.**
Buna uygun bir şey olsun.
boonah ooy**goon** beer shay olsoon

**Do you have a 'lighter / darker' shade?**
'Daha açık / Daha koyu' tonda bir şey var mı?
'dah**hah** ah-chık / dah**hah** koyoo' tondah beer shay **vahr** mı

I'd like something in …   … bir şey istiyorum.
                          … beer shay eesteeyoroom

| beige | Bej | behzh |
| black | Siyah | seeyahh |
| blue | Mavi | maavee |
| brown | Kahverengi | kahhvehrehng(y)ee |
| gold | Altın rengi | ahltın rehng(y)ee |
| green | Yeşil | yehsheel |
| grey | Gri | gree |
| mauve | Açık mor | ahchık mor |
| orange | Portakal rengi | portahkahl rehng(y)ee |
| pink | Pembe | pehmbeh |
| purple | Mor | mor |
| red | Kırmızı | kırmızı |
| silver | Gümüş rengi | gewmewsh rehng(y)ee |
| turquoise | Turkuvaz | toorkoovahz |
| white | Beyaz | beh-yahz |
| yellow | Sarı | sahrı |

## *Complaints*   Şikâyetler

**I want to return this.**
**Bunu geri vermek istiyorum.**
boonoo g(y)ehree vehrmehk eesteeyoroom

**I bought this yesterday.**
**Bunu dün satın aldım.**
boonoo **dewn** sahtın ahldım

**It doesn't 'work/fit'.**
**Çalışmıyor./Uymuyor.**
chahlıshmıyor/**ooy**mooyor

**I'd like a refund.**
**Paranın geri ödenmesini istiyorum.**
pahrahnın g(y)eh**ree** ödehnmehseenee eesteeyoroom

**Here's the receipt.**
**İşte makbuz.**
eeshteh mahkbooz

**Can you exchange this, please?**
**Bunu değiştirebilir misiniz, lütfen?**
boo**noo** deh-yeeshteerehbee**leer**
meesee-neez **lewt**fehn

## *Paying* Ödeme

**How much is this?**
**Bu ne kadar?**
boo **neh** kahdahr

**Can I pay by traveller's check?**
**Seyahat çeki ile ödeyebilir miyim?**
seh-yah**haht** chek(y)ee eeleh ödeh-yehbee**leer** mee-yeem

**I think there's a mistake in the bill.**
**Sanırım hesapta bir yanlışlık var.**
sah**nı**rım hehsahptah beer yahnlıshlık vahr

**May I have a receipt, please?**
**Makbuz alabilir miyim, lütfen?**
mahkbooz ahlahbee**leer** mee-yeem, **lewt**fehn

**You've given me too 'much/little' change.**
**Çok 'fazla/az' bozukluk verdiniz.**
**choke** 'fahzlah/ahz' bozooklook vehrdeeneez

**Please pay the cashier.**
**Kasiyere ödeme yapın, lütfen.**
kahseeyeh**reh** ödehmeh yahpın **lewt**fehn

# Clothes Giysiler

**Where's the 'coats/underwear/haberdashery' department?**
'Ceket/İç çamaşırı/Tuhafiye' bölümü nerede?
'jeh**k(y)eht**/**eech** chahmahshırı/toohahfee**yeh**'
bölewmew **neh**rehdeh

**I'd like … for a (eight-year-old) 'boy/girl'.**
(Sekiz yaşındaki) Bir 'erkek / kız' çocuk için …
istiyorum.
[seh**keez** yahshındahk(y)ee] beer 'ehr**k(y)ehk** / **kız**'
chojook eecheen … eesteeyoroom

**Where are the beach clothes?**
Plaj giysileri nerededir?
**plahzh** g(y)eeyseelehree
**neh**rehdehdeer

**Where can I find 'socks/
stockings'?**
Nerede çorap bulabilirim?
**neh**rehdeh cho-rahp boolahbeeleereem

**Do you have anything in …?**
… kumaşından (yapılmış) bir şey var mı?
… koomahshındahn (yahpılmısh) beer shay **vahr** mı

**Do you have anything of better quality?**
Daha kaliteli bir şeyiniz var mı?
dah**hah** kahleetehlee beer sheh-yeeneez **vahr** mı

**I'd like something finer.**
Daha ince bir şey rica ediyorum.
dah**hah** eenjeh beer shay ree-**jah** ehdeeyoroom

**ALIŞVERİŞ & HİZMETLER**

### Is this 'pure cotton / pure wool / synthetic'?
Saf pamuklu mu / Saf yünlü mü / Sentetik mi?
sahf pahmookloo moo / sahf
yewnlew mew / sehntehteek mee

### Where's the 'mirror / fitting room'?
'Ayna / Giyinme kabini' nerededir?
'ai-nah / g(y)ee-yeenmeh kahbeenee' nehrehdehdeer

### Can I try it on?
Deneyebilir miyim?
dehneh-yehbeeleer mee-yeem

### It doesn't fit.
Uymadı.
ooymahdı

### It fits very well.
Çok iyi uydu.
choke ee-yee ooydoo

### What's it made of?
Neden yapılmıştır?
nehdehn yahpılmıshtır

| English | Turkish | Pronunciation |
|---|---|---|
| cambric | patiska | pahteeskah |
| chiffon | şifon | sheefon |
| corduroy | fitilli kadife | feeteellee kahdeefeh |
| cotton | pamuklu | pahmookloo |
| denim | blucin kumaşı | bloojeen koomahshı |
| lace | dantel | dahntehl |
| gabardine | gabardin | gahbahrdeen |
| leather | deri | dehree |
| linen | keten | kehtehn |
| poplin | poplin | popleen |
| satin | saten | sahtehn |
| silk | ipek | eepehk |
| suede | süet | seweht |
| towelling | havlu kumaş | hahvloo koomahsh |
| velvet | kadife | kahdeefeh |
| velveteen | pamuklu kadife | pahmookloo kahdeefeh |
| wool | yün | yewn |

**SHOPPING & SERVICES**

## *Clothes and accessories*
*Giysiler ve Aksesuarlar*

| | | |
|---|---|---|
| anorak | anorak | ahno**rahk** |
| bathing cap | bone | **bo**neh |
| bathing suit, swimsuit | mayo | **mah**-yo |
| bathrobe | sabahlık | sahbahh**lık** |
| belt | kemer | k(y)eh**mehr** |
| blouse | bluz | blooz |
| bra | sutyen | soot**yehn** |
| button | düğme | dew(y)**meh** |
| cap | kasket | kahs**k(y)eht** |
| cardigan | hırka | **hır**kah |
| coat | manto, palto | **mahn**to, **pahl**to |
| dress | elbise | ehlbee**seh** |
| evening dress | gece elbisesi | g(y)eh**jeh** ehlbeesehssee |
| girdle | korse | **kor**seh |
| gloves | eldiven | ehldee**vehn** |
| handbag | el çantası | **ehl** chahntahsı |
| hat | şapka | **shahp**kah |
| jacket | ceket | jehk**(y)eht** |
| jeans | kot, blucin | kot, bloo**jeen** |
| jersey, pullover | kazak | kah**zahk** |
| kneesocks | uzun çorap | oo**zoon** cho-rahp |
| nightdress | gecelik | g(y)ehjeh**leek** |
| panties | bayan külotu | bah-**yahn** k(y)ewlotoo |
| pants, trousers | pantolon | pahnto**lon** |
| pantyhose | külotlu çorap | k(y)ewlot**loo** cho-rahp |
| raincoat | yağmurluk | yahwmoor**look** |
| scarf | atkı | **aht**kı |
| shirt | gömlek | göm**lehk** |
| shorts | şort | short |
| skirt | etek | eh**tehk** |
| slip | erkek külotu | ehr**k(y)ehk** k(y)ewlotoo |

| socks | erkek çorabı | ehrk(y)ehk cho-rahbı |
|---|---|---|
| sports jacket | spor ceket | **spor** jehk(y)eht |
| stockings | çorap | cho-**rahp** |
| suit (man's) | erkek elbisesi | ehr**k(y)ehk** ehlbeesehsee |
| suit (woman's) | tayyör | tai-**yör** |
| sweater | kazak | kah**zahk** |
| swimming trunks | erkek mayosu | ehr**k(y)ehk** mah-yosoo |
| tie | kravat | krah**vaht** |
| tracksuit | eşofman | ehshof**mahn** |
| umbrella | şemsiye | shehmsee-**yeh** |
| underpants | don | don |
| undershirt | fanila | fah**nee**lah |
| waistcoat, vest | yelek | yeh**lehk** |
| zip | fermuar | fehrmoo**ahr** |

## *Size* Beden

**I don't know the 'English/American' sizes.**
'İngiliz/Amerikan' bedenlerini bilmiyorum.
'een**g(y)ee**leez/ahmehree**kahn**' behdehnlehreenee **beel**meeyoroom

**I don't know what size I take.**
Hangi beden kullandığımı bilmiyorum.
**hun**gyee behdehn koollahndıımı **beel**meeyoroom

**Could you measure me?**
Ölçülerimi alır mısınız, lütfen?
ölchewlehreemee ah**lır** mısınız **lewt**fehn

## I take a size thirty-eight.
**Otuz sekiz beden kullanıyorum.**
otooz seh**k(y)eez** behdehn koollahnıyoroom

### Women's Dresses, etc. — Kadın Elbiseleri, vb.

| Turkish | 36 | 38 | 40 | 42 | 44 | 46 |
|---|---|---|---|---|---|---|
| British | 10 | 12 | 14 | 16 | 18 | 20 |
| American | 8 | 10 | 12 | 14 | 16 | 18 |

### Men's suits, etc. — Erkek elbiseleri, vb.

| Turkish | 46 | 48 | 50 | 52 | 54 | 56 |
|---|---|---|---|---|---|---|
| British / American | 36 | 38 | 40 | 42 | 44 | 46 |

### Men's shirts — Erkek gömlekleri

| Turkish | 35 | 36 | 38 | 41 | 43 | 45 |
|---|---|---|---|---|---|---|
| British / American | 13 ½ | 14 | 15 | 16 | 17 | 18 |

### Men's socks — Erkek çorapları

| Turkish | 39/40 | 41/42 | 43/44 | 45/46 | 47/48 |
|---|---|---|---|---|---|
| British / American | 10 | 10 ½ | 11 | 11 ½ | 12 |

### Stockings — Kadın çorapları

| Turkish | 0 | 1 | 2 | 3 | 4 | 5 | 6 |
|---|---|---|---|---|---|---|---|
| British / American | 8 | 8 ½ | 9 | 9 ½ | 10 | 10 ½ | 11 |

## Shoes Ayakkabılar

### I'd like a pair of …
**Bir çift ... rica ediyorum.**
**beer** cheeft ... ree-**jah** ehdeeyoroom

| **boots** | **çizme** | chee**zmeh** |
|---|---|---|
| **plimsolls (sneakers)** | **tenis ayakkabısı** | |
| | teh**neess** ah-yahkkahbısı | |
| **sandals** | **sandalet** | sahndah**leht** |

| shoes | ayakkabı | ah-**yahk**kahbı |
| flat | düz | dewz |
| with rubber soles | kauçuk tabanlı | |
| | kahoo**chook** tahbahnlı | |
| with leather soles | kösele tabanlı | |
| | kö**seh**leh tahbahnlı | |
| with a heel | ökçeli | ökche**lee** |
| slippers | terlik | tehr**leek** |

## Do you have it another colour?
**Başka bir renk var mı?**
bahsh**kah** beer rehnk **vahr** mı

## Do you have the same in black?
**Aynısının siyahı var mı?**
ai-nısının seeyah**hı** **vahr** mı

## These are too 'small/big'.
**Bunlar çok 'küçük/büyük'.**
boonlahr **choke** 'k(y)ewchewk/bewyewk'

## Do you have a 'larger/smaller' size?
**'Daha büyük/Daha küçük' bir numara var mı?**
'dah**hah** bewyewk/dah**hah** k(y)ewchewk' beer noomahrah **vahr** mı

## I need some 'shoe polish/shoelaces'.
**Biraz 'Ayakkabı boyası / Ayakkabı bağı'na ihtiyacım var.**
beerahz 'ah-**yahk**kahbı boyahsı/ah-**yahk**kahbı bahwı'nah eehteeyahjım vahr

| leather | deri | deh**ree** |
| rubber | kauçuk | kahoo**chook** |
| cloth | kumaş | koo**mahsh** |
| suede | süet | sew**eht** |

| Women's shoes | | | Kadın ayakkabıları | | |
|---|---|---|---|---|---|
| Turkish | 36 | 37 | 38 | 39 | 40 |
| British | 4.5 | 5 | 5.5-6.5 | 7 | 7.5 |
| American | 6 | 6.5 | 7-8 | 8.5 | 9 |

| Men's shoes | | | Erkek ayakkabıları | | |
|---|---|---|---|---|---|
| Turkish | 40 | 41 | 42 | 43 | 44 | 45 |
| British | 6 | 7 | 8 | 9 | 10 | 11 |
| American | 6.5 | 7.5 | 8.5 | 9.5 | 10.5 | 11.5 |

# Chemist's (Drugstore) Eczane

**Where's the nearest (all-night) chemist's?**
En yakın (nöbetçi) eczane nerededir?
**ehn** yahkın (nöbeht**chee**) ehjzaaneh **neh**rehdehdeer

**What time does the chemist's close?**
Eczane ne zaman kapanır?
ehjzaaneh **neh** zahmahn kahpahnır

## *Pharmaceutical* Eczacılıkla ilgili

**Do you have a small first-aid kit?**
Sizde, küçük bir ilk-yardım çantası bulunur mu?
seezdeh, k(y)ew**chewk** beer eelk-yahr**dım** chahntahsı booloo**noor** moo

**Can you prepare this prescription for me, please?**
Bana bu reçeteyi hazırlayabilir misiniz, lütfen?
bahnah boo reh**che**teh-yee hahzırlah-yahbee**leer** meeseeneez, **lewt**fehn

ALIŞVERİŞ & HİZMETLER

### I'd like some 'aspirin/sun cream'.
'Aspirin/Güneş kremi' rica ediyorum.
'ahspee**reen**/gew**nehsh** krehmee' ree-**jah** ehdeeyoroom

### Can I have 'a/an/some' …
'Bir/Biraz' … alabilir miyim?
'beer/beerahz' … ahlahbee**leer** mee-yeem

| | | |
|---|---|---|
| analgesic | ağrı kesici | ahwrı k(y)ehseejee |
| aspirin | aspirin | ahspee**reen** |
| antiseptic cream | yara merhemi | yah**rah** mehrhehmee |
| baby food | bebek maması | beh**behk** mahmahsı |
| band-aids | plaster | plah**stehr** |
| condoms | prezervatif | prehzehrvah**teef** |
| cotton wool | pamuk | pah**mook** |
| cough drops | boğaz pastili | boh**wahz** pahsteelee |
| disinfectant | dezenfektan | dehzehnfehk**tahn** |
| ear drops | kulak damlası | koo**lahk** dahmlahsı |
| eye drops | göz damlası | göz dahmlahsı |
| feeding bottle | biberon | beebeh**ron** |
| insect repellent | böcek ilacı | bö**jehk** eelahjı |
| iodine | tentürdiyot | tehntewrdee**yot** |
| iron tablets | demir hapı | deh**meer** hahpı |
| laxative | müshil | mew**seel** |
| mouthwash | gargara | gahrgah**rah** |
| nose drops | burun damlası | boo**roon** dahmlahsı |
| powder | talk pudrası | **tahlk** poodrahsı |
| sleeping pills | uyku ilacı | ooy**koo** eel(y)ahjı |
| vitamin pills | vitamin | veetah**meen** |
| thermometer | termometre | tehrmo**meht**reh |
| tissues | kâğıt mendil | k(y)aaıt mehndeel |
| tranquillizers | yatıştırıcı | yahtıshtırıjı |

### Can you give me something for …
Bana … için bir şey verebilir misiniz?
bahnah … eecheen beer shay vehrehbee**leer** meeseeneez

SHOPPING & SERVICES

| a hangover | içki mahmurluğu | |
| --- | --- | --- |
| | eechk(y)ee mahhmoorloohwoo | |
| constipation | peklik | pehkleek |
| a cough | öksürük | öksewrewk |
| diarrhoea | ishal | eeshahl |
| a headache | baş ağrısı | bahsh ahwrısı |
| insect bites | böcek sokması | böjehk sokmahsı |
| indigestion | mide bozukluğu | meedeh bozookloohwoo |
| sea sickness | deniz tutması | dehneez tootmahsı |
| sunburn | güneş yanığı | gewnehsh yahnıı |
| travel sickness | yol tutması | yol tootmahsı |

## *Toiletries*   *Güzellik ürünleri*

| aftershave lotion | tıraş losyonu | tırahsh losyonoo |
| --- | --- | --- |
| astringent lotion | yüz losyonu | yewz losyonoo |
| blusher | allık | ahllık |
| body lotion | vücut losyonu | vewjoot losyonoo |
| comb | tarak | tahrahk |

cream (for 'dry/greasy' skin)
krem (kuru/yağlı cilt için)
krehm (kooroo/yahwlı jeelt eecheen)

| curlers | bigudi | beegoodee |
| --- | --- | --- |
| dye | saç boyası | sahch boyahsı |
| emery board | manikür takımı | mahneek(y)ewr tahkımı |
| eye shadow | far | fahr |
| eyeliner | göz kalemi | göz kahlehmee |
| face powder | yüz pudrası | yewz poodrahsı |
| hair gel | saç jölesi | sahch zhölehsee |
| hair slide | saç tokası | sahch tokahsı |
| hair slide | toka | tokah |
| hairbrush | saç fırçası | sahch fırchahsı |
| hairspray | saç spreyi | sahch spreh-yee |
| hand cream | el kremi | ehl krehmee |
| lipstick | ruj | roozh |
| mascara | rimel | reemehl |
| moisturizing cream | nemlendirici krem | |
| | nehmlehndeereejee krehm | |

| nail clippers | tırnak makası | tırnahk mahkahsı |
|---|---|---|
| nail polish remover | aseton | ahsehton |
| perfume | parfüm | pahrfewm |
| razor blades | tıraş bıçağı | tırahsh bıchahwı |

**shampoo (for dry hair)**
**şampuan (kuru saç için)**
shahmpooahn (kooroo sahch eecheen)

**shampoo (for greasy hair)**
**şampuan (yağlı saç için)**
shahmpooahn (yahwlı sahch eecheen)

| shaving brush | tıraş fırçası | tırahsh fırchahsı |
|---|---|---|
| shaving cream | tıraş kremi | tırahsh krehmee |
| soap | sabun | sahboon |
| suntan cream/oil | güneş kremi/yağı | |
| | gewnehsh krehmee/yahwı | |
| toilet paper | tuvalet kağıdı | toovahleht k(y)ahwıdı |
| toilet water | kolonya | ko-lon-yah |
| toothbrush | diş fırçası | deesh fırchahsı |
| toothpaste | diş macunu | deesh mahjoonoo |

# Buying food and drink
Yiyecek ve içecek satın alma

**Do you have any bread?**
**Ekmek var mı?**
ehkmehk **vahr** mı

**A loaf of bread, please.**
**Bir (somun) ekmek, lütfen.**
**beer** (somoon) ehk**mehk lewt**fehn

**Can I help myself?**
**Kendim alabilir miyim?**
k(y)ehndeem ahlahbee**leer**
mee-yeem

**Do you sell frozen foods?**
**Dondurulmuş yiyecek satıyor musunuz?**
dondoorool**moosh** yeeyehjehk sah**t**ıyor moosoonooz

**What sort of cheese do you have?**
**Ne tür peyniriniz var?**
**neh** tewr payneereeneez vahr

**A bottle of 'milk / beer / wine', please.**
**Bir şişe 'süt / bira / şarap', lütfen.**
beer shee**sheh** 'sewt / bee**rah** / shah**rahp**' **lewt**fehn

**I'd like ...    ... rica ediyorum / istiyorum.**
          .... ree-**jah** ehdeeyoroom / eesteeyoroom

| | |
|---|---|
| a box of chocolates beer | **Bir kutu çikolata**<br>beer kootoo cheekolah**tah** |
| a jar of jam | **Bir kavanoz reçel**<br>beer kahvahnoz reh**chel** |
| a packet of tea | **Bir paket çay**<br>beer pahk(y)eht **chai** |
| a tube of mustard | **Bir tüp hardal**<br>beer tewp hahr**dahl** |
| six eggs | **Altı yumurta**<br>ahltı yoomoor**tah** |
| ten slices of salami | **On dilim salam**<br>on deeleem sah**lahm** |

**Give me 'half a kilo / a kilo / two kilos' of ..., please.**
**Bana 'yarım / bir / iki' kilo ... verin, lütfen.**
bahnah 'yah**rım** / **beer** / ee**k(y)ee**' k(y)eelo ... vehreen **lewt**fehn

| apples | elma | ehl**mah** |
|---|---|---|
| bananas | muz | mooz |
| grapes | üzüm | ew**zewm** |
| mandarins | mandalina | mahndah**lee**nah |
| onions | soğan | soh**wahn** |

| oranges | portakal | portah**kahl** |
| pears | armut | ahr**moot** |
| potatoes | patates | pah**tah**tehss |
| tomatoes | domates | do**mah**tehss |

**How much a 'bottle/kilo'?**
**'Şişesi/Kilosu' ne kadar?**
'sheeseh**see**/k(y)eelo**soo**' neh kahdahr

## Bookshop, Newsstand and Stationer's
Kitapçı, Gazete Bayii ve Kırtasiyeci

**Where is the nearest bookshop?**
**En yakın kitapçı nerededir?**
**ehn** yah**kın** k(y)eetahpchı **neh**rehdehdeer

**Where's the guidebook section?**
**Rehber kitaplar bölümü nerede?**
rehh**behr** k(y)eetahplahr bölewmew **neh**rehdeh

**Where can I buy an English-language newspaper?**
**Nereden İngilizce bir gazete satın alabilirim?**
**neh**rehdehn eeng(y)ee**leez**jeh beer gahzehteh sahtın ahlahbeeleereem

**Do you sell 'Turkish/English/American' magazines?**
**'Türk/İngiliz/Amerikan' dergileri satıyor musunuz?**
'**tewrk/een**g(y)eeleez/ahmehree**kahn**' dehrg(y)eelehree sah**t**ıyor moosoonooz

**Do you have second-hand books?**
Sizde kullanılmış kitaplar bulunur mu?
seezdeh koollahnıl**mısh** k(y)eetahplahr booloo**noor** moo

**Do you have a photocopier?**
Sizde fotokopi makinesi var mı?
seezdeh fotoko**pee** mahk(y)eenehsee **vahr** mı

**I'd like a 'road map/map of the city'.**
Bir 'karayolları haritası/şehir haritası' istiyorum.
beer 'kah**rah-**yollahrı hahreetahsı / sheh-**heer**
hahreetahsı' eesteeyoroom

**Do you have any of …'s books in English?**
…'in İngilizce kitapları var mı?
…'een eeng**(y)ee**leezjeh k(y)eetahplahrı **vahr** mı

**I'd like a dictionary.**
Bir sözlük rica ediyorum.
beer söz**lewk** ree-**jah** ehdeeyoroom

| **Pocket dictionary.** | **Turkish - English** |
|---|---|
| Cep sözlüğü | Türkçe - İngilizce |
| jehp sözlewew | **tewrk**-che - eeng(y)ee**leez**jeh |

**I'd like 'a/an/some' …**
'Bir/Birkaç (Biraz)'... rica ediyorum.
'beer/beerkahch (beerahz)' … ree-**jah** ehdeeyoroom

| address book | adres defteri | ahd**rehss** dehftehree |
|---|---|---|
| adhesive tape | seloteyp | sehlo-**tape** |
| ballpoint pen | tükenmez kalem | tu-k(y)ehn**mehz** kahlehm |
| calendar | takvim | tahk**veem** |
| carbon paper | karbon kâğıdı | kahr**bon** k(y)aaıdı |
| crayons | mum boya | **moom** boyah |
| drawing pins | raptiye | rahptee**yeh** |
| envelopes | mektup zarfı | mehk**toop** zahrfı |

| eraser | silgi | seelg(y)ee |
| exercise book | defter | dehftehr |
| felt-tip pen | keçeli kalem | k(y)ehchelee kahlehm |
| fountain pen | dolmakalem | dolmahkahlehm |
| glue | yapıştırıcı | yahpıshtırıjı |
| grammar book | dilbilgisi kitabı | deelbeelg(y)eesee k(y)eetahbı |
| ink | mürekkep | mewrehkk(y)ehp |
| notebook | not defteri | not dehftehree |
| notepaper | mektup kâğıdı | mehktoop k(y)aaıdı |
| paintbox | boya kutusu | bo-yah kootoosoo |
| paper | kâğıt | k(y)aaıt |
| paperclips | ataç | ahtahch |
| pencil sharpener | kalemtıraş | kahlehmtırahsh |
| pencil | kurşun kalem | koorshoon kahlehm |
| playing cards | oyun kağıdı | oyoon k(y)ahwıdı |
| postcard | kartpostal | kahrtpostahl |
| ruler | cetvel | jehtvehl |
| tracing paper | kopya kâğıdı | kop-yah k(y)ahğıdı |
| writing pad | bloknot | bloknot |

# Music, CD, DVD, Video
Müzik, CD, DVD, Video

**Do you have any CDs by ...?**
Sizde ...'nin CD'leri var mı?
seezdeh ...'neen cd'lehree **vahr** mı

**Are there any new CDs by ...?**
...'nin yeni CD'leri bulunur mu?
...'neen yeh**nee** cd'lehree booloo**noor** moo

**I'd like a CD/DVD.**
Bir CD/DVD rica ediyorum.
beer cd/dvd ree-**jah** ehdee**yo**room

**ALIŞVERİŞ & HİZMETLER**

**Can I listen to this CD?**
Bu CD'yi dinleyebilir miyim?
**boo** cd'yee deenleh-yeh**bee**leer mee-yeem

**Do you have any recordings of local music?**
Sizde yöresel müzik kayıtları var mı?
seezdeh yöreh**sehl** mew**zeek** kah-yıtlahrı **vahr** mı

| | | |
|---|---|---|
| **chamber music** | oda müziği | o**dah** mewzee(y)ee |
| **classical music** | klasik müzik | klah**seek** mewzeek |
| **instrumental music** | enstrümantal müzik | |
| | | ehnstrewmahn**tahl** mewzeek |
| **jazz** | caz | jahz |
| **light music** | hafif müzik | hah**feef** mewzeek |
| **folk music** | halk müziği | **hahlk** mewzee(y)ee |
| **orchestral music** | orkestra müziği | |
| | | ork**(y)eh**strah mewzee(y)ee |
| **pop music** | pop müzik | **pop** mewzeek |
| **vocal music** | çok sesli müzik | |
| | | **choke** sehslee mewzeek |

## Laundry & Dry-cleaner's
Çamaşırhane & Kuru temizleyici

**I'd like these clothes ...**
Bu elbiseleri ... istiyorum.
**boo** ehlbeesehlehree ... eesteeyoroom

| | | |
|---|---|---|
| **cleaned** | temizletmek | tehmeezleht**mehk** |
| **ironed/pressed** | ütületmek | ewtu-leht**mehk** |
| **washed** | yıkatmak | yıkaht**mahk** |

**I need them ...** ... **gerekiyor.** ... g(y)ehrehk(y)eeyor

| | | |
|---|---|---|
| **today** | Bugün | **boo**-gewn |
| **tomorrow** | Yarın | **ya**hrın |
| **as soon as possible** | En kısa zamanda | |
| | **ehn** kısah zahmahndah | |

**SHOPPING & SERVICES**

tonight                **Bu akşam**   **boo** ahkshahm
**before Sunday** **Pazar'dan önce**  pahzahr**dahn** önjeh

### Can you get this stain out?
**Bu lekeyi çıkarabilir misiniz?**
**boo** lehk(y)eh-yee chıkahrahbee**leer** meesee-neez

### Can you 'stitch/mend' this?
**Bunu 'dikebilir misiniz/onarabilir misiniz'?**
boo**noo** 'deek(y)ehbee**leer** meesee-neez/
ohnahrahbee**leer** meesee-neez

### When will they be ready?
**Ne zaman hazır olur?**
**neh** zahmahn hahzır ohloor

### This isn't mine.
**Bu benimki değil.**
boo behneemk(y)ee **deh**-yeel

### There's something missing.
**Bir şey kayıp.**
beer **shay** kah-yıp

## Hairdresser and Barber
Kuaför ve Berber

### May I make an appointment for this morning ?
**Bu sabah için bir randevu alabilir miyim?**
**boo** sahbahh  eecheen beer rahndehvoo ahlahbee**leer**
mee-yeem

### I want my hair cut.
**Saçımı kestirmek istiyorum.**
sahch**ımı** k(y)ehsteermehk eesteeyoroom

**I want my hair trimmed.**
**Saçımı biraz kısaltmak istiyorum.**
sahchımı beerahz kısahlt**mahk** eesteeyoroom

**Not too short at the sides.**
**Kenarlar çok kısa olmasın.**
k(y)ehnahrlahr **choke** kısah **ol**mahsın

**A little more off the 'top/back'.**
**'Üstten/Arkadan' biraz daha (alın).**
'ewsttehn/ahrkahdahn' beerahz dah**hah** (ahlın)

**Please do not use any hairspray.**
**Saç spreyi kullanmayın, lütfen.**
**sahch** spreh-yee kool**lahn**mah-yın **lewt**fehn

**Do you have a colour chart?**
**Bir renk kataloğunuz var mı?**
beer **rehnk** kahtahlooonooz **vahr** mı

**My hair is 'greasy/dry/normal'.**
**Saçım 'yağlı/kuru/normal'.**
sahchım '**yahw**lı/koo**roo**/nor**mahl**'

**The water is too 'cold/hot'.**
**Su çok 'soğuk/sıcak'.**
soo **choke** 'sohwook/sıjahk'

**I'd like a shave.**
**Bir sakal tıraşı rica ediyorum.**
beer sah**kahl** tırahshı ree-**jah** ehdeeyoroom

**Would you trim my 'beard/moustache'?**
**'Sakalımı/Bıyığımı' düzeltir misiniz, lütfen?**
'sahkahlımı/bıyıımı' dewzehl**teer** meesee-neez
**lewt**fehn

Thank you. I like it very much.
Teşekkür ederim. Çok beğendim.
teh-shehk-**kewrr** ehdehreem. **choke** beh-yehndeem

| bleach | renk açma | **rehnk** ahch-mah |
| blow dry | fönleme | fönleh**meh** |
| dye | boyama | boyah**mah** |
| manicure | manikür | mahnee**kewrr** |
| permanent wave | perma | **pehr**mah |
| shampoo and set | mizanpli | meezahn**plee** |

# Electrical appliances
Elektrikli aletler

What's the voltage?
Voltaj nedir?
vol**tahzh** nehdeer

Do you have a battery for this?
Bunun için bir piliniz var mı?
boo**noon** eecheen beer peeleeneez **vahr** mı

Can you show me how it works?
Bana onun nasıl çalıştığını gösterebilir misiniz?
bahnah ohnoon **nah**sıl chahlıshtıını göstehrehbee**leer**
meesee-neez

I'd like 'a / an / some' ...
'Bir / Birkaç' ... rica ediyorum.
'beer / beerkahch' ... ree-**jah** ehdeeyoroom

| adaptor | adaptör | ahdahp**tör** |
| amplifier | amplifikatör | ahmpleefeekah**tör** |
| light bulb | ampul | ahm**pool** |
| calculator | hesap makinesi | heh**sahp** mahk(y)eenehsee |
| car radio | oto radyosu | oto rahdyosoo |

| extension lead | uzatma kordonu | oozah**t**mah kordonoo |
| fuse | **sigorta** | see**gor**tah |
| headphones | **kulaklık** | koolah**klık** |
| plug | **fiş** | **feesh** |
| radio | **radyo** | **rah**dyo |
| shaver | **tıraş makinesi** | tı**rahsh** mahk(y)eenehsee |
| speakers | **hoparlör** | hopah**rlör** |
| (portable) television | (portatif) **televizyon** | |
| | (portahteef) tehlehveez**yon** | |
| video recorder | **video** | vee**deo** |

# Camping equipment & Hardware
## Kamp malzemeleri & Hırdavat

**Where's the camping equipment ?**
**Kamp malzemeleri nerededir?**
**kahmp** mahlzehmehlehree
**neh**rehdehdeer

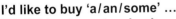

**I'd like to buy 'a/an/some' …**
**'Bir/Birkaç'** … satın almak
istiyorum.
'beer/beerkahch' … sahtın ahlmahk eesteeyoroom

| axe | **balta** | bah**ltah** |
| blanket | **battaniye** | bahttahnee**yeh** |
| bottle-opener | **şişe açacağı** | shee**sheh** ah-chahjahwı |
| bucket | **kova** | ko**vah** |
| butane gas | **bütan gaz** | bew**tahn** gahz |
| camp bed | **kamp yatağı** | **kahmp** yahtahwı |
| candle(s) | **mum** | **moom** |
| can-opener | **konserve açacağı** | |
| | konseh**rveh** ah-chahjahwı | |
| compass | **pusula** | poosoo**lah** |
| cool box | **soğutucu** | sohwootoo**joo** |
| corkscrew | **tirbuşon** | teerboo**shon** |

| crockery | tabak çanak takımı | |
| | tahbahk chahnahk tahkımı | |
| cup(s) | fincan | feenjahn |
| cutlery | çatal bıçak takımı | |
| | chahtahl bıchahk tahkımı | |
| deck chair | şezlong | shehzlong |
| | eelk yahrdım chahntahsı | |
| first-aid kit | ilk yardım çantası | |
| fishing tackle | olta | oltah |
| flashlight | cep feneri | jehp fehnehree |
| folding chair | portatif sandalye | portahteef sahndahl-yeh |
| folding table | portatif masa | portahteef mah-sah |
| food box | yiyecek kutusu | yeeyehjehk kootoosoo |
| fork(s) | çatal | chahtahl |
| frying pan | tava | tahvah |
| glass | bardak | bahrdahk |
| groundsheet | çadır zemini | chahdır zehmeenee |
| hammer | çekiç | chek(y)eech |
| hammock | hamak | hahmahk |
| ice pack | buz torbası | booz torbahsı |
| kettle | çaydanlık | chai-dahnlık |
| knives | bıçak | bıchahk |
| lamp | lamba | lahmbah |
| lantern | fener | fehnehr |
| matches | kibrit | k(y)eebreet |
| mattress | minder, şilte | meendehr, sheelteh |
| mosquito net | cibinlik | jeebeenleek |
| mug(s) | maşrapa | mahshrahpah |
| paraffin (kerosene) | gazyağı | gahzyahwı |
| penknife | çakı | chahkı |
| picnic basket | piknik sepeti | peekneek sehpehtee |
| pillow | yastık | yahstık |
| plastic bag | plastik torba | plahsteek torbah |
| plate(s) | tabak | tahbahk |
| rope | halat | hahlaht |
| rucksack | sırt çantası | sırt chahntahsı |
| saucepan | tencere | tehnjehreh |
| saucer(s) | fincan tabağı | feenjahn tahbahwı |

| scissors | makas | mah**kahs** |
| screwdriver | tornavida | tornah**vee**dah |
| sleeping bag | uyku tulumu | oo**ykoo** tooloomoo |
| spoon(s) | kaşık | kah**shık** |
| string | ip, sicim | eep, see**jeem** |
| teaspoon(s) | çay kaşığı | **chai** kahshıı |
| tent peg(s) | çadır çubuğu | chah**dır** chooboohwoo |
| tent pole | çadır direği | chah**dır** deereh-yee |
| tent | çadır | chah**dır** |
| tool kit | alet çantası | aa**leht** chahntahsı |
| torch | cep feneri | **jehp** fehnehree |
| tumbler(s) | bardak | bahr**dahk** |
| vacuum flask | termos | tehr**mos** |
| washing powder | çamaşır tozu | chahmah**shır** tozoo |
| water carrier | su bidonu | **soo** beedonoo |
| water flask | matara | mah**tah**rah |

## Photography  Fotoğrafçılık

**I'd like to have some passport photos taken.**
**Vesikalık fotoğraf çektirmek istiyorum.**
vehseekahlık fotohw-**rahf** chekteermehk eesteeyoroom

**I'd like to buy a camera.**
**Bir fotoğraf makinesi satın almak istiyorum.**
beer fotohw-**rahf** mahk(y)eenehsee sahtın ahlmahk eesteeyoroom

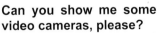

**Can you show me some video cameras, please?**
**Video kameraları gösterebilir misiniz, lütfen?**
**vi**deo kahmehrahlahrı göstehrehbee**leer** meesee-neez **lewt**fehn

## Do you have a 'four/five'-megapixel digital camera?
**'Dört /Beş' megapiksel bir dijital kamera var mı?**
'**dört/behsh**' mehgahpeeksehl beer deezheetahl kahmehrah **vahr** mı

## I'd like to buy 'a sixty-four MB/an extra' memory card for my digital camera.
**Dijital fotoğraf makinem için 'altmış dört MB/ek' bir hafıza kartı satın almak istiyorum.**
deezhee**tahl** fotohw-rahf mahk(y)eenehm eecheen '**ahltmısh dört** mb / **ehk**' beer hahfızah kahrtı sahtın ahlmahk eesteeyoroom

## I'd like to buy a digital camera with ...
..........lı/li/lu/lü bir dijital fotoğraf makinesi satın almak istiyorum.
.........lı/lee/loo/lew beer deezhee**tahl** fotohw-**rahf** mahk(y)eenehsee sahtın ahlmahk eesteeyoroom

| | | |
|---|---|---|
| **flash** | Flaş | flahsh |
| **a CCD sensor** | CCD sensor (algılayıcı) | |
| | ccd sehnsor (ahlgılah-yıjı) | |
| **a resolution of five megapixels** | | |
| Beş megapiksel çözünürlük | | |
| behsh mehgahpeeksehl chözewnewrlewk | | |
| **a thirty-two MB memory** | Otuz iki MB hafıza | |
| | otooz eek(y)ee mb hahfızah | |
| **a USB cable** | USB kablo | usb kahblo |
| **a wide-angle lens** | Geniş açılı objektif | |
| | g(y)ehneesh ah-chılı ohb-zhehk**teef** | |
| **LCD screen** | LCD ekran | lcd ehkrahn |
| **'optical/digital' zoom lens** | | |
| 'Optik/Dijital' uzaklık ayarlı mercek | | |
| 'op**teek**/deezhee**tahl**' oozahklık ah-yahrlı mehrjehk | | |

**I'd like 'a/an' ...**   Bir ... istiyorum.
beer ... eesteeyoroom

| | | |
|---|---|---|
| **battery** | pil | **peel** |
| **battery charger** | pil şarj aleti | peel **shahrzh** aalehtee |
| **cable release** | deklanşör | dehklahn**shör** |
| **digital camera printer** | | |
| dijital fotoğraf makinesi yazıcısı | | |
| deezheetahl fotohw-**rahf** mahk(y)eenehsee yahzijisi | | |
| **flash** | flaş | flahsh |
| **lens** | objektif | obzhehk**teef** |
| **lens cap** | objektif kapağı | obzhehk**teef** kahpahwı |

**Will you enlarge this, please?**
Bunu büyültebilir misiniz, lütfen?
boo**noo** bewyewltehbee**leer** meesee-neez **lewt**fehn

**When will they be ready?**
Ne zaman hazır olur?
**neh** zahmahn hahzır ohloor

**There's something wrong with the ...**
... arızalı.   ... aarızahlı

| | | |
|---|---|---|
| **flash** | Flaş | flahsh |
| **LCD screen** | LCD ekran | lcd ehkrahn |
| **lens** | Objektif/Mercek | obzhehk**teef**/mehr**jehk** |
| **USB cable** | USB kablosu | usb kahblosoo |
| **shutter** | Obtüratör / Kapak | ob-tu-rah**tör** / kah**pahk** |

# Tobacconist's Sigara, Tütün

**A packet of … (cigarettes), please.**
**Bir paket … (sigarası), lütfen.**
**beer** pahk(y)eht … (seegahrahsı) **lewt**fehn

**Do you have 'English/American/Turkish' cigarettes?**
**'İngiliz/Amerikan/Türk' sigaraları var mı?**
'**een**g(y)eeleez/ahmehree**kahn**/**tewrk**' seegahrahlahrı **vahr** mı

**I'd like a carton.**
**Bir karton rica ediyorum.**
**beer** kahr**ton** ree-**jah** ehdeeyoroom

**I'd like to buy a lighter.**
**Bir çakmak satın almak istiyorum.**
beer chahk**mahk** sahtın ahl**mahk** eesteeyoroom

| cigarette holder | sigara ağızlığı | see**gah**rah aaızlıı |
| filter-tipped | filtreli | **feelt**rehlee |
| king size | uzun | oo**zoon** |
| matches | kibrit | k(y)ee**breet** |
| menthol | mentollü | mehntol**lew** |
| mild/strong | hafif (yumuşak)/sert | |
| | hah-feef (yoomoo**shahk**)/sehrt | |
| pipe tobacco | pipo tütünü | **pee**po tutunu |
| pipe | pipo | **pee**po |
| snuff | enfiye | ehnfee**yeh** |
| without filter | filtresiz | **feelt**rehseez |

# Spectacles & Contact lenses
## Gözlük & Lens

**I've broken my glasses. Can you repair them?**
**Gözlüğümü kırdım. Tamir edebilir misiniz?**
gözlewew**mew** kırdım.  taameer ehdehbee**leer**
meesee-neez

**The frame is broken.**
**Çerçeve kırık.**
cherr-che**veh** kırık

**Can you change the lenses?**
**Camları değiştirebilir misiniz?**
jahmlahrı deh-yeeshteerehbee**leer** meesee-neez

**I'd like tinted lenses.**
**Hafif renkli cam istiyorum.**
hah**feef** rehnklee **jahm** eesteeyoroom

**When will they be ready?**
**Ne zaman hazır olur?**
**neh** zahmahn hahzır ohloor

**I'd like a pair of sunglasses.**
**Güneş gözlüğü rica ediyorum.**
gew**nehsh** gözlewew ree-**jah** ehdeeyoroom

**Please give me a spectacle case.**
**Bir gözlük kılıfı verir misiniz, lütfen?**
beer göz**lewk** kılıfı veh**reer** meesee-neez **lewt**fehn

**I'm 'short-sighted / longsighted'.**
**Ben 'miyobum / hipermetrobum'.**
behn 'mee**yo**boom / heepehrmeht**ro**boom'

**May I look in a mirror?**
**Aynaya bakabilir miyim?**
ai-nah-yah bahkahbee**leer** mee-yeem

**I'd like some contact lenses.**
**Kontakt lens rica ediyorum.**
con**tact lenss** ree-**jah** ehdeeyoroom

**Do you have any contact lens solution?**
**Kontakt lens solüsyonu var mı?**
con**tact lenss** solewsyonoo **vahr** mı

## Jeweller's Kuyumcu dükkânı

**Do you have anything in 'gold/silver'?**
**'Altın/Gümüş' bir şeyiniz var mı?**
'ahl**tın**/gew**mewsh**' beer sheh-yeeneez **vahr** mı

**Could I see that, please?**
**Şunu görebilir miyim, lütfen?**
shoo**noo** göreh bee**leer** mee-yeem **lewt**fehn

**Is this real 'gold/silver?**
**Bu gerçek 'altın mıdır/gümüş müdür'?**
boo g(y)ehr-**chehk** 'ahl**tın** mıdır/gew**mewsh** mewdewr'

**How many carats is this?**
**Bu kaç ayar (kırat)?**
boo **kahch** ah-yahr (kıraht)

**I'd like 'a/an/some' ...**
**'Bir/Birkaç' ... rica ediyorum.**
'beer/beerkahch' ... ree-**jah** ehdeeyoroom

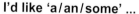

| bracelet | bilezik | beeleh**zeek** |
| brooch | broş | brosh |
| chain | zincir | zeen**jeer** |

| | | |
|---|---|---|
| **clip, pin** | iğne | ee(y)**neh** |
| **cross** | haç | hahch |
| **cufflinks** | kol düğmesi | **kol** dewmehsee |
| **cutlery** | çatal-bıçak takımı | chah**tahl**-bı**chahk** tahkımı |
| **earrings** | küpe | k(y)ew**peh** |
| **engagement ring** | nişan yüzüğü | nee**shahn** yewzewew |
| **gem** | mücevher | mewjeh**vhehr** |
| **jewel box** | mücevher kutusu | mewjeh**vhehr** kootoosoo |
| **necklace** | kolye | **kol**yeh |
| **ring** | yüzük | yew**zewk** |
| **rosary** | tespih | tehs**peeh** |
| **wedding ring** | alyans | ahl**yahnss** |

| | | |
|---|---|---|
| **Amber** | Kehribar | k(y)ehhree**bahr** |
| **Amethyst** | Ametist, Mor yakut | ahmeh**teest**, **mor** yaakoot |
| **Chromium** | Krom | **krom** |
| **Copper** | Bakır | bah**kır** |
| **Coral** | Mercan | mehr**jahn** |
| **Crystal** | Kristal | krees**tahl** |
| **Cut glass** | Kesme cam | k(y)ehs**meh** jahm |
| **Diamond** | Elmas | ehl**mahss** |
| **Emerald** | Zümrüt | zewm**rewt** |
| **Enamel** | Mine | mee**neh** |
| **Gold** | Altın | ahl**tın** |
| **Gold-plated** | Altın kaplama | ahl**tın** kahplah**mah** |
| **Ivory** | Fildişi | **feel**deeshee |
| **Jade** | Yeşim | yeh**sheem** |
| **Onyx** | Oniks | ohn**eex** |
| **Pearl** | İnci | een**jee** |
| **Platinum** | Platin | plah**teen** |
| **Ruby** | Yakut | yah**koot** |
| **Sapphire** | Safir | sah**feer** |
| **Silver-plated** | Gümüş kaplama | g(y)ew**mewsh** kahplah**mah** |
| **Stainless steel** | Paslanmaz çelik | pahslahn**mahz** cheleek |
| **Topaz** | Topaz (sarı yakut) | to**pahz** (sahrı yahkoot) |
| **Turquoise** | Firuze | feeroo**zeh** |

ALIŞVERİŞ & HİZMETLER

## Watch-maker's  Saatçi

I'd like 'a/an' ...　　(Bir) ... rica ediyorum.
　　　　　　　　　　(beer) ... ree-**jah** ehdeeyoroom

| alarm clock | çalar saat | chah**lahr** sah-aht |
| battery | pil | **peel** |
| clock | saat | sah-**aht** |
| pocket watch | cep saati | **jehp** sah-ah-tee |
| watch | saat | sah-**aht** |
|   quartz | kuvars | **koo**vahrss |
|   digital | dijital | deezhee**tahl** |
|   automatic | otomatik | otomah**teek** |
| waterproof | su geçirmez | soo g(y)ehcheer**mehz** |
| wristwatch | kol saati | **kol** sah-ah-tee |

**The 'winder/spring/strap/glass' is broken.**
'Pim/Yay/Kayış/Cam' kırık.
'**peem**/**yay**/kah-yı**sh**/**jahm**' kırık

**When will it be ready?**
Ne zaman hazır olur?
**neh** zahmahn hahzır ohloor

## Toys  Oyuncaklar

**I'd like a toy for a five-year-old girl.**
Beş yaşında bir kız (çocuk) için bir oyuncak istiyorum.
**behsh** yahshındah beer **kız** (chojook) eecheen beer oyoon**jahk** eesteeyoroom

**I'd like a game for a six-year-old boy.**
Altı yaşında bir erkek çocuk için bir oyun istiyorum.
ahl**tı** yahshındah beer ehr**k(y)ehk** chojook eecheen beer o**yoon** eesteeyoroom

SHOPPING & SERVICES

| ball | top | top |
|---|---|---|
| beach ball | deniz topu | deh**neez** topoo |
| book | kitap | k(y)ee**tahp** |
| building blocks | oyun blokları | o**yoon** bloklah-rı |
| card game | iskambil oyunu | eeskahm**beel** oyoonoo |
| chess set | satranç takımı | saht**rahnch** tahkımı |
| colouring book | boyama kitabı | boyah**mah** k(y)eetahbı |
| doll | oyuncak bebek | oyoon**jahk** behbehk |
| flippers | palet(ler) | pah**leht(lehr)** |
| pail (bucket ) | kova | ko**vah** |
| shovel (spade) | kürek | k(y)ew**rehk** |
| skate | paten | pah**tehn** |
| snorkel | şnorkel | shnohr-**k(y)ehl** |
| toy car | oyuncak araba | oyoon**jahk** ahrahbah |
| videogame | video oyunu | vee**deo** oyoonoo |

# Repairs Tamir

**I'd like to have these shoes repaired.**
Bu ayakkabıları tamir ettirmek istiyorum.
**boo** ah-yahkkahbılahrı taameer ehtteermehk
eesteeyoroom

**I'd like new soles and heels.**
Yeni taban ve ökçe istiyorum.
yeh**nee** tahbahn veh ök**che**
eesteeyoroom

**Can you stitch this?**
Bunu dikebilir misiniz?
boo**noo** deek(y)ehbee**leer**
meesee-neez

**Can you sew on this button?**
Bu düğmeyi dikebilir misiniz?
**boo** dewmeh-yee deek(y)ehbee**leer** meesee-neez

**This is broken. Can you repair it?**
Bu bozuk. Tamir edebilir misiniz?
boo bo**zook**. tahmeer ehdehbee**leer** meesee-neez

**Can you repair this camera?**
Bu fotoğraf makinesini tamir edebilir misiniz?
**boo** fotohw-rahf mahk(y)eenehseenee taameer
ehdehbee**leer** meesee-neez

**Can you repair this watch?**
Bu saati tamir edebilir misiniz?
**boo** sah-ah-tee taameer ehdehbee**leer** meesee-neez

**It's 'slow/fast'.**
Geri kalıyor/İleri gidiyor.
g(y)eh**ree** kahlıyor/eeleh**ree**
g(y)eedeeyor

**When will they be ready?**
Ne zaman hazır olur?
**neh** zahmahn hahzır ohloor

## At the post office   Postanede

**Where's the nearest post office?**
En yakın postane nerededir?
**ehn** yahkın postahneh **neh**rehdehdeer

**What time does the post office 'open/close'?**
Postane ne zaman 'açılıyor/kapanıyor'?
postahneh **neh** zahmahn 'ahchılıyor/kahpahnıyor'

**Where's the letter (mail) box?**
Posta kutusu nerededir?
pos**tah** kootoosoo **neh**rehdehdeer

**I'd like to send this parcel.**
**Bu paketi göndermek istiyorum.**
**boo** pahk(y)ehtee göndehr**mehk** eesteeyoroom

**Do I need to fill in a customs declaration form?**
**Gümrük beyannamesi doldurmalı mıyım?**
gewm**rewk** beh-yahnnahmehsee doldoormahlı mıyım

**A stamp for this 'card/letter', please.**
**Bu 'kart/mektup' için bir pul, lütfen.**
boo '**kahrt**/mehk**toop**' eecheen beer **pool lewt**fehn

**What's the postage for a letter to London?**
**Londra'ya mektup ücreti nedir?**
**lon**drah-yah mehktoop ewjrehtee **neh**deer

**How much is it to send a letter surface mail to Australia?**
**Avustralya'ya adi postayla bir mektup göndermek ne kadar?**
ahvoos**trahl**-yah-yah aa**dee** pos-tai-lah beer mehk**toop** göndehrmehk **neh** kahdahr

**What's the airmail to the USA ?**
**ABD'ye (Amerika Birleşik Devletleri'ne) uçak postası ne kadar?**
ah-beh-deh-yeh (ahmehreekah beerlehsheek dehvlehtlehreeneh) oochahk postahsı **neh** kahdahr

**May I have a form, please?**
**Bir form alabilir miyim, lütfen?**
beer form ahlahbee**leer** mee-yeem **lewt**fehn

| Abroad | Yurt dışı | **yoort** dıshı |
| Airmail | Uçak postası | oo**chahk** postahsı |
| Express | Ekspres | ex**press** |
| Inland | Yurt içi | **yoort** eechee |
| Local | Şehir içi | sheh-**heer** eechee |
| Money order | Havale | hahvaa**leh** |
| Registered mail | Taahhütlü | taahhewt**lew** |
| Surface mail | Adi posta | aa**dee** postah |

## Telephoning  Telefon etme

**Where's the nearest telephone (booth)?**
En yakın telefon (kulübesi) nerededir?
**ehn** yahkın tele**phone** (koolewbehsee) **neh**rehdehdeer

**May I use your phone?**
Telefonunuzu kullanabilir miyim?
tehlehfonoonoozoo koollahnahbee**leer**
mee-yeem

**I'd like to telephone Italy.**
İtalya'ya telefon etmek istiyorum.
ee**tahl**-yah-yah tele**phone** ehtmehk eesteeyoroom

**Please give me an international telephone card.**
Bana uluslararası bir telefon kartı verin, lütfen.
bahnah ooloos**lahr**ahrahsı beer tele**phone** kahrtı
vehreen, **lewt**fehn

**Will you get me this number?**
Bana bu numarayı bağlar mısınız?
bahnah boo noomahrah-yı bahw**lahr** mısınız

**Do you have a telephone directory?**
Bir telefon rehberiniz var mı?
beer tele**phone** rehhbehreeneez **vahr** mı

**I'd like to reverse the charges.**
Ödemeli aramak istiyorum.
ödehmeh**lee** ahrahmahk eesteeyoroom

**Hello, this is … speaking.**
Alo, ben …
**ah**lo, behn …

**Is that …?**
Siz …'misiniz?
seez …'meesee-neez

**I'd like to speak to …**
… ile konuşmak istiyorum.
… eeleh konooshmahk eesteeyoroom

**Please speak 'louder / more slowly'.**
'Daha yüksek sesle / Daha yavaş' konuşur musunuz, lütfen.
'dah**hah** yewksehk sehsleh / dah**hah** yahvahsh' konoo**shoor** moosoonooz **lewt**fehn

**I was cut off; can you reconnect me?**
Konuşmam kesildi; beni yeniden bağlayabilir misiniz?
konoosh**mahm** k(y)ehseeldee; behnee yehneedehn bahwlah-yahbee**leer** meesee-neez

**Hold the line, please.**
Hattan ayrılmayın, lütfen.
hahttahn ai-**rıl**mah-yın **lewt**fehn

**Would you try again later, please?**
Daha sonra tekrar dener misiniz, lütfen?
dah**hah** sonrah tehkrahr deh**nehr** meesee-neez **lewt**fehn

**What was the cost of that call?**
Bu görüşmenin fiyatı ne kadar?
boo görewshmehneen feeyahtı **neh** kahdahr

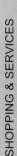

EĞLENCE & DİNLENCE

# ENTERTAINMENT & RELAXING
## EĞLENCE & DİNLENCE

ENTERTAINMENT & RELAXING

## **Cinema and Theatre**   Sinema ve Tiyatro

**What's on at the cinema tonight?**
Bu akşam sinemada ne oynuyor?
boo ahkshahm seenehmahdah **neh** oynooyor

**Where's that new film directed by … being shown?**
...'nin yönettiği yeni film nerede gösteriliyor?
...'neen yöneht-tee(y)ee yehnee feelm **neh**rehdeh göstehreeleeyor

**Can you recommend 'a good film / a comedy'?**
'İyi bir film / Bir komedi' önerebilir misiniz?
'ee-**yee** beer feelm / beer komehdee' önehrehbee**leer** meesee-neez

**Who's in it?**
Kimler oynuyor?
k(y)eem**lehr** oynooyor

**Who's the director?**
Yönetmen kim?
yöneht**mehn** k(y)eem

**Who's playing the lead ?**
Başrolde kim oynuyor?
bahshroldeh **k(y)eem** oynooyor

**What's playing at the theatre?**
Tiyatroda ne oynuyor?
teeyahtrodah **neh** oynooyor

**What sort of play is it? / Who is it by?**
Ne tür bir oyun? / Kimin eseri?
**neh** tewr beer oyoon / k(y)ee**meen** ehsehree

**EĞLENCE & DİNLENCE**

**What time does it begin?**
Saat kaçta başlıyor?
sah-aht kahch**tah** bahshlıyor

**Are there any seats for 'tonight/tomorrow evening'?**
'Bu gece/Yarın akşam' için yer var mı?
'**boo** g(y)ehjeh / **ya**hrın ahkshahm' eecheen yehr **vahr** mı

**How much are the tickets?**
Biletler ne kadar?
beeleht**lehr neh** kahdahr

**I'd like to book seats for Saturday.**
Cumartesi için yer ayırtmak istiyorum.
joo**mahr**tehsee eecheen **yehr** ah-yırtmahk eesteeyoroom

**Please give me two tickets for the matinée on Sunday.**
Pazar günkü matine için iki bilet verir misiniz, lütfen?
pah**zahr** gewnk(y)ew mahteeneh eecheen eek**(y)ee** beeleht veh**reer** meesee-neez **lewt**fehn

**I'm sorry, we're sold out.**
Üzgünüm; hepsi satıldı.
ewz-**gew**newm; **hehp**see sahtıldı

**How much are the seats in 'stalls/circle'?**
'Salondaki/Balkondaki' yerler ne kadar?
'sahlondah**k(y)ee**/bahlkondah**k(y)ee**' yehrlehr **neh** kahdahr

**ENTERTAINMENT & RELAXING**

**Not too far back.**
Çok arkada olmasın.
**choke** ahrkahdah **ol**mahsın

**Somewhere in the middle.**
Ortalarda olsun.
ortahlahr**dah** olsoon

**May I have a programme, please?**
Bir program alabilir miyim, lütfen?
beer programh ahlahbee**leer** mee-yeem **lewt**fehn

**Where are these seats?**
Bu yerler (koltuklar) nerededir?
boo yehrlehr (koltooklahr) **neh**rehdehdeer

**May I see your ticket?**
Biletinizi görebilir miyim?
beelehteeneezee görehbee**leer** mee-yeem

**This is your seat.**
Yeriniz burası.
yehreeneez **boo**rahsı

## Concert, Ballet and Opera
Konser, Bale ve Opera

**Where is the 'opera house / concert hall'?**
'Opera binası / Konser salonu' nerededir?
'opeh**rah** beenahsı / kon**sehr** sahlonoo '**neh**rehdehdeer

**Can you recommend 'a concert / a ballet / an opera'?**
Bir 'konser / bale / opera' önerebilir misiniz?
beer 'kon**sehr** / **bah**leh / ohpeh**rah**' önehrehbee**leer**
meesee-neez

**EĞLENCE & DİNLENCE**

**Who's the 'soloist/conductor'?**
'Solist/Orkestra şefi' kim?
'so**leest**/ork(y)ehst**rah** shehfee' k(y)eem

**Which orchestra is playing?**
Hangi orkestra çalıyor?
**hun**gyee ork(y)ehstrah chahlıyor

**What are they playing?**
Hangi eseri çalıyorlar?
**hun**gyee ehsehree
chahlıyorlahr

**Who's 'singing/dancing'?**
Kim 'şarkı söylüyor/dans ediyor'?
**k(y)eem** 'shahrkı söylewyor/dahnss ehdeeyor'

## Nightclubs and Discos
Gece kulüpleri ve Diskotekler

You ought to visit a nightclub with belly dancing during your stay. You can also enjoy some traditional folk dancing, like the Sword and Shield Dance or the Spoon Dance.

**Can you recommend a good 'nightclub/show'?**
İyi bir 'gece kulübü/gösteri' önerebilir misiniz?
ee-**yee** beer 'g(y)ehjeh koolewbew/göstehree'
önehrehbee**leer** meesee-neez

**Is there a good 'discotheque/jazz club' here?**
Burada iyi bir 'diskotek/caz kulübü' var mı?
boorahdah ee-**yee** beer 'deeskotehk/**jahz** koolewbew'
**vahr** mı

ENTERTAINMENT & RELAXING

**Do you know a good discotheque?**
**İyi bir diskotek biliyor musunuz?**
ee-**yee** beer deeskotehk bee**lee**yor moosoonooz

**Would you like to dance?**
**Dans etmek ister misiniz?**
**dahnss** ehtmehk ees**tehr** meesee-neez

**What time is the 'show / floorshow'?**
**'Gösteri / Eğlence programı' ne zaman?**
'göstehree / aylehn**jeh** prograhmı' **neh** zahmahn

## Sports and Games
Spor ve Oyunlar

There are a variety of sports facilities
in big cities. All major hotels provide
private swimming pools, tennis
courts and fitness centres.

**Where is the nearest 'tennis court / golf course'?**
**En yakın 'tenis kortu/golf sahası' nerededir?**
**ehn** yahkın 'teh**neess** kortoo/**golf** sahhahsı' **neh**rehdehdeer

**What's the charge per 'game/day/hour'?**
**'Oyun başına/Günlük/Saatlik' ücret ne kadar?**
'o**yoon** bahshınah/gewn**lewk**/sah-aht-**leek**' ewjreht **neh** kahdahr

**Can we hire rackets?**
**Raket kiralayabilir miyiz?**
rahk(y)eht k(y)eerahlah-yahbee**leer** mee-yeez

EĞLENCE & DİNLENCE

ENTERTAINMENT & RELAXING

**Where can we go 'swimming/fishing'?**
**Nerede 'yüzmeye/balık tutmaya' gidebiliriz?**
neh rehdeh 'yewzmeh-yeh/bahlık tootmah-yah'
g(y)eedehbeeleereez

**Where's the stadium?**
**Stadyum neresdedir?**
stahdyoom **neh**rehdehdeer

**I want to go to a 'football match/tennis tournament'.**
**Bir 'futbol maçına / tenis turnuvasına' gitmek istiyorum.**
beer 'foot**bol** mahchınah/teh**neess** toornoovahsınah'
g(y)eetmehk eesteeyoroom

**Who's playing?/When does it start?**
**Kim (Kimler) oynuyor?/Ne zaman başlıyor?**
k(y)eem [k(y)eem**lehr**] oynooyor/**neh** zahmahn
bahshlıyor

| **What's the score?** | **Who's winning?** |
|---|---|
| **Skor nedir?** | **Kim kazanıyor?** |
| **skor** nehdeer | k(y)eem kahzahnıyor |

**Is there a swimming pool here?**
**Burada bir yüzme havuzu var mı?**
**boo**rahdah beer yewzmeh hahvoozoo **vahr** mı

| **Is it 'indoor/open air'?** | **Is it heated?** |
|---|---|
| **'Kapalı mı/Açık mı'?** | **Isıtması var mı?** |
| 'kahpah**lı** mı/ah-ch**ık** mı' | ısıtmahsı **vahr** mı |

**What's the admission charge?**
**Giriş ücreti ne kadar?**
g(y)ee**reesh** ewjrehtee **neh** kahdahr

**Can you swim in the 'lake / river'?**
**'Gölde / Nehirde' yüzülüyor mu?**
'göldeh / nehheerdeh' yewzew**lew**yor moo

**Where is the race course?**
**Hipodrom nerede?**
heepod**rom neh**rehdeh

**Who's the jockey?**
**Jokey kim?**
zho**kay** k(y)eem

**Can I hire (rent) 'skates / ski equipment'?**
**'Paten / Kayak malzemesi' kiralayabilir miyim?**
'pah**tehn** / kah-**yahk** mahlzehmehsee' k(y)eerahlah-
yahbee**leer** mee-yeem

**Is there a 'ski slope / skating rink'?**
**Bir 'kayak yapma yeri / paten sahası' var mı?**
beer 'kah-**yahk** yahpmah yehree / pah**tehn** sahhahsı'
**vahr** mı

## On the beach   Plajda

**Is the beach 'sand / pebbles / rocks'?**
**Plaj 'kum mu / çakıl mı / kayalık mı'?**
pl(y)ahzh '**koom** moo / chah**kıl** mı / kah-yah**lık** mı'

**Can I hire a ...?**
**Bir ... kiralayabilir miyim?**
beer ... k(y)eerahlah-yahbee**leer** mee-yeem

| cabin | cabin | kah**been** |
| deckchair | şezlong | shehz**long** |
| motor boat | motorbotu | motor**botoo** |
| rowing boat | sandal | sahn**dahl** |
| sailing boat | yelkenli tekne | yehlk(y)ehn**lee** tehkneh |
| sunshade | güneş şemsiyesi | gew**nehsh** shehmseeyehsee |

### Can I hire diving equipment?
**Dalış malzemesi kiralayabilir miyim?**
dah**lısh** mahlzehmehsee k(y)eerahlah-yahbee**leer**
mee-yeem

### What does it cost by the hour?
**Saati ne kadar?**
sah-ah-tee **neh** kahdahr

### Is there a lifeguard?
**Cankurtaran var mı?**
jahnkoortahrahn **vahr** mı

### Is it safe for small children?
**Küçük çocuklar için güvenli midir?**
k(y)ew**chewk** chojook**lahr** eecheen gewvehn**lee**
meedeer

### Is it safe to swim here?
**Burada yüzmek güvenli midir?**
**boo**rahdah yewzmehk gewvehn**lee** meedeer

### Bathing 'prohibited / dangerous'.
**Denize girmek 'yasaklanmıştır / tehlikelidir'.**
dehnee**zeh** g(y)eermehk 'yahsahklahn**mısh**tır /
tehhleek(y)eh**lee**deer'

### It's very deep here.
**Burası çok derindir.**
**boo**rahsı **choke**
dehreendeer

### Can we water ski here?
**Burada su kayağı yapabilir miyiz?**
**boo**rahdah **soo** kah-yahwı yahpahbee**leer** mee-yeez

# HEALTH
## SAĞLIK

## General Genel

**I must see a doctor.**
**Bir doktora görünmem gerekiyor.**
beer dohktoh**rah** görewnmehm g(y)ehrehk(y)eeyor

**Where's the doctor's surgery?**
**Doktorun muayenehanesi neprededir?**
dohktohroon moo-ah-yehneh-hahneh-see **neh**rehdeh-deer

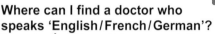

**Where can I find a doctor who speaks 'English/French/German'?**
**Nerede 'İngilizce / Fransızca / Almanca' konuşan bir doktor bulabilirim?**
**neh**rehdeh 'eeng(y)ee**leez**jeh/frahn**sız**jah/ahl**mahn**-jah' konooshahn beer dohk**tohr** boolahbeeleereem

**Can you recommend 'a/an' …?**
**Bir … önerebilir misiniz?**
beer … önehrehbee**leer** meesee-neez

| | | |
|---|---|---|
| **children's doctor** | çocuk doktoru | cho**jook** dohktohroo |
| **general practitioner** | dahiliyeci | dahheeleeyeh**jee** |
| **eye specialist** | göz doktoru | **göz** dohktohroo |
| **gynaecologist** | jinekolog | zheenehko**log** |

**What are the surgery hours?**
**Muayene saatleri nelerdir?**
moo-ah-yeh**neh** sah-aht-lehree nehlehrdeer

**Could the doctor come to see me here?**
**Doktor beni görmeye buraya gelebilir mi?**
dohktohr behnee görmeh-yeh **boo**rah-yah g(y)ehlehbee**leer** mee

**Can I have an appointment for tomorrow?**
**Yarına bir randevu alabilir miyim?**
yahrı**nah** beer rahndehvoo ahlahbee**leer** mee-yeem

## Ailments   Hastalıklar

**I'm ill.**
**Hastayım.**
hahs**tah**-yım

**I feel unwell.**
**Kendimi kötü hissediyorum.**
k(y)ehndeemee kö-**tu** heess-sehdeeyoroom

**I feel nauseous.**
**Midem bulanıyor.**
mee**dehm** boolahnıyor

**I feel shivery.**
**Titriyorum.**
teet**ree**yoroom

**I feel dizzy.**
**Başım dönüyor.**
bahs**hım** dönewyor

**I've got a fever.**
**Ateşim var.**
ahteh**sheem** vahr

**My temperature is thirty-nine degrees Centigrade.**
**Ateşim otuz dokuz derece.**
ahtehsheem otooz do**kooz** dehrehjeh

**I've been vomiting.**
**Kusuyorum.**
koos**oo**yoroom

**My stomach is upset**
**Midem bozuk.**
mee**dehm** bozook

**I've got diarrhoea.**
**İshalim var.**
eeshah**leem** vahr

**I'm constipated.**
**Kabızım.**
kah**bız**ım

**I've got a cold.**
**Soğuk algınlığım var/Üşüttüm.**
sohw**ook** ahlgınlıım vahr/ewshewt-**tewm**

**I've got a pain in my 'right/left' arm.**
**'Sağ/Sol' kolumda bir ağrı var.**
'**sahw/sol**' koloomdah beer aarı vahr

**My nose keeps bleeding.**
**Sürekli burnum kanıyor.**
**sew**rehklee boor**noom** kahnıyor

**I have difficulty in breathing.**
**Soluma güçlüğüm var.**
soloo**mah** gewchlewewm vahr

**I can't sleep.**
**Uyuyamıyorum.**
ooyoo**yah**mıyoroom

**I can't eat.**
**Yemek yiyemiyorum.**
yehmehk yee**yeh**meeyoroom

**My stomach hurts.**
**Midem ağrıyor.**
mee**dehm** ahwrıyor

**I've got a backache.**
**Belim ağrıyor.**
beh**leem** ahwrıyor

**I have an earache.**
**Kulağım ağrıyor.**
koolaa**ım** ahwrıyor

**I have a headache.**
**Başım ağrıyor.**
bah**shım** ahwrıyor

**I have sunstroke.**
**Güneş çarptı.**
gew**nehsh** chahrptı

**I have a sore throat.**
**Boğazım ağrıyor.**
bohwah**zım** ahwrıyor

**I have a bad cough.**
**Kötü bir öksürüğüm var.**
kö-**tu** beer öksewrew**ewm** vahr

**I'm allergic to …**
…'ye alerjim var.
…'yeh ahlehr**zheem** vahr

**I'm diabetic.**
Şeker hastasıyım.
sheh**k(y)ehr** hahstahsıyım

**My blood pressure is too 'low / high'.**
Tansiyonum çok 'düşük / yüksek'.
tahnseeyonoom **choke** 'dewshewk / yewksehk'

| abscess | çıban (apse) | chı**bahn** (ahp**seh**) |
|---|---|---|
| appendicitis | apandisit | ahpahndees**eet** |
| asthma | astım | **ahst**ım |
| infection | enfeksiyon | ehnfehksee**yon** |
| influenza | grip | g**reep** |
| insomnia | uykusuzluk | ooykoosooz**look** |
| itch | kaşıntı | kahs**hınt**ı |
| jaundice | sarılık | sah**rıl**ık |
| measles | kızamık | kıza**hm**ık |
| pneumonia | zatürree | zah-tewr-reh-**eh** |
| sunburn | güneş yanığı | gew**nehsh** yahnıı |
| tonsillitis | bademcik iltihabı | bahdehm**jeek** eelteehahbı |
| ulcer | ülser | ewl**sehr** |

**I think I have food poisoning.**
Zehirlendiğimi sanıyorum.
zehheerlehndee(y)ee**mee** sahnıyoroom

**There's been an accident.**
Bir kaza oldu.
beer kah**zah** oldoo

**My child has had a fall.**
Çocuğum düştü.
chojoohw**oom** dewsh-tu

**'He/She' has hurt 'his/her' head.**
**Başından yaralandı.**
bahshın**dahn** yahrahlahndı

**I've 'cut/burned' my hand.**
**Elimi 'kestim/yaktım'.**
ehlee**mee** 'k(y)ehsteem/yahktım'

**My wrist hurts.**
**Bileğim acıyor.**
beeleh-**yeem** ahjıyor

**I think I've sprained my ankle.**
**Sanırım, ayak bileğimi incittim.**
sah**nı**rım, ah-**yahk** beeleh-yeemee eenjeetteem

**I fell down and hurt my arm.**
**Düştüm ve kolumu incittim.**
dewsh**tewm** veh koloo**moo** eenjeetteem

**My 'ankle/leg' is swollen.**
**'Ayak bileğim/Bacağım' şişti.**
'ah-**yahk** beeleh-yeem/bahjahw**ım**' sheeshtee

**I can't move my 'leg/arm'.**
**'Bacağımı/Kolumu' kımıldatamıyorum.**
'bahjahwı**mı**/koloo**moo**' kımıldah**tah**mıyoroom

**There's something in my eye.**
**Gözümde bir şey var.**
gözewm**deh** beer **shay** vahr

**I have a 'wound/boil/bruise/graze/rash'.**
**Bir 'yara/çıban/çürük/sıyrık/isilik' var.**
beer 'yah**rah**/chı**bahn**/chew**rewk**/sıyrık/eesee**leek**'
vahr

**I have an insect bite.**
**Böcek soktu.**
bö**jehk** soktoo

**I have a blister.**
**Su topladı.**
**soo** toplahdı

**I've been bitten by a dog.**
**Bir köpek tarafından ısırıldım.**
beer kö**pehk** tahrahfındahn ısırıl**dım**

## Parts of the body
Vücudun organları

| | | |
|---|---|---|
| arm | kol | kol |
| back | sırt | sırt |
| bladder | idrar torbası (mesane) | |
| | eed**rahr** torbahsı (meh**saa**neh) | |
| bone | kemik | k(y)eh**meek** |
| bowel | bağırsak | bahwır**sahk** |
| breast | meme | meh**meh** |
| cheek | yanak | yah**nahk** |
| chest | göğüs | gö**ewss** |
| ear | kulak | koo**lahk** |
| elbow | dirsek | deer**sehk** |
| eye | göz | göz |
| face | yüz | yewz |
| finger | parmak | pahr**mahk** |
| genitals | cinsel organlar | jeen**sehl** orgahnlahr |
| gums | diş etleri | **deesh** ehtlehree |
| hand | el | ehl |
| head | baş | bahsh |
| heart | kalp | kahlp |
| heel | topuk | to**pook** |
| hip | kalça | kahl**chah** |
| jaw, chin | çene | cheneh |
| joint | eklem | ehk**lehm** |
| kidney | böbrek | böb**rehk** |

SAĞLIK

| knee | diz | deez |
|------|-----|------|
| kneecap | diz kapağı | **deez** kahpahwı |
| leg | **bacak** | bah**jahk** |
| lip | **dudak** | doo**dahk** |
| liver | karaciğer | kah**rah**jee(y)ehr |
| lung | akciğer | **ahk**jee(y)ehr |
| mouth | ağız | ahwz |
| muscle | kas | kahs |
| nail | tırnak | tır**nahk** |
| neck | boyun | bo**yoon** |
| nerve | sinir | see**neer** |
| nervous system | sinir sistemi | see**neer** seestehmee |
| nose | burun | boo**roon** |
| rib | kaburga kemiği | kah**boor**gah k(y)ehmee(y)ee |
| shoulder | omuz | o**mooz** |
| skin | deri | deh**ree** |
| spine | bel kemiği | **behl** k(y)ehmee(y)ee |
| spine | omurga | o**moor**gah |
| stomach | mide | mee**deh** |
| temple | şakak | shah**kahk** |
| throat | boğaz | boh**wahz** |
| thumb | başparmak | **bahsh**pahrmahk |
| toe | ayak parmağı | ah-**yahk** pahrmahwı |
| tongue | dil | deel |
| tonsils | bademcikler | bahdehmjeek**lehr** |
| vein | damar | dah**mahr** |
| wrist | bilek | bee**lehk** |

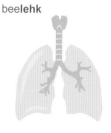

HEALTH

# **Treatment** Tedavi

**This is my usual medication.**
Bu her zaman kullandığım ilaçtır.
boo **hehr** zahmahn koollahndıım eelahchtır

**Could you give me another prescription?**
Başka bir reçete yazabilir misiniz?
bahsh**kah** beer rehcheteh yahzahbee**leer** meesee-neez

**I don't want anything too strong.**
Çok kuvvetli bir ilaç istemiyorum.
**choke** koovvehtlee beer eelahch ees**teh**meeyoroom

**Can you prescribe an antidepressant?**
Bir yatıştırıcı yazabilir misiniz?
beer yahtıshtırıjı yahzahbee**leer** meesee-neez

**Can you prescribe a 'painkiller / sedative'?**
Bir 'ağrı kesici / sakinleştirici' yazabilir misiniz?
beer 'ahwrı k(y)ehseejee / sahk(y)eenlehshteereejee'
yahzahbee**leer** meesee-neez

**How many times a day should I take it?**
Bunu günde kaç kez almalıyım?
boo**noo** gewndeh **kahch** k(y)ehz ahlmahlıyım

**Must I stay in bed?**
Yatakta kalmam gerekiyor mu?
yahtahk**tah** kahlmahm g(y)ehreh**k(y)ee**yor moo

**When can I travel again?**
Tekrar ne zaman yolculuk edebilirim?
tehkrahr **neh** zahmahn yoljoolook ehdehbeeleereem

**I feel better now.**
**Şimdi kendimi daha iyi hissediyorum.**
**sheem**dee k(y)ehndeemee dah**hah** ee-yee heess-sehdeeyoroom

**I'll take your 'temperature/blood pressure'.**
**'Ateşinizi/Tansiyonunuzu' ölçeceğim.**
'ahtehshenee**zee**/tahnseeyonoonoo**zoo**' ölchejeh-yeem

**Where does it hurt?**
**Neresi acıyor (ağrıyor)?**
**neh**rehsee ahjıyor (ahwrıyor)

**Do you have a pain here?**
**Burası acıyor mu (ağrıyor mu)?**
boorahsı ah**j**ıyor moo (ahwrıyor moo)

**How long have you had the pain?**
**Ne kadar zamandır ağrınız var?**
**neh** kahdahr zahmahndır ahwrınız vahr

**I want you to have an x-ray taken.**
**Bir röntgen çektirmenizi istiyorum.**
beer rönt**g(y)ehn** chekteermehneezee eesteeyoroom

**I'd like a specimen of your 'blood/urine'.**
**Bir 'kan/idrar' örneğinizi istiyorum.**
beer '**kahn**/eed**rahr**' örneh-yeeneezee eesteeyoroom

| Open your mouth. | Put out your tongue. |
|---|---|
| **Ağzınızı açın.** | **Dilinizi çıkarın.** |
| ahwzını**zı** ah-chın | deeleenee**zee** chıkahrın |

| Breathe 'in/out'. | Please lie down. |
|---|---|
| **Nefes 'alın/verin'.** | **Lütfen yatın.** |
| neh**fehss** 'ahlın/vehreen' | **lewt**fehn yahtın |

**It's infected.**
**Mikrop kapmış.**
meek**rop** kahpmısh

**You have food poisoning.**
**Yemekten zehirlenmişsiniz.**
yehmehk**tehn** zehheerlehn**meesh**seeneez

**I'll have to put it in plaster.**
**Alçıya koymam gerekecek.**
ahlchı-**yah** koymahm g(y)ehrehk(y)ehjehk

**I'll give you some antibiotics.**
**Size bir antibiyotik vereceğim.**
seezeh beer ahnteebeeyo**teek** vehrehjeh-yeem

**Take this three times a day.**
**Bunu günde üç kez alın.**
boo**noo** gewndeh **ewch** k(y)ehz ahlın

**I'll give you an injection.**
**Size bir iğne yazacağım.**
seezeh beer ee(y)**neh** yahzahjahwım

## Women's section   Kadın bölümü

**I haven't had my period for two months.**
**İki aydır regl (aybaşı) olmadım.**
eek**(y)ee** ai-dır rehgl (ai-bahshı) ol**mah**dım

**I have period pains.**
**Regl ağrılarım var.**
**rehgl** ahwrılahrım vahr

**I have a vaginal infection.**
**Vajinal bir enfeksiyonum var.**
vahzhee**nahl** beer ehnfehkseeyonoom vahr

SAĞLIK

**I'm two months' pregnant.**
**İki aylık hamileyim.**
eek(y)ee ai-lık hahmee**leh**-yeem

**I'm on the pill.**
**Doğum kontrol hapı alıyorum.**
dohwoom kon**trol** hahpı ahlıyoroom

## Dentist  Diş hekimi

**Can you recommend a good dentist?**
**İyi bir diş hekimi önerebilir misiniz?**
ee-**yee** beer **deesh** hehk(y)eemee önehrehbee**leer**
meesee-neez

**I must see a dentist.**
**Bir diş hekimine görünmem gerekiyor.**
beer **deesh** hehk(y)eemeeneh görewnmehm
g(y)ehrehk(y)eeyor

**I have a toothache.**
**Dişim ağrıyor.**
dee**sheem** ahwrıyor

**Can you fix it temporarily?**
**Şimdilik düzeltebilir misiniz?**
sheemdeeleek dewzehltehbee**leer** meesee-neez

**This tooth 'has broken off/hurts'.**
**Bu diş 'kırıldı/ağrıyor'.**
**boo** deesh 'kırıl**dı**/ahwrıyor'

| at the back | arkadaki | ahrkahdah**k(y)ee** |
| at the bottom | aşağıdaki | ahshahwdah**k(y)ee** |
| at the front | öndeki | öndeh**k(y)ee** |
| at the top | yukarıdaki | yookahrıdah**k(y)ee** |

HEALTH

# REFERENCE SECTION
## BAŞVURU BÖLÜMÜ

BAŞVURU BÖLÜMÜ

REFERENCE SECTION

## Numbers Sayılar

| | | | |
|---|---|---|---|
| 0 | zero | sıfır | sıfır |
| 1 | one | bir | beer |
| 2 | two | iki | eek(y)ee |
| 3 | three | üç | ewch |
| 4 | four | dört | dört |
| 5 | five | beş | behsh |
| 6 | six | altı | ahltı |
| 7 | seven | yedi | yehdee |
| 8 | eight | sekiz | sehk(y)eez |
| 9 | nine | dokuz | dokooz |
| 10 | ten | on | on |
| 11 | eleven | on bir | on beer |
| 12 | twelve | on iki | on eek(y)ee |
| 13 | thirteen | on üç | on ewch |
| 14 | fourteen | on dört | on dört |
| 15 | fifteen | on beş | on behsh |
| 16 | sixteen | on altı | on ahltı |
| 17 | seventeen | on yedi | on yehdee |
| 18 | eighteen | on sekiz | on sehk(y)eez |
| 19 | nineteen | on dokuz | on dokooz |
| 20 | twenty | yirmi | yeermee |
| 21 | twenty-one | yirmi bir | yeermee beer |
| 22 | twenty-two | yirmi iki | yeermee eek(y)ee |
| 23 | twenty-three | yirmi üç | yeermee ewch |
| 30 | thirty | otuz | otooz |
| 40 | forty | kırk | kırk |
| 50 | fifty | elli | ehllee |
| 60 | sixty | altmış | ahltmısh |
| 70 | seventy | yetmiş | yehtmeesh |
| 80 | eighty | seksen | seksehn |
| 90 | ninety | doksan | doksahn |
| 99 | ninety-nine | doksan dokuz | doksahn dokooz |

| | | | |
|---|---|---|---|
| 100 | hundred | yüz | yewz |
| 200 | two hundred | iki yüz | ee**k(y)ee** yewz |
| 1,000 | thousand | bin | been |
| 2,000 | two thousand | iki bin | ee**k(y)ee** been |
| 10,000 | ten thousand | on bin | **on** been |
| 20,000 | twenty thousand | yirmi bin | yeer**mee** been |
| 100,000 | a hundred thousand | yüz bin | yewz been |
| 200,000 | two hundred thousand | iki yüz bin | |
| | | | ee**k(y)ee** yewz been |

| | | | |
|---|---|---|---|
| 1,000,000 | a million | bir milyon | **beer** meelyon |
| 1,000,000,000 | a billion | bir milyar | **beer** meelyahr |

## ORDINAL NUMBERS     SIRA SAYILARI

| | | |
|---|---|---|
| first | birinci | beereen**jee** |
| second | ikinci | ek(y)een**jee** |
| third | üçüncü | ewchewn**jew** |
| fourth | dördüncü | dördewn**jew** |
| fifth | beşinci | behsheen**jee** |
| sixth | altıncı | ahltın**jı** |
| seventh | yedinci | yehdeen**jee** |
| eighth | sekizinci | sehk(y)eezeen**jee** |
| ninth | dokuzuncu | dokoozoon**joo** |
| tenth | onuncu | onoon**joo** |

| | | |
|---|---|---|
| one book, a book | bir kitap | **beer** k(y)eetahp |
| (the) two books | iki kitap | ee**k(y)ee** k(y)eetahp |
| one time, once | bir kez | **beer** k(y)ehz |
| two times, twice | iki kez | ee**k(y)ee** k(y)ehz |
| three times | üç kez | **ewch** k(y)ehz |
| half an hour | yarım saat | yah**rım** sah-aht |
| half a kilo | yarım kilo | yah**rım** k(y)eelo |
| half an apple | yarım elma | yah**rım** ehlmah |
| one and a half kilos | bir buçuk kilo | |
| | | **beer** boochook k(y)eelo |

| **two and a half hours** | **iki buçuk saat** | |
| | eek(y)ee boochook sah-aht | |
| **one percent** | **yüzde bir** | yewzdeh **beer** |
| **one by one** | **birer birer** | bee**rehr** beerehr |

**1991** bin dokuz yüz doksan bir
been do**kuz** yewz doksan **beer**

**1987** bin dokuz yüz seksen yedi
been do**kuz** yewz seksehn yeh**dee**

**2005** iki bin beş
eek(y)ee been **behsh**

## Conversion tables
Dönüştürme tabloları

### Length Measures    Uzunluk Ölçüleri

1 **inch** = 2.54 cm (santimetre)
1 **foot** = 30.479 cm (santimetre)
1 **yard** = 0.914 m (metre)
1 **mile** = 1 mil = 1609.34 m (metre)
1 **nautical mile** : 1 deniz mili = 1852 m (metre)
1 **kilometre** (kilometer) = 1 kilometre

### Weight Measures    Ağırlık Ölçüleri

1 **ounce** = 28.35 gr (gram)
1 **pound** = 0.454 kg (kilogram)
1 **stone** = 6.35 kg (kilogram)
1 **hundredweight** = 50.80 kg (kilogram)
1 **metric ton** (tonne) = 1000 kg (kilogram)
1 **short ton** (**American**) = 907,185 kg (kilogram)
1 **long ton** (**English**) = 1016 kg (kilogram)

## **Fluid Measures**   Sıvı Ölçüleri

1 gallon :
**American** = 3.79 litre
**English** = 4.54 litre

1 quart (1/4 gallon):
**American** = 0.946 litre
**English** = 1.136 litre

1 pint (1/8 gallon):
**American** = 0.473 litre
**English** = 0.568 litre

## **Temperature Measures**   Sıvı Ölçüleri

1 centigrade = $[(1 \times 1.8) + 32]$ degrees **Fahrenheit**

| Centigrade (Santigrat) | Fahrenheit (Fahrenhayt) |
|---|---|
| - 25 | - 13 |
| - 20 | - 4 |
| - 5 | 23 |
| 0 | 32 |
| 5 | 39.5 |
| 10 | 50 |
| 25 | 77 |

## **Days**   Günler

| Monday | Pazartesi | pah**zahr**tehsee |
| Tuesday | Salı | sah**lı** |
| Wednesday | Çarşamba | chahrshahm**bah** |
| Thursday | Perşembe | pehrshehm**beh** |
| Friday | Cuma | joo**mah** |
| Saturday | Cumartesi | joo**mah**rtehsee |
| Sunday | Pazar | pah**zahr** |

BAŞVURU BÖLÜMÜ

| on Monday | Pazartesi günü |  |
| --- | --- | --- |
|  | pah**zahr**tehsee gewnew |  |
| on Tuesday | Salı günü | sahlı gewnew |
| yesterday | dün | dewn |
| today | bugün | **boo**-gewn |
| tomorrow | yarın | **yah**rın |
| the day before yesterday | önceki gün |  |
|  | önjeh**k(y)ee** gewn |  |
| the day after tomorrow | öbür gün | ö**bewr** gewn |
| morning | sabah | sah**bahh** |
| in the morning | sabahleyin | sah**bahh**leh-yeen |
| afternoon | öğleden sonra |  |
|  | ööleh**dehn** sonrah |  |
| in the afternoon | öğleden sonra(ları) |  |
|  | ööleh**dehn** sonrah(lahrı) |  |
| evening | akşam | ahk**shahm** |
| in the evening | akşamleyin | ahk**shahm**-leh-yeen |
| night | gece | g(y)eh**jeh** |
| at night | geceleyin | g(y)eh**jeh**-leh-yeen |

## Months and Seasons Aylar ve Mevsimler

| January | Ocak | o-**jahk** |
| --- | --- | --- |
| February | Şubat | shoo**baht** |
| March | Mart | mahrt |
| April | Nisan | nee**sahn** |
| May | Mayıs | mah-**yıs** |
| June | Haziran | hahzee**rahn** |
| July | Temmuz | tehm**mooz** |
| August | Ağustos | ahwoos**tos** |
| September | Eylül | ay**lewl** |
| October | Ekim | ehk(y)eem |
| November | Kasım | kah**sım** |
| December | Aralık | ahrah**lık** |

REFERENCE SECTION

| | | |
|---|---|---|
| in March | **Martta, Mart ayında** | |
| | mahrt**tah**, **mahrt** ah-yındah | |
| the first of February | **Şubatın biri** | |
| | shoobah**tın** bee**ree** | |
| on the second of April | **Nisanın ikisinde** | |
| | neesah**nın** eek(y)eeseen**deh** | |
| on the fifth of February | **Şubatın beşinde** | |
| | shoobah**tın** behsheen**deh** | |
| the sixth of May | **Mayısın altısı** | |
| | mah-yı**sın** ahl**tı**sı | |
| the beginning of October | **Ekimin başı** | |
| | ehk(y)ee**meen** bah**shı** | |
| the end of November | **Kasımın sonu** | |
| | kahsı**mın** so**noo** | |

| | | |
|---|---|---|
| **Winter** | **Kış** | kısh |
| **Spring** | **İlkbahar** | **eelk**bahhahr |
| **Summer** | **Yaz** | yahz |
| **Autumn** | **Sonbahar** | **son**bahhahr |
| **in autumn** | **sonbaharda** | **son**bahhahrdah |
| **in spring** | **ilkbaharda** | **eelk**bahhahrdah |
| **during the winter** | **kış boyunca** | **kısh** boyoonjah |

## Countries  Ülkeler

| | | |
|---|---|---|
| **Afghanistan** | **Afganistan** | ahfgahnees**tahn** |
| **Albania** | **Arnavutluk** | ahrnahvoot**look** |
| **Algeria** | **Cezayir** | jeh**zaa**-yeer |
| **Argentina** | **Arjantin** | ahr-**zhahn**-teen |
| **Armenia** | **Ermenistan** | ehrmehnees**tahn** |
| **Azerbaijan** | **Azerbaycan** | ahzehr-bai-**jahn** |
| **Bolivia** | **Bolivya** | bo**leev**yah |
| **Brazil** | **Brezilya** | breh**zeel**yah |
| **Bulgaria** | **Bulgaristan** | boolgahrees**tahn** |

BAŞVURU BÖLÜMÜ

| Canada | Kanada | kah**nah**dah |
|---|---|---|
| China | Çin | cheen |
| Cuba | Küba | **k(y)ew**bah |
| Cyprus | Kıbrıs | **kıb**rıss |
| Denmark | Danimarka | dahnee**mahr**kah |
| Egypt | Mısır | **mı**sır |
| England | İngiltere | eeng(y)eel**teh**reh |
| Finland | Finlandiya | feen**lahn**-dee-yah |
| France | Fransa | **frahn**sah |
| Georgia | Gürcistan | gewrjees**tahn** |
| Germany | Almanya | ahl-**mahn**-yah |
| Great Britain | Büyük Britanya | bew**yewk** breetahn-yah |
| India | Hindistan | heendees**tahn** |
| Iran | İran | **ee**rahn |
| Iraq | Irak | ı**rahk** |
| Ireland | İrlanda | eer**lahn**dah |
| Israel | İsrail | eess-**rah**-eel |
| Italy | İtalya | ee**tahl**-yah |
| Japan | Japonya | zhah-**pon**yah |
| Jordan | Ürdün | **ewr**dewn |
| Kenya | Kenya | **k(y)ehn**yah |
| Korea | Kore | **ko**reh |
| Kuwait | Kuveyt | **koo**vait |
| Lebanon | Lübnan | **lewb**nahn |
| Libya | Libya | **leeb**yah |
| Luxembourg | Lüksembourg | lewk**sehm**booorg |
| Hungary | Macaristan | mahjahrees**tahn** |
| Malaysia | Malezya | mah**lehz**yah |
| Mexico | Meksika | mehk**see**kah |
| Netherlands | Hollanda | hol**lahn**dah |
| New Zealand | Yeni Zelanda | yeh**nee** zehlahndah |
| Greece | Yunanistan | yoonahnees**tahn** |
| Nicaragua | Nikaragua | neekahrah**goo**ah |
| Nigeria | Nijerya | nee**zhehr**-yah |
| Norway | Norveç | **nor**vehch |
| Pakistan | Pakistan | pahk(y)ees**tahn** |
| Panama | Panama | pah**nah**mah |
| Palestine | Filistin | fee**lees**teen |

REFERENCE SECTION

| Paraguay | Paraguay | pahrah**goo**-ai |
|---|---|---|
| Peru | Peru | **peh**roo |
| Philippines | Filipinler | feelee**peen**lehr |
| Poland | Polonya | po**lon**yah |
| Portugal | Portekiz | **por**tehk(y)eez |
| Romania | Romanya | ro**mahn**yah |
| Russia | Rusya | **roos**yah |
| Saudi Arabia | Suudi Arabistan | soooo**dee** ahrahbeestahn |
| Scotland | İskoçya | ees**koch**yah |
| Somalia | Somali | so**mah**lee |
| South Africa | Güney Afrika | gew**nay** ahfreekah |
| Spain | İspanya | ees**pahn**yah |
| Sudan | Sudan | **soo**dahn |
| Sweden | İsveç | **ees**vehch |
| Switzerland | İsviçre | ees**veech**reh |
| Syria | Suriye | **soo**ree-yeh |
| Taiwan | Tayvan | **tai**-vahn |
| Thailand | Tayland | **tai**-lahnd |
| Tunisia | Tunus | **too**nooss |
| Turkey | Türkiye | **tewr**-k(y)eeyeh |
| Uganda | Uganda | oo**gahn**dah |
| United States | A. B. D. (Amerika Birleşik Devletleri) | |
| ah beh deh (ahmeh**ree**kah beerleh**sheek** dehvleht-lehree) | | |
| Uruguay | Uruguay | ooroo**goo**-ai |
| Venezuela | Venezuela | vehnehzoo**ehlah** |
| Vietnam | Vietnam | vee-**eht**nahm |
| Wales | Galler | **gahl**lehr |
| Yemen | Yemen | **yeh**mehn |
| Zambia | Zambiya | **zahm**beeyah |

## Kıtalar Continents

| Asia | Asya | **ahss**-yah |
|---|---|---|
| Europe | Avrupa | ahv**roo**pah |
| Africa | Afrika | ah**free**kah |
| Australia | Avustralya | ahvoo**strahl**yah |
| North America | Kuzey Amerika | koo**zay** ahmehreekah |
| South America | Güney Amerika | gew**nay** ahmehreekah |

# BASIC TURKISH GRAMMAR

## TEMEL TÜRKÇE DİLBİLGİSİ

## Subject Pronouns

| ben | I |
|-----|---|
| sen | you (informal, familiar singular) |
| o | he, she, it |
| biz | we |
| siz | you (formal, polite singular and plural) |
| onlar | they |

## Demonstratives

| bu | this | bunlar | these |
|----|------|--------|-------|
| şu | that | şunlar | those |
| o | that | onlar | those |

## Syllabification

Turkish has six syllable patterns. Each syllable begins with a single consonant or a single vowel.

| genç | young | el | hand |
|------|-------|----|------|
| alt | bottom | ne | what |
| sen | you | o | he, she, it, that |
| | | | (demonstrative) |

## Vowel Harmony Rule

There are two groups of vowels in the Turkish alphabet :

**A) a , ı , o , u**      **B) e , i , ö , ü**

### Vowel Harmony Rule

All the vowels in original Turkish words tend to be in the same group. The final vowel of the word is called a 'dominant vowel'. The group of the final vowel in the word determines the group of the vowel in the suffix. Study the following examples and try to understand how the harmony rule works.

- **kedidir**        ...... is (a) cat
- **yaşlıdır**        ...... is old
- **yoldur**        ...... (a) road
- **köydür**        ...... (a) village

## Adjectives & Indefinite Article

**Adjective + noun** is used as in English.
The adjective modifies the noun it precedes.

- **güzel kız**        (the) pretty girl
- **ilginç kitap**        (the) interesting book
- **uzun (boylu) çocuk**        (the) tall child

☛ Note that there is no definite article (the) in Turkish. Any noun may be understood with or without 'the'.

♦ When the indefinite article and adjective(s) modify one noun, the indefinite article is followed by the noun.

- **güzel bir kız**        a pretty girl

■ '**mı/mi/mu/mü**' is the interrogative particle.
It is written as an independent word.

| | | | |
|---|---|---|---|
| • ..... güzel **mi**(dir)**?** | is ..... pretty? |
| • ..... akıllı **mı**(dır)**?** | is ..... intelligent? |
| • ..... büyük **mü**(dür)**?** | is ..... big? |
| • ..... ucuz **mu**(dur)**?** | is ..... cheap? |

## The Plural

The plural is formed by adding the suffix '**ler/lar**' to
the singular.

| | |
|---|---|
| After **e, i, o, ü** in the last syllable : | **-ler** |
| After **a, ı, o, u** in the last syllable : | **-lar** |

| | |
|---|---|
| • **çocuk** | (the) child |
| • çocuk**lar** | (the) children |
| • **defter** | (the) notebook |
| • defter**ler** | (the) notebooks |

## Verbs

The infinitive is formed by adding the suffix
'**mek/mak**' to the simple verb (verb stem) which is the
singular imperative.

| Infinitive | | Verb stem | |
|---|---|---|---|
| **gel**mek | coming, to come | **gel** | come |
| **git**mek | going, to go | **git** | go |

### Negative Form

A verb is turned into the negative by attaching the
negative sign '**me/ma**' directly to the verb stem. In the
negative form the stress falls on the last syllable of the
verb stem.

- gitme**mek**     **not** going, **not** to go
- gitme !         **don't** go!

## Possessive Case

| | | Possessive adjectives | |
|------|------------|----------|---------------|
| **Ben** | I | **Benim** | My |
| **Sen** | You | **Senin** | Your |
| **O** | He, She, It | **Onun** | His, Her, Its |
| **Biz** | We | **Bizim** | Our |
| **Siz** | You | **Sizin** | Your |
| **Onlar** | They | **Onların** | Their |
| **Kim?** | Who? | **Kimin?** | Whose? |

■ When the possessive adjective is followed by a noun, the noun takes the possessive suffix too.

- **benim** defter**im**    my notebook (**defter** : notebook)
- **senin** defter**in**     your notebook

■ The possessive pronouns may be omitted.

- **defterim**     my notebook
- **defterimiz**   our notebook

### Compounds

- Ali'**nin** kitabı    Ali's book; the book of Ali
- Tom'**un** defteri    Tom's notebook; the notebook of Tom
- adam**ın** yüz**ü**      the man's face; the face of the man
- kadın**ın** saçı       the woman's hair; the hair of the woman

## There is / are (not)

The words **var** and **yok** are always followed by the verb 'to be' which may be omitted in the present tense.

| var | : | extant, in existence |
| yok | : | non-extant, not in existence |

■ These words have two principal uses:

**1.** Their first function is to express possession.

- **(Benim) bir arabam var(dır)**.  I have (got) a car.

**2.** Their second function is to express the English 'there is/are (not)'

- **Masanın üstünde bir kitap var(dır)**.
  There is a book on the table.

## Simple Past Tense

The Turkish 'Simple Past Tense' is used to talk about an action that is finished or has been completed in the past. It can also be used as an equivalent to the English 'Present Perfect Tense'.

(*) **(ben) geldim**  I came, I did come, I have come

(*) Personal pronouns may be omitted.

■ All the simple past tense suffixes (which are the past tense forms of 'to be') begin with the variable consonant **t/d**.

When the dominant vowel in the verb stem is 'e' or 'i':

gelmek to come          seçmek to choose, to select

| (Ben) | geldim | seçtim | eledim |
| (Sen) | geldin | seçtin | eledin |
| (O) | geldi | seçti | eledi |
| (Biz) | geldik | seçtik | eledik |
| (Siz) | geldiniz | seçtiniz | elediniz |
| (Onlar) | geldiler | seçtiler | elediler |

TÜRKÇE DİLBİLGİSİ

<u>When the dominant vowel is 'a' or 'ı':</u>

| | <u>da</u>lmak to dive | | <u>ba</u>kmak to look |
|---|---|---|---|
| **(Ben)** | dald**ım** | | bakt**ım** |
| **(Sen)** | dald**ın** | | bakt**ın** |

<u>When the dominant vowel is 'o' or 'u'</u>

| | <u>oku</u>mak to read | | <u>ko</u>şmak to run |
|---|---|---|---|
| **(Ben)** | oku**dum** | | koş**tum** |
| **(Sen)** | oku**dun** | | koş**tun** |

<u>When the dominant vowel is 'ö' or 'ü'</u>

| | <u>bö</u>lmek to separate, to divide | | <u>ö</u>pmek to kiss |
|---|---|---|---|
| **(Ben)** | böl**düm** | | öp**tüm** |
| **(Sen)** | böl**dün** | | öp**tün** |

### Negative

The simple past tense suffix is preceded by the negative syllable '**me/ma**'.

- gel**me**<u>dim</u>    I didn't come, I haven't come

### Interrogative

- gördün **mü**?    did you see?, have you seen?
- okudunuz **mu**?    did you read?, have you read?
- **Kim** geldi?    who came?, who has come?
- **Nasıl** geldiler?    how did (have) they come?

## Present Continuous Tense

| (Ben) | **verb stem +** (ı / i / u / ü) **+ yor + um** |
|---|---|
| **(Sen)** | **verb stem +** (ı / i / u / ü) **+ yor + sun** |
| **(O)** | **verb stem +** (ı / i / u / ü) **+ yor** |
| **(Biz)** | **verb stem +** (ı / i / u / ü) **+ yor + uz** |
| **(Siz)** | **verb stem +** (ı / i / u / ü) **+ yor + sunuz** |
| **(Onlar)** | **verb stem +** (ı / i / u / ü) **+ yor + lar** |

TURKISH GRAMMAR

**bak**mak    to look

| (Ben) | bak**ıyorum** | I am looking. |
| (Sen) | bak**ıyorsun** | You are looking. |
| (O) | bak**ıyor** | He (she, it) is looking. |

**gel**mek    to come

| (Biz) | gel**iyoruz** | We are coming. |
| (Siz) | gel**iyorsunuz** | You are coming. |
| (Onlar) | gel**iyorlar** | They are coming. |

## Negative

In the present continuous tense the negative sign is
**m(ı/i/u/ü)**.

| (Ben) | **verb stem** + m(ı / i / u / ü) + yor um |
| (Sen) | **verb stem** + m(ı / i / u / ü) + yor sun |
| (O) | **verb stem** + m(ı / i / u / ü) + yor |
| (Biz) | **verb stem** + m(ı / i / u / ü) + yor uz |
| (Siz) | **verb stem** + m(ı / i / u / ü) + yor sunuz |
| (Onlar) | **verb stem** + m(ı / i / u / ü) + yor lar |

- (Ben)    **gelmiyorum**       I am not coming
- (Sen)    **gelmiyorsun**      You are not coming

## Interrogative

| (Ben) | **verb stem** + (ı / i / u / ü) + yor mu yum? |
| (Sen) | **verb stem** + (ı / i / u / ü) + yor mu sun? |
| (O) | **verb stem** + (ı / i / u / ü) + yor mu? |
| (Biz) | **verb stem** + (ı / i / u / ü) + yor mu yuz? |
| (Siz) | **verb stem** + (ı / i / u / ü) + yor mu sunuz? |
| (Onlar) | **verb stem** + (ı / i / u / ü) + yor lar mı? |

- (Ben)    **geliyor muyum?**       Am I coming?
- (Sen)    **geliyor musun?**       Are you coming?

## Simple Present Tense

<u>When the verb stem ends in a consonant :</u>

| Verb Stem + | Tense particle (a/e/ı/i/ü/u)r + | Personal suffix | |
|---|---|---|---|
| gel | ir | im | I come |
| gel | ir | sin | you come |
| gel | ir | | he (she, it) comes |
| gel | ir | iz | we come |
| gel | ir | siniz | you come |
| gel | ir | ler | they come |

- Her sabah erken kalk**arım**.
  I get up early every morning.

- Yüzme havuzu 9.00'da açıl**ır**.
  The swimming pool opens at 9.00.

- Dünya güneşin çevresinde dön**er**.
  The world goes round the sun.

<u>When the verb stem ends in a vowel :</u>

| Verb Stem + | r + | Personal suffix | |
|---|---|---|---|
| oku | r | um | I read |
| oku | r | sun | you read |
| oku | r | | he (she, it) reads |
| oku | r | uz | we read |
| oku | r | sunuz | you read |
| oku | r | lar | they read |

- yürü**rüm**    I walk
- tara**rım**    I comb
- ezberle**rim**    I memorize

## Negative

| Verb Stem + | me(z)/ma(z) + | Personal suffix | |
|---|---|---|---|
| gel | me | m | I don't come |
| gel | mez | sin | you don't come |
| gel | mez | | he (she, it) doesn't come |
| gel | me | yiz | we don't come |
| gel | mez | siniz | you don't come |
| gel | mez | ler | they don't come |

## Interrogative

### mı/mi/mu/mü

| | | | |
|---|---|---|---|
| gelir | mi | yim? | do I come? |
| gelir | mi | sin? | do you come? |
| gelir | mi ? | | does he (she, it) come? |
| gelir | mi | yiz? | do we come? |
| gelir | mi | siniz? | do you come? |
| gelirler | mi ? | | do they come? |

## Future Tense

| | | Future tense particle | |
|---|---|---|---|
| | Verb stem + | (ecek / acak) + | Personal suffix |
| (ben) | gel | eceğ * | im |
| | I will (am going to) come | | |
| (sen) | gel | ecek | sin |
| | you will (are going to) come | | |
| (o) | gel | ecek | |
| | he/she/it will (is going to) come | | |

| | | | |
|---|---|---|---|
| **(biz)** | **gel** | **eceğ** * | **iz** |
| we will (are going to) come | | | |
| **(siz)** | **gel** | **ecek** | **siniz** |
| you will (are going to) come | | | |
| **(onlar)** | **gel** | **ecek** | **ler** |
| they will (are going to) come | | | |

\*The future tense particle is **'ecek/acak'**.

  **'k'** is a variable consonant (**k/ğ**).

- yaz**mak**    to write      yaz**acağım**    I will write

- yürü**mek**    to walk      yürü**yecek**    he/she will walk

## Negative

| | | | | |
|---|---|---|---|---|
| **gel** | **me** | ***yeceğ** | **im** | I won't come |
| **gel** | **me** | **yecek** | **sin** | you won't come |
| **gel** | **me** | **yecek** | | he/she/it won't come |
| **gel** | **me** | **yeceğ** | **iz** | we won't come |
| **gel** | **me** | **yecek** | **siniz** | you won't come |
| **gel** | **me** | **yecek** | **ler** | they won't come |

   * **'y'** is a buffer.

- yaz**mayacağım**      I won't write
- temiz**lemeyeceğiz**      we won't clean

## Interrogative

| | | | | |
|---|---|---|---|---|
| **gel** | **ecek** | **mi** | **yim?** | will I come? |
| **gel** | **ecek** | **mi** | **sin?** | will you come? |
| **gel** | **ecek** | **mi?** | | will he/she/it come? |
| **gel** | **ecek** | **mi** | **yiz?** | will we come? |
| **gel** | **ecek** | **mi** | **siniz?** | will you come? |
| **gel** | **ecek(ler)** | **mi?** | | will they come? |

- yaz**acak mıyım?**          will I write?
- yürü**yecek mi?**           will he / she walk?

## Necessity

### The particle 'meli/malı'

The particle '**meli/malı**' means 'must, have to, be obliged to...etc'. It is attached to the verb stem and followed by the required form of '**olmak**: to be'

| Gitmeliyim | I have to go | (gitmek : to go) |
|---|---|---|
| Okumalıyım | I have to read | (okumak : to read) |

### Negative

| (ben) gitmemeliyim  I mustn't go |
|---|

- yürü**memeli**yim      I mustn't walk
- yürü**memeli**sin      you mustn't walk

### Interrogative

- gitmeli **mi**yim?      do I have to go?
- gitmeli **mi**sin?      do you have to go?

### Zorunda olmak (be obliged to/have to)

| (Ben) **gitmek zorundayım**<br>I **am obliged to (have to) go** |
|---|

- (ben)   gitmek **zorunda**yım       I am obliged to go
- (sen)   gitmek **zorunda**sın       you are obliged to go
- (o)     gitmek **zorunda**(dır)     she is obliged to go
- (biz)   gitmek **zorunda**yız       we are obliged to go
- (siz)   gitmek **zorunda**sınız     you are obliged to go
- (onlar) gitmek **zorunda**(dır)lar  they are obliged to go

### Negative

- gitmek zorunda **değilim**          I don't have to go

### Interrogative

- gitmek zorunda **mı**yım?          do I have to go?

# TURKISH - ENGLISH
# **DICTIONARY**

## TÜRKÇE - İNGİLİZCE
## **SÖZLÜK**

| Kısaltmalar | Abbreviations |
|---|---|
| *n.* : noun | *pron.* : pronoun |
| *adj.* : adjective | *prep.* : preposition |
| *v.* : verb | *conj.* : conjunction |
| *adv.* : adverb | *interj.* : interjection |
| *pref.* : prefix | *suf.* : suffix |

## A - a

abartmak *v.* exaggerate.
abone *n.* subscriber.
acele etmek *v.* hurry.
acente *n.* agent.
acı *adj.* bitter; pain.
acı veren *adj.* painful.
acımak *v.* pity.
acıtmak *v.* hurt.
acil durum *n.* emergency.
acil *adj.* urgent.
aç *adj.* hungry.
açık *adj.* open, light, clear.
açıkça *adj.* obviously.
açıklama *n.* explanation.
açıklamak *v.* explain.
açlık *n.* hunger.
açmak *v.* open; turn on.
ad *n.* name.
ada *n.* island.
adalet *n.* justice.
adam *n.* man, fellow.
adım *n.* step.
adil *adj.* fair.
adres *n.* address.
af *n.* pardon; forgiveness.
affedersin(iz)! *interj.* excuse me!
affetmek *v.* excuse, forgive.
ağaç *n.* tree.
ağır *adj.* heavy.
ağırlığında olmak *v.* weigh.
ağırlık *n.* weight.

**ağız** *n.* mouth.
**ağlamak** *v.* cry.
**ağrı** *n.* pain.
**ağrımak** *v.* ache.
**ağustos** *n.* August.
**ah!** *interj.* ah, ouch!
**ahlaki** *adj.* moral.
**ahmak** *n.* fool.
**aile** *n.* family.
**ait olmak** *v.* belong to.
**akciğer** *n.* lung.
**akıl** *n.* mind, reason, sense.
**akıllı** *adj.* clever.
**akıllıca** *adj.* wise, *adv.*
  cleverly.
**akıntı** *n.* stream.
**akmak** *v.* flow, run.
**akraba** *n.* relative.
**akşam** *n.* evening.
**aktör** *n.* actor.
**aktris** *n.* actress.
**alan** *n.* area.
**alarm** *n.* alarm.
**aldatmak** *v.* cheat.
**aldırış etmek** *v.* mind.
**alet** *n.* tool, instrument.
**alev** *n.* flame.
**alfabetik** *adj.* alphabetical.
**alıkoymak** *v.* keep.
**alın** *n.* forehead.
**alışık olmak** *v.* be used to.
**alışılmış** *adj.* usual.
**alışkanlık** *n.* habit.
**alışmış** *adj.* used to.
**alıştırma** *n.* exercise, activity.
**alışveriş** *n.* shopping.
**alkol** *n.* alcohol.
**Allah** *n.* God.
**allahaısmarladık!** *interj.*
  goodbye!
**almak** *v.* get, receive, take.
**alt etmek** *v.* overcome.
**alt** *n.* bottom.

**alt kat(ta)** *prep.* downstairs.
**altı** *n. / adj.* six.
**altın** *n.* gold, *adj.* golden.
**ama** *conj.* but.
**amaç** *n.* aim.
**aman Allahım / Tanrım!** *interj.*
  oh dear!, good God!
**ambulans** *n.* ambulance.
**amca** *n.* uncle.
**ampul** *n.* bulb.
**an** *n.* moment.
**ana baba** *n.* parent(s).
**ana** *n. / adj.* main.
**anahtar** *n.* key, switch.
**anı** *n.* memory.
**anıt** *n.* monument.
**anlam** *n.* meaning, sense.
**anlamak** *v.* understand,
  realize; see.
**anlamı olmak** *v.* mean.
**anlaşma** *n.* agreement.
**anlatmak** *v.* tell.
**anlayış** *n.* understanding.
**anne** *n.* mother, mummy.
**ansızın** *adv.* suddenly.
**antrenman** *n.* training.
**apaçık** *adj.* plain, obvious.
**apartman dairesi** *n.* flat.
**aptal** *adj.* stupid, *n.* fool.
**ara** *n.* break.
**ara sıra (arada sırada)** *adv.*
  sometimes, occasionally.
**araba** *n.* car, automobile.
**araç** *n.* vehicle.
**aralık** *n.* interval, half-open; *n.*
  December.
**aramak** *v.* search for, look in,
  look for; call.
**arasında** *prep.* between,
  among.
**araştırma** *n.* research.
**arı** *n.* bee.
**arıza yapmak** *v.* break down.

arka *n.* back.
arkada / arkasında *prep.* behind.
arkadaş *n.* friend.
arkadaşlık *n.* friendship.
armağan *n.* gift, present.
armut *n.* pear.
artmak *v.* increase.
asansör *n.* lift, elevator.
asıl *adj.* original.
asılsız *adj.* false, baseless.
asit *n.* acid.
asker *n.* soldier.
askeri *adj.* military.
askerler *n.* troops.
asla *adv.* never.
aslan *n.* lion.
asmak *v.* hang.
aşağı *prep. / adv.* down.
aşağıda below.
aşağıya doğru *prep.* downwards.
aşçı *n.* cook.
aşık olmak *v.* be in love, fall in love.
aşırı *adj.* extreme.
aşırmak *v.* steal.
aşina (tanıdık) *adj.* familiar.
at arabası *n.* cart.
at *n.* horse.
ata binmek *v.* ride.
atamak *v.* appoint.
ateş etmek *v.* shoot.
ateş *n.* fire; temperature.
ateş yakmak *v.* fire.
atış *n.* shoot, throw.
atlamak *v.* jump.
atmak *v.* throw.
atölye *n.* workshop.
av *n.* hunt.
avcı *n.* hunter.
avlanmak *v.* hunt.
avlu *n.* yard.

avukat *n.* lawyer.
ay *n.* moon; month.
ayağa kalkmak *v.* stand up.
ayak basmak *v.* arrive.
ayak bileği *n.* ankle.
ayak *n.* foot.
ayak parmağı *n.* toe.
ayakkabı *n.* shoe.
ayçiçeği *n.* sunflower.
aydınlatma *n.* lighting.
aydınlatmak *v.* flash.
ayırmak *v.* separate; reserve.
ayırt etmek *v.* distinguish.
aylık *adj.* monthly; salary.
ayna *n.* mirror.
aynı *adj.* same.
ayrı *adj.* separate.
ayrılma *n.* separation.
ayrılmak *v.* leave, depart.
ayrıntı *n.* detail.
az *adj.* little, few.
azaltmak *v.* reduce.

## B - b

baba *n.* father, dad(dy).
baca *n.* chimney.
bacak *n.* leg.
bagaj *n.* baggage, luggage.
bağ *n.* link.
bağımlı *adj.* dependent.
bağımsız *adj.* independent.
bağırmak *v.* shout, cry.
bağışlamak *v.* forgive, pardon.
bağlamak *v.* connect, tie.
bağlı olmak *v.* depend, be due to.
bahane *n.* excuse.
bahçe *n.* garden.
bahçıvan *n.* gardener.
bahis *n.* bet.
bahse girmek *v.* bet.

TÜRKÇE – İNGİLİZCE SÖZLÜK

TURKISH – ENGLISH DICTIONARY

**bakan** *n.* minister; secretary.
**bakıcı** *n.* attendant, nurse.
**bakır** *n.* copper.
**bakkal** *n.* grocer.
**bakmak** *v.* look at, take care of; look after.
**bal** *n.* honey.
**baldız** *n.* sister-in-law.
**balık** *n.* fish.
**balık tutmak** *v.* fish.
**balo** *n.* ball.
**balon** *n.* balloon.
**bando** *n.* band.
**banka** *n.* bank.
**banknot** *n.* banknote.
**banyo** *n.* bath, bathroom.
**banyo yapmak** *v.* bathe.
**bar** *n.* bar.
**bardak** *n.* glass.
**barış** *n.* peace.
**basamak** *n.* step.
**basın** *n.* press.
**basit** *adj.* simple.
**baskı** *n.* print, pressure.
**basmak** *v.* press, print.
**baş ağrısı** *n.* headache.
**baş aşağı** *n.* upside down.
**baş** *n.* head *n. / adj.* top.
**baş parmak** *n.* thumb.
**başarı** *n.* success.
**başarılı** *adj.* successful.
**başarısızlık** *n.* failure.
**başarmak** *v.* succeed; achieve.
**başka** *prep.* else, *adj.* other.
**başkan** *n.* president, chairman; head.
**başkent** *n.* capital.
**başlamak** *v.* begin, start.
**başlangıç** *n.* beginning, start.
**başlık** *n.* cap; headline.
**başvuru** *n.* application.
**batı** *n.* west.

**batıya ait** *adj.* western.
**batmak** *v.* sink.
**battaniye** *n.* blanket.
**bavul** *n.* suitcase.
**bay** *n.* Mister, Mr.
**bayan** (bekar) *n.* Miss /Ms., Mrs.
**bayılmak** *v.* faint.
**bayrak** *n.* flag.
**bazen** *adv.* sometimes.
**bebek** *n.* baby.
**beceri** *n.* skill.
**becerikli** *adj.* skilful.
**bedava** *adj.* free.
**bekâr** *adj.* single.
**bekçi** *n.* guard.
**bekleme odası** *n.* waiting room.
**beklemek** *v.* wait, keep waiting, await.
**belediye binası** *n.* city hall.
**belge** *n.* document.
**belirtmek** *v.* remark, determine.
**bellek** *n.* memory.
**belli başlı** *adj.* chief.
**ben** *pron.* I.
**benim** *adj.* my.
**benzer** *prep.* like *adj.* similar.
**benzin** *n.* gas *n.* petrol.
**benzin istasyonu** *n.* gas station.
**berbat etmek** *v.* spoil.
**berbat** *adj.* terrible, miserable, awful.
**berber** *n.* barber, hairdresser.
**berrak** *adj.* clear.
**besin** *n.* food.
**beslemek** *v.* feed.
**beyaz** *adj.* white.
**beyefendi** *n.* sir, gentleman.
**beyin** *n.* brain.
**bezelye** *n.* pea.

bıçak *n.* knife.
bıkmak *v.* get bored with.
bırakmak *v.* leave, release.
biber *n.* pepper.
biçim *n.* form, shape.
biçimlendirmek *v.* shape.
bildirmek *v.* declare, inform.
bilek *n.* wrist.
bilemek *v.* sharpen.
bilet gişesi *n.* booking office.
bilet *n.* ticket.
bilgelik *n.* wisdom.
bilgi *n.* information, knowledge.
bilgili *adj.* learned.
bilgisayar *n.* computer.
bilhassa *adv.* especially.
bilmek *v.* know.
bina *n.* building.
binmek *v.* ride.
bir *adj.* one; *indefinite article* a, an.
biraz *adj.* little, a little.
birçok *adj.* lot, many, a lot of, lots of, various.
birdenbire *adv.* suddenly.
bireysel *adj.* individual.
biricik *adj.* only.
biriktirmek *v.* save, collect.
birinci (ilk) *adj.* first.
birinci sınıf *adj.* first-class.
birisi *pron.* somebody, someone, anybody.
birleşmek *v.* unite.
birleştirmek *v.* join, combine.
birlik *n.* union.
bisiklet *n.* bicycle, bike.
bitirmek *v.* finish.
bitki *n.* plant.
bitmek *v.* end, finish.
bluz *n.* blouse.
bodrum *n.* basement.
boğa *n.* bull.

boğaz ağrısı *n.* sore throat.
boğaz *n.* throat.
bomba *n.* bomb.
borcu olmak *v.* owe.
borç *n.* debt.
boru *n.* pipe, horn.
boş *adj.* empty.
boşaltmak *v.* discharge.
boşluk *n.* space.
boşuna *adj.* in vain.
bot *n.* boat.
boy *n.* size.
boya *n.* paint.
boyamak *v.* paint; colour.
boynuz *n.* horn.
boyun *n.* neck.
bozuk para *n.* change.
bozuk *adj.* destroyed, out of order.
böcek *n.* insect.
bölge *n.* region, district.
bölmek *v.* divide, separate.
bölüm (şube) *n.* department, branch.
böyle *adj.* such, *adv.* like this.
böylece *adv.* thus.
bu arada *adv.* meanwhile.
bu *pron.* this.
buçuk *n.* / *adj.* half; half past.
budala *n.* fool.
bugün *adv.* today.
bugünlerde *adv.* nowadays.
buğday *n.* wheat.
buhar *n.* steam.
bulaşık(lar) *n.* dishes.
bulmaca *n.* puzzle.
bulmak *v.* find.
buluş *n.* invention.
buluşmak *v.* meet.
bulut *n.* cloud.
bulutlu *adj.* cloudy.
bununla birlikte *conj.* however.

TÜRKÇE – İNGİLİZCE SÖZLÜK

**burada / burası / buraya** *adv.* here.
**burun** *n.* nose.
**buz** *n.* ice.
**buzağı** *n.* calf.
**buzdolabı** *n.* fridge, refrigerator.
**bükmek** *v.* bend.
**bükülmek** *v.* curl.
**bütün** *adj.* all, total, whole.
**büyücü** *n.* wizard.
**büyük** *adj.* big, great.
**büyükanne** *n.* grandmother.
**büyükbaba** *n.* grandfather.
**büyüme** *n.* growth.
**büyümek** *v.* grow, grow up.

## C - c

**cadde** *n.* avenue.
**cadı** *n.* witch.
**cam** *n.* glass.
**can** *n.* soul, life.
**can sıkıcı** *adj.* boring.
**cankurtaran** *n.* ambulance.
**casus** *n.* spy.
**cehennem** *n.* hell.
**ceket** *n.* jacket.
**cennet** *n.* heaven.
**cep** *n.* pocket.
**cerrah** *n.* surgeon.
**cesaret etmek** *v.* dare.
**cesaret** *n.* courage.
**cesaretlendirmek** *v.* encourage.
**ceset** *n.* corpse, dead body.
**cetvel** *n.* ruler.
**cevap** *n.* answer, reply.
**cevaplamak** *v.* answer, reply.
**ceza** *n.* punishment.
**cezalandırmak** *v.* punish.
**cezp etmek** *v.* attract.
**cırcır böceği** *n.* cricket.

**ciddi** *adj.* serious.
**cilâ** *n.* shine.
**cilt** *n.* skin; binding.
**cinayet** *n.* murder.
**cins** *n.* kind, category.
**cinsiyet** *n.* sex.
**cisim** *n.* substance.
**civarda** *prep.* about.
**coğrafya** *n.* geography.
**cömert** *adj.* generous.
**cuma** *n.* Friday.
**cumartesi** *n.* Saturday.
**cumhuriyet** *n.* republic.
**cümle** *n.* sentence.

## Ç - ç

**çabucak** *adv.* quickly.
**çabuk** *adj.* fast, prompt, quick.
**çadır** *n.* tent.
**çağrı** *n.* call.
**çakmak** *n.* lighter.
**çalar saat** *n.* alarm clock.
**çalı** *n.* bush.
**çalışma** *n.* labour.
**çalışmak** *v.* work, practise.
**çalıştırmak** *v.* employ.
**çalkalamak** *v.* shake.
**çalmak** *v.* ring; play; steal.
**çamaşır** laundry.
**çamaşır makinesi** *n.* washing machine.
**çamaşırhane** *n.* laundry.
**çamur** *n.* mud.
**çan** *n.* bell.
**çanak** *n.* bowl.
**çanta** *n.* bag.
**çapraz bulmaca** *adj.* crossword.
**çare** *n.* remedy.
**çarpı işareti** *n.* cross.
**çarpışmak** *v.* collide; fight.
**çarpmak** *v.* crash; multiply.

TURKISH – ENGLISH DICTIONARY

çarşamba *n.* Wednesday.
çatal *n.* fork.
çatı *n.* roof; framework.
çatlak *n.* crack, break.
çavdar *n.* rye.
çay (dere, su yolu) *n.* watercourse; tea.
çaydanlık *n.* teapot, kettle.
çayır *n.* grass, field.
çek *n.* cheque / check; draft.
çekiç *n.* hammer.
çekiliş *n.* draw, drawing.
çekinmek *v.* shy away; avoid.
çekmece *n.* drawer.
çekmek *v.* pull, extend.
çelik *n.* steel.
çene *n.* chin, jaw.
çengel *n.* grapple, hanger.
çerçeve *n.* mat, rim; frame.
çeşit *n.* style, type, kind; class.
çeviri *n.* translation, interpretation.
çevirmek *v.* change into, turn over; translate.
çeyrek geçe quarter past.
çeyrek kala quarter to.
çeyrek *adj.* quarterly, quarter.
çığlık *n.* cry.
çıkartmak *v.* take off.
çıkış *n.* exit.
çıkmak *v.* come out; climb.
çılgın *adj.* crazy.
çıplak *adj.* bare.
çiçek açmak *v.* bloom.
çiçek *n.* flower.
çift *adj.* double; *n.* pair, couple.
çiftçi *n.* farmer.
çiftlik *n.* farm.
çiğ *adj.* raw, uncooked, raw.
çikolata *n.* chocolate.
çirkin *adj.* ugly.

çivi *n.* nail.
çizelge *n.* table, timetable.
çizgi *n.* line, stripe.
çizme *n.* boot.
çizmek *v.* draw, cross out.
çocuk *n.* child, boy.
çocukluk *n.* childhood.
çoğunluk *n.* majority.
çoğunlukla *adv.* mostly.
çok *adj.* very; very much; many; much.
çorap *n.* stocking.
çorba *n.* soup.
çökmek *v.* collapse; **yere çökmek** crouch; **diz çökmek** kneel.
çöl *n.* desert.
çömlek *n.* pot*n.* pottery.
çömlekçilik *n.* pottery.
çöp *n.* garbage, waste.
çöp kutusu *n.* dustbin.
çözmek *n.* unfasten; solve; melt.
çubuk *n.* rod, bar; pipe.
çukur *n.* pit, hole, hollow.
çuval *n.* sack, bag.
çünkü *conj.* because, for, since.

## D - d

dağ *n.* mountain.
dağıtmak *v.* scatter; distribute; spread.
dağlık *adj.* mountainous.
daha *adv.* more, yet.
dahi (de, da) *adv.* also, too; *conj.* as well.
dahi *n.* genius.
dahil *adj.* included.
daima *adv.* always.
daire (büro) *n.* office.
daire *n.* circle.

**dakika** *n.* minute.
**daktilo etmek** *v.* type.
**daktilo** *n.* typewriter.
**daktilocu** *n.* typist.
**dal** *n.* branch.
**dalga** *n.* wave.
**dalgalı** *adj.* rough, wavy.
**damat** *n.* groom, bridegroom.
**damga** *n.* stamp.
**damla** *n.* drop.
**dana** *n.* calf.
**dans etmek** *v.* dance.
**dans** *n.* dance.
**dansçı** *n.* dancer.
**dar** *adj.* narrow; tight.
**darıltmak** *v.* offend.
**davet etmek** *v.* invite.
**davet** *n.* invitation.
**davranış** *n.* behaviour, act.
**davranmak** *v.* behave, act; treat.
**dayanmak** *v.* lean; resist.
**de, da** *prep.* in, at, on.
**dede** *n.* grandfather.
**dedikodu** *n.* tittle-tattle, *n.* rumour.
**defne** *n.* Daphne.
**defter** *n.* writing book.
**değer** *n.* worth, value, cost price.
**değerli** *adj.* valuable, precious.
**değil** *pref.* non-, *pref.* un-; *adj.* no.
**değin** *prep.* until, up to.
**değirmen** *n.* mill; grinder.
**değişiklik** *n.* change, modification.
**değiştirmek** *v.* change, shift, modify.
**değnek** *n.* stick.
**dehşet** *n.* horror, panic.
**deli** *adj.* crazy, madman.

**delik** *n.* hole, opening; *adj.* hollow.
**delikanlı** *n.* youngster.
**delil** *n.* proof, evidence.
**delmek** *v.* hole; perforate.
**demeç** *n.* speech, declaration.
**demek** *v.* say, tell.
**demek ki** *conj.* so, then.
**demet** *n.* bunch, bundle.
**demir** *n. / adj.* iron.
**demiryolu** *n.* railroad, railway.
**demokrasi** *n.* democracy.
**denek** *v.* try.
**deneme** *n.* trial.
**deney** *n.* experiment.
**deneyim** *n.* experience.
**denge** *n.* balance.
**deniz** *n.* sea.
**deniz kuvvetleri** *n.* navy.
**dere** *n.* brook, stream.
**derece** *n.* degree *n.* level.
**dergi** *n.* magazine.
**derhal** *adv.* immediately *adv.* once, at once.
**deri** *n.* skin; leather**derin** *adj.* deep.
**derinlik** *n.* depth.
**derli toplu** *adj.* tidy.
**dernek** *n.* association.
**ders** *n.* lesson.
**ders kitabı** *n.* textbook.
**destek** *v.* support.
**devam etmek** *v.* continue, go on, last.
**devlet** *n.* government, state.
**devre** *n.* period; stage; circuit.
**devrilmek** *v.* fall down, turn over.
**devrim** *n.* revolution.
**dış** *adj.* out.
**dışarı** *adj.* outdoor.
**dışarıda** *adv.* out, outside.
**dışişleri** *n.* foreign, affairs.

diğer *adj.* other, *adj. / pron.* another.

diken *n.* thorn; spine.

dikkat *n.* care, notice, caution; attention!

dikmek *v.* sew; raise.

dil *n.* tongue; language, speech.

dilekçe *n.* application; request.

dilemek *v.* wish, desire.

dilenci *n.* beggar.

dilim *n.* slice; segment.

din *n.* religion.

dindar *adj.* religious.

dinlemek *v.* listen.

dinlenmek *v.* rest.

dinleyici(ler) *n.* audience.

dip *n.* bottom.

-dir / dır *v.* is, are.

direk *n.* post.

direnç *n.* resistance.

dirsek *n.* elbow.

diş ağrısı *n.* toothache.

diş fırçası *n.* toothbrush.

diş *n.* tooth.

diş macunu *n.* toothpaste.

dişçi *n.* dentist.

diz çökmek *v.* kneel.

diz *n.* knee.

doğa *n.* nature.

doğal *adj.* natural.

doğmak *v.* be born; rise.

doğmuş born doğru *adj.* correct, right, true.

doğrudan *adj.* direct; *adv.* directly.

doğu *n.* east.

doğum günü *n.* birthday.

doğum *n.* birth.

doğuya ait *adj.* eastern.

doktor *n.* doctor, physician.

doku *n.* tissue.

dokuma *n.* fabric, texture, woven.

dokumacılık *n.* weaving.

dokunmak *v.* touch, handle.

dolandırıcı *n.* swindler; faker.

dolandırmak *v.* defraud, cheat.

dolap *n.* cupboard.

dolar *n.* dollar.

dolayı *conj.* because of; consequently.

doldurmak *v.* pour; fill in; charge.

dolmakalem *n.* fountain pen.

dolu *adj.* full, loaded.

dolunay *n.* full moon.

domates *adj.*

domuz *n.* pig.

domuz eti *n.* pork.

donanım *n.* installation; gear.

donanma *n.* armada; fleet.

dondurma *n.* ice cream.

donmak *v.* freeze; chill.

donuk *adj.* dim; faint.

dost *n.* fellow; friend; comrade.

dökmek *v.* pour; sprinkle.

dönem *n.* term, period, era.

dönemeç *n.* turning, bend.

dönmek *v.* turn; circle; turn back.

dört *adj.* four.

döşemek *v.* furnish.

döviz bozdurmak *v.* exchange.

döviz *n.* foreign currency.

dövmek *v.* beat.

dövüşmek *v.* fight.

dua etmek *v.* pray.

dua *n.* prayer.

dudak *n.* lip.

duman *n.* smoke.

durak *n.* stop.

**duraksamak** *v.* hesitate.
**durdurmak** *v.* stop.
**durmak** *v.* stop, stand.
**durum** *n.* case, situation, state.
**duruşma** *n.* trial.
**duş** *n.* shower.
**duvar** *n.* wall.
**duygu** *n.* feeling.
**duymak** *v.* hear.
**duyu** *n.* sense.
**düdük** *n.* whistle.
**düğme** *n.* button; switch.
**düğüm** *n.* tie; node.
**düğün** *n.* wedding.
**dükkan** *n.* shop, store, market.
**dümdüz** *adj.* straight, flat.
**dün** *n. / adj.* yesterday.
**dünya** *n.* world, earth.
**dünyevi** *adj.* secular, *adj. / adv.* worldly.
**dürbün** *n.* field glasses.
**dürüst** *adj.* honest, faithful.
**düşman** *n.* enemy, foe.
**düşmek** *v.* fall down, drop; decrease.
**düşünce** *n.* thought, comment, idea.
**düşünmek** *v.* think, consider.
**düşürmek** *v.* drop; reduce.
**düzeltmek** *v.* correct, put in order.
**düzenlemek** *v.* organize, arrange, settle.
**düzenli** *adj.* tidy, in order; regular.
**düzensiz** *adj.* untidy; irregular.
**düzey** *n.* level; grade.
**düzine** *n.* dozen.

**E - e**

**ebeveyn** *n.* parents.
**eczane** *n.* drugstore.
**efendim!** *interj.* pardon!
**efsane** *n.* legend.
**eğer** *conj.* if.
**eğilmek** *v.* bow, lean.
**eğimli yüzey** *n.* slope.
**eğirmek** *v.* spin.
**eğitim** *n.* education, training.
**eğlence** *n.* fun, amusement.
**eğlendirmek** *v.* amuse, entertain.
**ekim** *n.* October.
**eklem** *n.* joint.
**eklemek** *v.* add;join on.
**ekmek** *n.* bread; *v.* sow.
**ekmekçi** *n.* baker.
**ekran** *n.* screen.
**eksiği olmak** *v.* lack.
**eksik** *adj.* missing;absent *n.* lack.
**ekstra** *adj.* extra, additional.
**ekşi** *adj.* sour.
**el feneri** *n.* torch.
**el** *n.* hand.
**elbette** *adv.* certainly, definitely; of course;.
**elbise** *n.* clothes, dress.
**elde etmek** *v.* obtain, achieve.
**eldiven** *n.* glove.
**elektrik** *n.* electricity; *adj.* electric.
**eleman** *n.* staff, member, element.
**elemek** *v.* eliminate; sift.
**elma** *n.* apple.
**elmas** *adj.* diamond.
**emanet** *n.* keeping; trust.
**emek** *n.* work, labour; effort.
**emin** *adj.* sure, certain; safe, secure.
**emir** *n.* order, command.
**emlak** *n.* property, real estate.

emniyet *n.* security, safety.
emretmek *v.* order, command.
emzirmek *v.* breast feed.
en az least, fewest, minimum.
en *suf.* -most, *adv.* most *adv.* very.
endişeli *adj.* worried; doubtful.
enerji *n.* energy.
engellemek *v.* prevent; interrupt.
epey(ce) *adj.* considerable.
er *n.* soldier.
erik *n.* plum.
erimek *v.* dissolve, melt.
erişmek *v.* reach.
eritmek *v.* dissolve.
erkek arkadaş *n.* boyfriend.
erkek kardeş *n.* brother.
erkek *adj.* male.
erken *adj. / adv.* early.
ertelemek *n.* delay.
erzak *n.* provisions.
eser *n.* work.
esir *n.* slave.
eski *adj.* old.
esmek *v.* blow.
esnemek *v.* yawn.
eş (hanım) *n.* wife.
eş (koca) *n.* husband.
eşek *n.* donkey.
eşit *adj.* equal.
eşlik etmek *v.* accompany.
eşlik *n.* company.
eşya *n.* furniture, goods, belongings.
et *n.* meat; flesh.
et suyu *n.* meat broth.
etek *n.* skirt.
etiket *n.* label, ticket, stamp.
etki *n.* effect, influence; impression.
etkilemek *v.* effect, influence; impress.

etkinlik *n.* activity; function, efficiency.
etraf *n.* environment, surroundings.
etrafında *prep. / adv.* around, *adv.* round.
ev halkı *n.* household.
ev *n.* house; home.
ev ödevi *n.* homework.
ev sahibi *n.* householder, host.
evcil hayvan *n.* pet, domestic animal.
evet *adv.* yes, okay, yeah.
evlat *n.* child; son, daughter.
evlenmek *v.* get married.
evlilik *n.* marriage.
evren *n.* universe, cosmos.
evrim *n.* evolution.
evvel *adv.* before, *adj.* first.
evvelki *adj.* previous.
eyalet *n.* state.
eylem *n.* action, deed.
eylül *n.* September.
ezberlemek *v.* learn by heart, memorize.
ezgi *n.* melody, tune.

## F - f

fabrika *n.* factory.
faiz *n.* interest.
faizli *adj.* at interest.
faizsiz *adj.* free of interest.
fakir *adj.* poor.
fare *n.* mouse.
fark *n.* difference.
farkına varmak *v.* notice.
farklı olmak *v.* differ.
farklı *adj.* different, various.
fayda *n.* use.
faydalı *adj.* useful.
faydasız *adj.* useless.

**fazla** *adj.* extra *adj.* / *adv.* much.
**felaket** *n.* disaster.
**fermuar** *n.* zipper.
**feryat** *n.* shout.
**fethetmek** *v.* conquer.
**fıçı** *n.* barrel.
**fıkra** *n.* joke.
**fırça** *n.* brush.
**fırın** *n.* oven, bakery.
**fırlamak** *v.* rush.
**fırlatmak** *v.* throw.
**fırsat** *n.* opportunity.
**fırtına** *n.* storm.
**fısıldamak** *v.* whisper.
**fıskiye** *n.* fountain.
**fiil** *n.* act; verb.
**fikir** *n.* idea, opinion.
**fil** *n.* elephant.
**film** *n.* film.
**firar etmek** *v.* escape, run away.
**firar** *n.* break.
**firavun** *n.* pharaoh.
**firma** *n.* firm, company.
**fiş** *n.* plug; bill.
**fiyasko** *n.* failure, fiasco.
**fiyat** *n.* cost, price.
**fiziksel** *adj.* material, physical.
**folluk** *n.* nest box.
**formalite** *n.* formality, process.
**fosil** *n.* fossil.
**fotoğraf** *n.* picture, photograph.
**fuar** *n.* fair, exposition.
**futbol** *n.* football, soccer.

## G - g

**galiba** *adv.* probably, apparently.
**garaj** *n.* garage.

**garanti** *n.* guarantee, warrant; certain.
**garantili** *adj.* guaranteed.
**gardırop** *n.* dressing room.
**garip** *adj.* strange, odd.
**garson** *n.* waiter, waitress.
**gayret** *n.* attempt, effort.
**gaz** *n.* gas, oil gas.
**gazete** *n.* newspaper.
**gazi** *n.* ghazi.
**gece** *n.* night, evening.
**gecikme** *n.* delay.
**gecikmek** *v.* be late; delay.
**geç** *adj.* late; delayed.
**geçen** *adj.* former, last.
**geçerli** *adj.* current; *adv.* in circulation.
**geçiş** *n.* transition, *n.* passage.
**geçmek** *v.* surpass; exceed; pass beyond.
**geçmiş** *n.* (the) past, *adj.* past, former, back.
**gelecek** *adj.* next; *n.* (the) future.
**gelenek** *n.* tradition, custom, convention.
**gelin** *n.* bride; daughter in law.
**gelinlik** *n.* wedding dress.
**gelişigüzel** *adj.* at random, by chance.
**gelişme** *n.* development, growth; reformation.
**gelişmek** *v.* grow, improve.
**gelmek** *v.* come, arrive.
**gemi** *n.* ship, vessel.
**genç** *adj.* young, adolescent.
**genel** *adj.* standard, common.
**geniş** *adj.* broad, large, wide.
**genişlemek** *v.* extend, expand.
**gerçek sim** truth, fact.

**gereç(ler)** *n.* materials, implements.
**gerekli** *adj.* necessary, essential.
**gerekmek** *v.* must, need.
**gerektirmek** *v.* require, necessitate.
**geri almak** *v.* withdraw, reclaim.
**geri dönmek** *v.* go back, turn back.
**geri** *n.* back; *prep.* behind, *adj.* backward.
**gerinmek** *v.* stretch.
**germek** *v.* stretch, tense.
**getirmek** *v.* bring, get.
**geveze** *n.* talkative, babbler.
**geyik** *n.* deer.
**gezegen** *n.* planet.
**gezi** *n.* trip, tour, journey.
**gezmek** *v.* wander, walk around.
**gıda** *n.* food, diet.
**gırtlak** *n. n.* larynx, throat.
**gibi** *prep.* like, such as, *adv.* as.
**gider** *n.* outgoings, expense.
**giriş** *n.* entry, gateway.
**girişken** *adj.* enterprising, pushing.
**girmek** *v.* enter, come in.
**gişe** booking office, ticket window.
**gitar** *n.* guitar.
**gitmek** *v.* go (away); last.
**giyecek** *n.* clothes, wearing.
**giyinmek** *v.* dress.
**gizem** *n.* secret.
**gizlemek** *v.* hide, conceal.
**golf** *n.* golf.
**gonca** *n.* bud.
**göğüs** *n.* breast, chest.
**gök gürültüsü** *n.* thunder.

**gökbilim** *n.* astronomy.
**gökdelen** *n.* skyscraper, tower block.
**gökyüzü** *n.* sky.
**göl** *n.* lake.
**gölge** *n.* shadow; shade.
**gömlek** *n.* shirt, blouse.
**göndermek** *v.* send, forward.
**gönüllü** *n.* volunteer; *adj.* voluntary.
**görenek** *n.* convention, tradition, custom.
**görev** *n.* duty, function, mission.
**görgü** *n.* manner, experience.
**görkemli** *adj.* gorgeous; splendid.
**görmek** *v.* see; notice, consider.
**görünmek** *v.* appear, seem.
**görüş** *n.* opinion, view, argument.
**gösteri** *n.* show, performance.
**götürmek** *v.* take, transport; lead.
**gövde** *n.* body, stem.
**göz** *n.* eye, optic.
**gözcü** *n.* watchman; observer.
**gözenek** *n.* pore, stoma.
**gözetmek** *v.* take care of, look after.
**gözlük** *n.* glasses, eyeglasses.
**gözyaşı** *n.* tear.
**grafik** *n.* diagram, graph(ics).
**gravür** *n.* gravure, engraving.
**grev** *n.* strike.
**grup** *n.* group, category.
**gurur** *n.* pride, vanity.
**gübre** *n.* dung, fertilizer.
**gücendirmek** *v.* offend, hurt.
**gücenmek** *v.* be offended.

**güç** *n.* strength, power; *adj.* hard.
**güçlü** *adj.* strong, powerful.
**güçlük** *n.* difficulty, trouble.
**güle güle!** *interj.* goodbye, bye bye.
**gül** *n.* rose.
**gülmek** *v.* laugh, smile.
**gülümseme** *n.* smile.
**gümrük** *n.* customs.
**gümrüksüz** *adj.* duty-free.
**gümüş** *adj. / n.* silver.
**gün** *n.* day.
**günah** *n.* sin, evil.
**günaydın!** *interj.* good morning.
**gündem** *n.* agenda.
**güneş** *n.* sun; *adj.* solar.
**güney** *n. / adj.* south.
**günlük** *n.* diary; *adj.* daily.
**güven** *n.* trust; confidence.
**güvence** *n.* guarantee; indemnity.
**güvenlik** *n.* security, safety.
**güvercin** *n.* pigeon.
**güverte** *n.* deck.
**güz** *n.* fall, autumn.
**güzel** *adj.* beautiful, pretty, good; *adj.* delightful.

## H - h

**haber** *n.* news, information, report.
**hafıza** *n.* memory.
**hafif** *adj.* light, *adv.* lightly.
**hafta** *n.* week.
**hafta sonu** weekend.
**hak etmek** *v.* deserve.
**hak** *n.* right; claim; just.
**hakem** *n.* referee, judge.
**haklı** *adj.* right, just; justifiable.
**haksız** *adj.* unjust, unfair.

**hal** *n.* state, situation.
**hala** *n.* aunt.
**hâlâ** *adv.* still, yet.
**halı** *n.* carpet.
**halk** *n.* society, public; folks.
**han** *n.* hostel, inn.
**hangi** *pron.* which; *adj.* whatever.
**hanımefendi** *n.* lady, ma'am.
**hapishane** *n.* jail, prison.
**harabe** *n.* ruin, remains.
**harcamak** *v.* spend.
**hareket etmek** *v.* act, move.
**hareket** *n.* action, movement.
**harf** *n.* letter.
**hariç** *prep.* excluding, except.
**harita** *n.* map.
**hasar** *n.* damage, harm.
**hassas** *adj.* sensitive, keen.
**hasta bakıcı** *n.* nurse.
**hasta** *n.* patient, *adj.* sick, ill.
**hasta olmak** *v.* become ill, feel ill.
**hastane** *n.* hospital.
**hata** *n.* error, mistake, fault.
**hatalı** *adj.* wrong, false.
**hatıra** *n.* memory; souvenir.
**hatta** *adv.* even, in fact.
**hava** *n. / adj.* air, atmosphere; weather.
**havaalanı** *n.* airport, airdrome.
**havlu** *n.* towel.
**havuz** *n.* pool.
**hayal** *n.* imagination, daydream; fiction.
**hayalet** *n.* ghost.
**hayat** *n.* life, living.
**hayır** *adv.* no; *n.* help, goodness.
**hayran olmak** *v.* admire.
**hayret etmek** *v.* be astonished, be surprised.
**hayvan** *n.* animal, creature.

hayvanat bahçesi *n.* zoo.
hazır *adj.* ready; prepared.
hazırlamak *v.* arrange,
  prepare, fix.
hazine *n.* treasure, mine.
haziran *n.* June.
hedef *n.* target, aim.
hediye *n.* present, gift.
hemen *prep.* at once, *adv.*
  immediately.
hemşire *n.* nurse; sister.
henüz değil *adv.* not yet,.
henüz *adv.* still; yet.
hep *adv.* all, whole; always.
hepsi *prep.* all.
her nasılsa *adv.* somehow.
her neyse *adv.* anyhow.
her *adj.* each, every, all.
herkes *n. / pron.* all, *pron.*
  everybody.
hesap *v.* calculate.
hesap *n.* account, bill;
  calculation.
hevesli *adj.* keen, willing.
heyecan *n.* excitement,
  enthusiasm.
heyecanlı *adj.* exciting.
heyecanlanmak *v.* get
  excited.
heykel *n.* statue, sculpture.
hırsız *n.* thief, burglar.
hız *n. / adj.* speed, *n.*
  momentum.
hızlanmak *v.* gain speed.
hızlı *adj.* quick, rapid.
hiç kimse *pron.* nobody.
hiç *adv.* any, *pron.* nothing.
hikaye *n.* story, tale.
hile *n.* trick, fraud.
hile yapmak *v.* trick, cheat.
hisse *n.* share, portion.
hissetmek *v.* feel, sense.
hizmet etmek *v.* serve.

hobi *n.* hobby.
horoz *n.* rooster, cock.
hostes *n.* hostess,
  stewardess.
hoş *adj.* fine, pleasant;
  charming.
Hristiyan *n. / adj.* Christian.
hububat *n.* cereal.
hücum *n.* assault, attack.
hüküm *n.* command, decree,
  verdict.
hükümlü *n.* convict,
  condemned.
hüner *n.* talent, skill.

## I - ı

ılıca *n.* hot spring.
ırk *n.* race.
ısı *n.* heath.
ısıtmak *v.* heath, warm.
ısırmak *v.* bite.
ıslak *adj.* wet; *adj.* soaked.
ıslık *n.* whistle.
ısrar etmek *v.* insist on,
  persist in.
ıssız *adj.* deserted, lonely ışık
  *n.* light;lamp.
ışın *n.* ray, radius ızgara *n.*
  grill, barbecue.

## İ - i

iade etmek *v.* return.
ibadet *n.* worship.
iç *adj.* in, interior, internal.
içermek *v.* include, involve.
içki *n.* liquor, drink.
içmek *v.* drink; smoke.
iddia *n.* bet; claim.
ifade etmek explain.
ifade *n.* expression,
  explanation.

**ihmal** *n.* neglect, default.
**ihracat** *n.* exportation.
**ihtiyaç** *n.* necessity, requirement.
**ikamet** *n.* habitation, stay;residence.
**ikaz** *n.* warning.
**iki** *adj.* two, *pref.* duo-.
**iklim** *n.* climate.
**ikna** *n.* persuasion.
**ilaç** *n.* medicine, drug.
**ilan** *n.* notice, announcement,.
**ilave etmek** *v.* add.
**ilave** *n.* addition.
**ile** *conj. / prep.* with, *prep.* by.
**ileri** *adj.* forward, *adv.* along; advanced.
**ilerlemek** *v.* go, go on; *v.* progress.
**ilgi** *n.* interest; relation, connection.
**ilham** *n.* inspiration.
**ilişki** *n.* connection; affair.
**ilk ad** *n.* first name.
**ilkbahar** *n. / adj.* spring.
**imdat!** *interj.* help!
**imkan** *n.* possibility; opportunity.
**imla** *n.* spelling.
**imzalamak** *v.* sign, underwrite.
**inanç** *n.* belief, faith.
**inanılmaz** *adj.* incredible.
**inanmak** *v.* believe (in).
**indirmek** *v.* lower; reduce.
**inek** *n.* cow.
**inkar etmek** *v.* deny, negate.
**inmek** *v.* descend, land; decrease.
**insafsız** *adj.* unjust, unfair.
**insan** *n.* people, man, human.
**insanlar** *n.* human being, folks.

**insanlık** *n.* humanity.
**inşa etmek** *v.* build.
**ip** *n.* rope, string.
**ipek** *n. / adj.* silk.
**iplik** *n.* thread, fabric.
**ipucu** *n.* clue, hint.
**irade** *n.* will, will power.
**ispat etmek** *v.* prove, confirm.
**istasyon** *n.* station.
**istek** *n.* wish, desire; demand.
**istemek** *v.* want, wish; ask for.
**istisna** *n.* exception.
**iş gücü** *n.* manpower.
**iş günü** *n. / adj.* workday, weekday.
**iş** *n.* job, work; labour.
**işaret** *n.* mark, signal.
**işaret etmek** *v.* mark, point out.
**işçi** *n.* workman, employee.
**işgal etmek** *v.* occupy.
**işitmek** *v.* learn.
**işlem** *n.* operation, procedure.
**işletmek** *v.* operate, run.
**işsiz** *adj.* out-of-work, unemployed.
**iştah** *n.* appetite.
**işveren** *n.* employer.
**ithalat** *n.* importation, importing, import.
**itiraf** *n.* confession.
**itiraz** *n.* objection, disapproval.
**itmek** *v.* push.
**iyi akşamlar!** *interj.* good evening!
**iyi geceler!** *interj.* good night!
**iyi günler!** *interj.* good afternoon; have a nice day!
**iyi sabahlar!** *interj.* good morning!
**iyi** *adj.* good, well; kind.
**iyi şanslar!** *interj.* good luck!

iz *n.* footprint; trace.
izin *n.* permission.
izin vermek *v.* let, allow, permit.
izlemek *v.* follow; watch.
izlenim *n.* impression.

## J - j

jambon *n.* ham.
Japon *n.* JapaneseJaponya *n.* Japan.
jelatin *n.* gelatine, jelly.
jeneratör *n.* generator, power unit, power plant.
jeton *n.* token; chip.
jilet *n.* razor blade.
jokey *n.* jockey.
jübile *n.* jubilee.

## K - k

kaba *adj.* rough, vulgar.
kabak *n.* squash.
kabiliyet *n.* ability.
kablo *n.* cable, cord.
kabuk *n.* crust, scurf.
kabul etmek *v.* admit, accept.
kaç tane? *adv.* how many?
kaçırmak *v.* miss;hijack.
kaçmak *v.* run away; escape.
kademe *n.* degree, stage.
kader *n.* fate, destiny.
kadın *n.* woman.
kafa *n.* head.
kafatası *n.* skull.
kağıt *n.* paper.
kağıt para *n.* note, bill.
kahkaha *n.* laugh, laughter.
kahraman *n.* hero, brave.
kahvaltı *n.* breakfast.
kahve *n.* coffee.
kahverengi *adj.* brown.

kalabalık *n.* crowd; *adj.* crowded.
kaldırmak *v.* lift, remove.
kalın *adj.* thick.
kalite *n.* quality.
kalkış *n.* departure; start.
kalkmak *v.* depart; ayağa kalkmak stand up.
kalmak *v.* stay; remain.
kalp *n.* heart.
kamp *n.* camp.
kamyon *n.* truck.
kanamak *v.* bleed.
kanat *n.* wing.
kanepe *n.* sofa.
kanıt *n.* evidence, proof.
kanıtlamak *v.* prove.
kap *n.* container, pot.
kapak *n.* cover.
kapalı *adj.* closed, shut, covered.
kapamak *v.* shut, close.
kapı *n.* door, gate.
kaplan *n.* tiger.
kapsamak *v.* include, involve.
kaptan *n.* captain, skipper.
kar *n.* snow.
kâr *n.* profit.
kara *n.* land, *n.* shore.
kara (siyah) *adj.* black.
karakol *n.* police station.
karanlık *n.* / *adj.* dark.
karar *n.* decision, resolution.
karar vermek *v.* decide, make a decision, resolve.
karın *n.* abdomen, tummy.
karış *n.* span.
karışık *adj.* mixed; confused.
karışıklık *n.* disorder, confusion.
karışım *n.* mixture.
karışmak *v.* interfere; be mixed; become confused.

**karşı** *prep.* against, *pref.* contra-, *adj.* opposed.
**karşı gelmek** *v.* oppose.
**karşı koymak** *v.* resist.
**kas** *n.* muscle.
**kasa** *n.* cash box, safe.
**kasaba** *n.* town.
**kasap** *n.* butcher.
**kase** *n.* bowl.
**Kasım** *n.* November.
**kasırga** *n.* tornado.
**kasıtlı** *adj.* intentional, purposeful.
**kaşık** *n.* spoon.
**kaşınmak** *v.* itch.
**kat** *n.* floor, storey; layer.
**katil** *n.* murderer, killer.
**kavga etmek** *v.* quarrel; fight.
**kaya** *n.* rock.
**kayak** *n.* ski.
**kaybetmek** *v.* lose.
**kaybolmak** *v.* be lost;disappear.
**kaygılanmak** *v.* worry.
**kayıp** *n.* lost.
**kayıt** *n.* registration.
**kaynak** *n.* source; wellspring.
**kaynamak** *v.* boil.
**kaza** *n.* accident.
**kazak** *n.* sweater, pullover.
**kazanç** *n.* profit, gain, earning.
**kazanmak** *v.* win; gain.
**kaz** *n.* goose.
**kazmak** *v.* dig.
**keçi** *n.* goat.
**kedi** *n.* cat, pussy.
**kek** *n.* cake.
**kelebek** *n.* butterfly.
**kelime** *n.* word.
**keman** *n.* violin.
**kemer** *n.* belt.
**kemik** *n. / adj.* bone.
**kenar** *n.* edging, border.

**kendi(si)** *n. / adj. / pref.* self.
**kere (kez, defa)** *n.* time(s); *prep.* by.
**kertenkele** *n.* lizard.
**kesinlikle** *adv.* certainly, definitively.
**keskin** *adj.* sharp;severe.
**kesmek** *v.* cut;interrupt.
**keşfetmek** *v.* explore, discover.
**kılavuz** *n.* guide, leader.
**kımıldamak** *v.* move.
**kırık** *adj.* broken.
**kırılmak** *v.* break; be offended.
**kırmızı** *adj.* red,.
**kısa** *adj.* short; brief.
**kısım** *n.* piece, part; section.
**kıskanç** *adj.* envious.
**kıskanmak** *v.* envy.
**kış** *n.* winter.
**kıta** *n.* continent; detachment.
**kıvırcık** *adj.* curly.
**kıyaslamak** *v.* compare.
**kıyı** *n.* shore, side.
**kız** *n.* girl; daughter.
**kız kardeş** *n.* sister.
**kızartmak** *v.* fry, bake.
**kızgın** *adj.* angry; hot.
**kibrit** *n.* match.
**kilise** *adj.* church.
**kilit** *n.* lock.
**kilitlemek** *v.* lock.
**kim** *pron.* who.
**kimya** *n.* chemistry.
**kin** *n.* grudge.
**kir** *n.* dirt.
**kira** *n.* hire, rent.
**kiralamak** *v.* hire.
**kişi** *n.* person, individual.
**kişisel** *adj.* personal, private, individual.
**kitap** *n.* book.

**koca (eş)** *n.* husband.
**koca(man)** *adj.* big, large.
**koklamak** *v.* smell, sniff.
**kokmak** *v.* smell.
**kol** *n.* arm; *n.* branch.
**kolay** *adj.* easy.
**koltuk** *n.* chair.
**komşu** *n.* neighbour.
**konser** *n.* concert.
**kontrol etmek** *v.* check.
**konu** *n.* subject, topic.
**konuk** *n.* guest.
**konuşmak** *v.* speak, talk.
**kopya** *n.* copy.
**koridor** *n.* aisle.
**korkak** *adj.* coward.
**korkmak** *v.* be afraid (of), fear.
**korsan** *n.* pirate.
**korumak** *v.* guard, keep.
**koşmak** *v.* run.
**koymak** *v.* put, set.
**koyun** *n.* sheep.
**kök** *n.* root, base; origin.
**köle** *n.* slave.
**köpek** *n.* dog.
**köprü** *n.* bridge.
**kör** *adj.* blind.
**körfez** *n.* gulf.
**köşe** *n.* corner, turning.
**kötü** *adj.* bad; evil.
**köy** *n.* village.
**kral** *n.* king.
**kravat** *n.* tie, necktie.
**kredi** *n.* credit.
**kreş** *n.* nursery, kindergarten.
**kuaför** *n.* hairdresser.
**kulak** *n.* ear.
**kule** *n.* tower.
**kullanışlı** *adj.* handy, practical.
**kullanmak** *v.* use; handle.
**kulübe** *n.* shed, cottage.

**kulüp** *n.* club.
**kumar** *n.* gambling.
**kumaş** *n.* fabric, cloth.
**kurabiye** *n.* cookie.
**kural** *n.* rule.
**kurs** *n.* course.
**kurtarmak** *v.* save, rescue.
**kuru** *adj.* dry; withered.
**kurum** *n.* association, society.
**kusur** *n.* fault, deficiency.
**kuş** *n.* bird.
**kuşku** *n.* suspicion, doubt.
**kutlamak** *v.* celebrate.
**kutsal** *adj.* holy.
**kutu** *n.* box, case.
**kutup** *n.* pole; axis.
**kuvvet** *n.* power, strength.
**kuvvetli** *adj.* strong, powerful.
**kuyruk** *n.* tail; queue.
**kuzey** *adj.* north.
**kuzu** *n.* lamb.
**küçük** *adj.* little, small.
**küfür** *n.* swear.
**kül** *n.* ash.
**kültür** *n.* culture.
**küpe** *n.* earring.
**küre** *n.* sphere.
**kürek** *n.* shovel.
**kürk** *n.* fur.
**kütüphane** *n.* library; bookcase.

## L - l

**lacivert** *adj.* dark blue.
**laik** *n.* laic, secular.
**lakap** *n.* nickname.
**lamba** *n.* lamp.
**lastik** *n.* rubber; tire.
**leke** *n.* stain, spot.
**lezzet** *n.* taste, flavour.
**lider** *n.* leader.
**limon** *n.* lemon.

**TÜRKÇE – İNGİLİZCE SÖZLÜK**

**TURKISH – ENGLISH DICTIONARY**

**listelemek** *v.* list.
**lokanta** *n.* restaurant.
**lokma** *n.* morsel.
**lokum** *n.* Turkish delight.
**lütfen** *interj.* please.

## M - m

**maaş** *n.* salary, wage.
**macera** *n.* adventure.
**maç** *n.* match, event.
**madde** *n.* matter, substance; item.
**maden** *n.* mine; mineral; metal.
**madeni para** *n.* coin.
**mağara** *n.* cave.
**mağaza** *n.* shop, store.
**mahkeme** *n.* law court.
**mahkum** *n.* prisoner.
**makas** *n.* scissors.
**makine** *n.* machine.
**makyaj** *n.* make-up.
**mal** *n.* goods; property.
**maliyet** *n.* cost, cost price.
**malzeme** *n.* material, *n.* supply.
**mevsim** *n.* season.
**mandal** *n.* catch, latch.
**mantar** *n.* mushroom.
**manzara** *n.* view, scene, landscape.
**mart** *n.* March.
**masa** *n.* table.
**masraf** *n.* expense.
**matem** *n. / adj.* mourning.
**mavi** *adj.* blue.
**mayıs** *n.* May.
**meblağ** *n.* sum, amount.
**mektup** *n.* letter.
**memur** *n.* officer, employee.
**mendil** *n.* handkerchief.
**menekşe** *n.* violet.

**merak etmek** *v.* be anxious, worry; wonder.
**merdiven** *n.* stair, *n.* ladder.
**merhaba** *interj.* hello!, hi!
**merkez** *n.* centre.
**mesela** *adv.* for instance, such as.
**meslek** *n.* job, career, occupation.
**meşgul** *adj.* busy; concerned.
**metro** *n.* metro, underground.
**mevcut** *adj.* present; existing.
**mevki** *n.* position, status.
**meydan** *n.* square, area, space.
**meyve** *n.* fruit.
**meyve suyu** *n.* fruit juice.
**mezar** *n.* tomb, grave.
**meze** *n.* appetizer, starter.
**mide** *n.* stomach.
**miktar** *n.* quantity.
**misafir** *n.* visitor.
**mobilya** *n.* furniture.
**moda** *adj.* fashion.
**mor** *adj.* purple, violet.
**motor** *n.* engine, motor.
**mum** *n.* candle.
**mutfak** *adj.* kitchen, cuisine.
**mutlu** *adj.* happy, pleased, glad,.
**muz** *n.* banana.
**mücadele** *n.* struggle.
**mücevher** *n.* jewel.
**mühendis** *n.* engineer.
**mükemmel** *adj.* perfect, great.
**mülakat** *n.* interview.
**mümkün** *adj.* possible.
**müsaade etmek** *v.* let, allow.
**müşteri** *n.* customer, buyer.
**müze** *n.* museum, gallery.
**müzik** *n.* music.

TÜRKÇE – İNGİLIZCE SÖZLÜK

## N - n

nadiren *adv.* scarcely.
nakit *n.* cash.
nasıl how.
nasılsınız how do you do.
nazik *adj.* polite.
neden *n.* cause; *pron.* why.
nefes *n.* breath.
nefret *n.* hatred, disgust.
nehir *n.* river.
nesne *n.* thing; *n.* object.
neşelenmek *v.* be joyful.
nicelik *n.* quantity.
nihayet *prep.* at last.
nisan *n.* April.
nitelik *n.* quality.
niyetlenmek *v.* intend.
nokta *n.* spot, dot.
normal *adj.* normal.
not *n.* note; grade.
numara *n.* number.
nüfus *n.* population.

## O - o

ocak cooker, oven; *n.* January.
oda *n.* room.
odun *n.* wood.
oğul *n.* son.
okul *n.* school.
okumak *v.* read, study.
okyanus *n.* ocean.
olağanüstü *adj.* extraordinary.
olanak *n.* possibility.
olay *n.* event.
olmak *v.* be, become; happen.
olta *n.* fishhook.
olumlu *adj.* positive.
olumsuz *adj.* negative.
oluşturmak *v.* constitute.
on *adj.* ten.

onarım *v.* repair, mend, restore.
onaylamak *v.* approve; confirm.
operasyon *n.* operation.
orada *adv.* there; over there.
ordu *n.* army.
orman *n.* forest, woods.
orta(sında) *adv. / prep.* (in the) middle.
ortak *n.* partner; common.
ortalama *n. / adj.* average.
otel *n.* hotel.
otobüs *n.* bus, omnibus.
otobüs durağı *n.* bus stop.
oturmak *v.* sit down; stay.
oy vermek *v.* vote.
oyun *n.* play.

## Ö - ö

ödemek *v.* pay.
ödül *n.* reward.
ödünç almak *v.* borrow.
ödünç vermek *v.* lend.
öfkelenmek *v.* get angry.
öğle *n.* noon, *adj.* midday.
öğrenci *n.* student.
öğüt vermek *v.* advise.
öksürmek *v.* cough.
ölçmek *v.* measure.
öldürmek *v.* kill, murder.
ön *n. / adj.* front.
önce *prep.* at first; *adj./adv.* ago.
öncülük *n.* leadership.
önemli *adj.* important.
öneri *n.* suggestion.
önlem *v.* prevent.
öpmek *v.* kiss.
örneğin *adv.* for example; for instance; such as.
örnek *n.* example; sample.
öteki *adj.* other.
övmek *v.* praise.

TURKISH – ENGLISH DICTIONARY

TÜRKÇE – İNGİLİZCE SÖZLÜK

özel *adj.* special.
özgür *adj. / adv.* free.
özgürlük *n.* freedom.
özlemek *v.* miss, long for.

## P - p

pahalı *adj.* expensive.
paketlemek *v.* wrap up.
palto *n.* overcoat.
pamuk *n. / adj.* cotton.
pansiyon *n.* pension, hostel.
pantolon *n.* trousers, pants.
para *n.* money.
parça *n.* part, piece.
park yapmak *v.* park.
parlak *adj.* brilliant.
parlamak *v.* shine.
parmak *n.* finger.
pasta *n.* cake, pastry.
patates *n.* potato.
patika *n.* footpath.
patlamak *v.* explode.
patron *n.* employer; pattern.
pay *n.* share; portion.
paylaşmak *v.* share.
pazar *n.* Sunday; *n.* bazaar.
pazarlık *n.* bargain.
pazartesi *n.* Monday.
pembe *adj.* pink.
pencere *n.* window.
perde *n.* curtain; screen.
peron *n.* platform.
personel *n.* personnel, staff.
perşembe *n.* Thursday.
petrol *n.* oil, petroleum.
peynir *n.* cheese.
pis *adj.* dirty.
pişirmek *v.* cook.
pişman olmak *v.* repent.
plaj *n.* each.
plaka *n.* license plate.
plan yapmak *v.* plan.

plastik *adj.* plastic.
polis *n.* policeman.
politika *n.* politics.
pompa *n.* pump.
popüler *adj.* popular.
posta *n.* mail.
postacı *n.* mailman.
postalamak *v.* mail, post.
postane *n.* post office.
pratik *adj.* handy.
profesyonel *n.* professional.
protesto etmek *v.* object.

## R - r

raf *n.* shelf.
rağmen *conj.* though; *prep.* despite.
rahat *adj.* comfortable.
rahip *n.* monk, priest.
rakam *n.* number.
rakip *n.* rival, opponent.
randevu *n.* appointment; rendezvous, date.
rapor *n.* report.
rastlamak *v.* coincide (with); run across.
rastlantı *n.* chance, coincidence.
reçel *n.* jam.
reddetmek *v.* reject, refuse.
rehber *n.* guide.
rekabet *n.* competition.
reklam *n.* advertisement.
rekor *n.* record.
renk *n.* colour.
resim *n.* picture, painting.
rica etmek *v.* ask (for), request.
roman *n.* novel.
rütbe *n.* degree; rank.
rüya *n.* dream.
rüzgar *n.* wind.

TURKISH – ENGLISH DICTIONARY

## S - s

saat *n.* clock, watch; *adv.* o'clock.

sabah *n.* morning.

sabırlı *n.* patient.

sabit *adj.* stable, fixed.

sabun *n.* soap.

saç *n.* hair.

saçma *adj.* ridiculous, nonsense.

sade *adj.* simple.

sadece *adv.* only, just.

sadık *adj.* faithful,.

sağır *adj.* deaf.

sağlamak *v.* supply,.

sağlık *n.* health.

sağ *adj.* right; alive.

sahil *n.* shore, sea-side.

sahip olmak *v.* own, possess.

sahne *n.* stage.

sahte *adj.* artificial, false.

sakal *n.* beard.

sakat *adj.* defective.

sakız *n.* chewing gum; mastic.

sakin *adj.* quiet; calm.

saklamak *v.* hide; preserve; keep secret.

salata *n.* salad.

salı *n.* Tuesday.

salıncak *n.* swing.

samimi *adj.* sincere.

sanat *n.* art.

sanatçı / sanatkar *n.* artist; craftsman.

sancımak *v.* ache.

sandal *n.* boat, rowboat.

saniye *n.* second; moment.

sanki *prep.* as if, as though.

sanmak *v.* suppose, think, imagine.

sap *n.* handle; stem.

sapmak *v.* turn.

saray *n.* palace.

sarhoş *adj.* drunk.

sarı *adj.* yellow.

sarılmak *v.* embrace; wrap up.

sarımsak *n.* garlic.

satın almak *v.* buy, purchase.

satmak *v.* sell.

savaş *n.* war, battle; struggle.

savunmak *v.* defend.

sayfa *n.* page.

saygı göstermek *v.* honour.

saygıdeğer *adj.* honourable.

sebep *n.* cause, reason.

sebze *n.* vegetable.

seçim *n.* selection; *n.* election.

seçmek *v.* select; elect.

sekreter *n.* secretary.

sel *n.* overflow.

selamlamak *v.* greet, salute.

sepet *n.* basket.

sergi *n.* exhibition, fair.

serin *adj.* cool.

sermaye *n.* capital.

sert *adj.* hard, rough.

servet *n.* fortune; assets.

servis yapmak *v.* service.

ses *n.* sound, noise.

seslenmek *v.* call, shout.

sevinmek *v.* be happy, be glad.

seviye *n.* level, grade.

sevmek *v.* like, enjoy; love.

seyahat *n.* travel, voyage, journey.

seyrek *adv.* seldom, rare.

sıcak *adj.* warm.

sıkıcı *adj.* boring.

sıkılmak *v.* be bored.

sık *adv.* frequently.

sınamak *v.* test, examine.

sınav *n.* test, examination.

**sınıf** *n.* class; category.
**sınır** *n.* frontier, border; limit.
**sıradan** *adj.* common.
**sır** *n.* secret.
**sırt** *n.* back.
**sıvı** *n. / adj.* liquid.
**sigorta** *n. / adj.* insurance.
**sihirbaz** *n.* illusionist, wizard.
**silmek** *v.* clean; erase.
**sinek** *n.* fly.
**sinema** *n.* cinema, movie.
**sinirlenmek** *v.* get nervous.
**sipariş** *v.* order.
**sis** *n.* fog.
**siyah** *adj.* black.
**soğuk almak** *v.* catch cold.
**soğuk** *n. / adj.* cold.
**sohbet** *n.* conversation, talk.
**sokak** *n.* road, street.
**sol** *adj.* left.
**solmak** *v.* fade.
**son** *n.* end; *adj.* last.
**sonbahar** *n.* autumn, fall.
**sonra** *adv.* then; after.
**sonuç** *n.* result; conclusion.
**sormak** *v.* ask (for).
**soru** *n.* question.
**sorumlu olmak** *v.* be responsible; be liable for.
**soruşturma** *n.* inquiry.
**sos** *n.* sauce.
**sosis** *n.* sausage.
**sosyal** *adj.* social.
**soyadı** *n.* surname.
**söylemek** *v.* say, tell.
**söz vermek** *v.* promise.
**spor** *n.* sport.
**stadyum** *n.* stadium.
**su** *n. / adj.* water.
**subay** *n.* officer.
**suç** *n.* crime.
**suçlamak** *v.* blame, accuse.
**suçlu** *adj.* guilty.

**sunmak** *v.* offer.
**susmak** *v.* be silent, be quiet.
**sünger** *n.* sponge.
**sürdürmek** *v.* continue, carry on.
**sürmek** *v.* continue; drive.
**sürpriz** *n. / adj.* surprise.
**sürücü** *n.* driver.
**süt** *n.* milk.
**sütun** *n.* column.

## Ş - ş

**şahane** *adj.* superb, great.
**şahıs** *n.* person, figure.
**şahit** *n.* witness.
**şair** *n.* poet.
**şaka** *n.* joke.
**şans** *n.* luck, chance.
**şapka** *n.* hat.
**şarkı** *n.* song.
**şarkıcı** *n.* singer.
**şaşırmak** *v.* be confused, be surprised.
**şefkatli** *adj.* affectionate, caring.
**şehir** *n.* city, town.
**şeker** *n.* sugar, candy.
**şemsiye** *n.* umbrella.
**şey** *n.* thing.
**şiddet** *n.* violence.
**şiir** *n.* poem, verse.
**şikayet etmek** *v.* complain.
**şimdi** *adv.* now, just.
**şirin** *adj.* pretty.
**şirket** *n.* company, incorporation.
**şişe** *n.* bottle.
**şişman** *adj.* fatty.
**şöhret** *n.* fame.
**şu** *adj. / prep.* that.
**şubat** *n.* February.

şüphelenmek *v.* doubt, suspect.

## T - t

tabak *n.* plate.
tabiat *n.* nature; character.
tahmin etmek *v.* guess; predict.
tahta *n.* wood; *adj.* wooden.
takım elbise *n.* suit.
takım *n.* team; troop.
takip etmek *n.* follow.
taklit etmek *v.* imitate; mock.
taksi *n.* taxi, cab.
talep etmek *v.* request, want.
tamam *prep.* all right, okay; *adj.* complete.
tamirat *n.* reparation.
tanık *n.* witness.
tanımak *v.* know; recognize.
tanınmayan *adj.* unknown.
tanışmak *v.* meet; be acquainted with.
tanıtmak *v.* introduce to; present.
tanrı *n.* God.
tanrıça *n.* goddess.
taramak *v.* comb.
tarif etmek describe.
tarih *n.* date; history.
tarla *n.* field.
tartı *n.* weigh.
tartışmak *v.* argue; discuss.
tartmak *v.* weigh.
tasarruf yapmak *v.* save.
taş *n.* stone.
taşımak *v.* carry; transport.
taşınmak *v.* move; move house.
taşıt *n.* vehicle; conveyance.
tatil *n.* vacation, holiday.
tatlı *adj.* tasty; sweet;.

tatmak *v.* taste.
tava *n.* pan, frying-pan.
tavan *n.* ceiling.
tavır *n.* attitude; behaviour.
tavsiye *v.* recommend, advise.
tavşan *n.* rabbit.
tavuk *n.* chicken; hen.
taze *adj.* fresh.
tebessüm *n.* smile.
tebrik etmek *v.* congratulate.
tecrübe *n.* experience, trial.
tedavi *n.* cure, treatment; therapy.
tedirgin *adj.* worried.
tehlike *n.* danger.
tek *n.* single; only.
tekerlek *n.* wheel.
teklif *v.* offer.
tekrar etmek *v.* repeat.
telaffuz *n.* pronunciation.
telaşlanmak *v.* get anxious.
telefon etmek *v.* telephone, call.
televizyon izlemek *v.* watch television.
tembel *adj.* lazy.
temiz *adj.* clear; clean.
temmuz *n.* July.
temsil etmek *v.* represent; act.
temsil *n.* performance; acting.
terazi *n.* scale.
tercih etmek *v.* prefer.
tercih *n.* choice.
tercüman *n.* translator.
tereddüt etmek *v.* hesitate; doubt.
terk etmek *v.* leave.
terlemek *v.* sweat.
terzi *n.* tailor.
teşekkür ederim! thank you!
teşekkür etmek *v.* thank.

TÜRKÇE – İNGİLİZCE SÖZLÜK

TURKISH – ENGLISH DICTIONARY

tıbbi *adj.* medical.
tıp *adj.* medicine, physic.
tıraş olmak *v.* shave.
tırmanmak *v.* climb.
ticaret *n.* trade, commerce.
ticari *adj.* commercial.
timsah *n.* alligator, crocodile.
titremek *v.* tremble; thrill.
tiyatro *n.* theatre, theater.
tohum *n.* seed, grain.
toplam *n.* total, sum.
toplantı *n.* meeting.
topluluk *n.* community; troop.
toprak *n.* soil; land; ground.
torun *n.* grandchild.
trafik *n.* traffic.
trafik kazası *n.* road accident.
trafik kuralları *n.* traffic-regulations.
tramvay *n.* tram.
tren istasyon *n.* railway station.
tuhaf *adj.* strange, odd.
turist *n.* tourist.
tutmak *v.* hold; catch; keep.
tutuklamak *v.* arrest.
tutuklu *n.* prisoner; under arrest.
tuvalet *n.* toilet, WC, bathroom, restroom, toilet, washroom, lavatory.
tuz *n.* salt.
tüccar *n.* merchant, trader.
tür *n.* type; *n.* species.

## U - u

ucuz *adj.* cheap.
uç *n.* tip, end, edge.
uçak *n.* airplane.
uçmak *v.* fly, wing.
uçurtma *n.* kite.
uçurum *n.* cliff.

uçuş *n.* flight.
uğramak *v.* come by.
uğraş *v.* cope; struggle.
ulaşmak *v.* reach; arrive at.
ulus *n.* nation.
ulusal *adj.* national.
uluslararası *adj.* international.
ummak *v.* hope, expect.
un *n.* flour.
unutmak *v.* forget.
usanmak *v.* be tired of.
usta *n.* craftsman; *adj.* skillful.
ustura *n.* razor.
uşak *n.* servant.
utanmak *v.* be ashamed.
uyandırmak *v.* awaken.
uyanmak *v.* awake.
uyarı *n.* warning.
uygulamak *v.* apply.
uygun *adj.* appropriate, fit.
uyumak *v.* sleep.
uzak *adj.* far, faraway.
uzatmak *v.* extend, expand; prolong.
uzay *n.* space.
uzman *n.* expert, specialist.
uzun *adj.* long; tall.

## Ü - ü

ücret *n.* charge; salary.
ücretsiz *adj.* free of charge.
üç *adj.* three.
ülke *adj.* country.
ümit etmek *v.* hope, expect.
ün *n.* fame.
ünlü *adj.* famous.
üretim *adj.* manufacturing.
üretmek *v.* produce.
ürün *n.* production; crop.
üst *n.* top.
üst kat *n.* upstairs.

**üstünlük** *n.* superiority **üye** *n.* member.
**üzerinde** *adv.* above; *prep.* upon, over.
**üzülmek** *v.* be sorry, be worried.

## V - v

**vagon** *n.* carriage.
**valiz** *n.* suitcase.
**varış** *n.* arrival.
**varmak** *v.* arrive, reach.
**vatandaş** *n.* citizen.
**vazo** *n.* vase.
**ve** *conj.* and.
**vergi** *n.* tax, duty.
**vermek** *v.* give.
**vesaire** *n.* et cetera *conj.* and so on, and so forth.
**veya** *conj.* or.
**vicdan** *n.* conscience.
**vurmak** *v.* strike; knock; shoot.
**vücut** *n.* body.

## Y - y

**yabancı** *n.* stranger, foreigner.
**yağ** *n.* fat, oil.
**yağmur** *n.* rain; *v.* rain.
**yakalamak** *v.* catch.
**yakın** *adj.* near, nearby.
**yaklaşık** *adv.* about; approximately.
**yakmak** *v.* burn, fire.
**yalan** *n.* lie, *adj.* false.
**yalan söylemek** *v.* lie, tell lies.
**yalnız** *adj.* lonely, alone.
**yalvarmak** *v.* beg.
**yangın** *n.* fire.
**yanı sıra** *adv.* besides.

**yanında** *adv.* next to; alongside.
**yanıtlamak** *v.* answer.
**yanlış** *n.* mistake; *adj.* incorrect.
**yanlış yapmak** make a mistake.
**yanmak** *v.* burn up; *v.* light.
**yapabilmek** *v.* be able to do; *v.* can.
**yapışmak** *v.* stick to, adhere.
**yapmak** *v.* do, make; build.
**yara** *n.* wound, cut; injury.
**yarar** *n.* benefit, profit.
**yaratık** *n.* creature.
**yardım etmek** *v.* help; assist; aid.
**yargılamak** *v.* judge.
**yarım** *adj.* half-.
**yarışmak** *v.* contest; compete.
**yasa** *n.* law.
**yasak** *adj.* prohibited, forbidden *n.* prohibition.
**yasaklamak** *v.* prohibit, forbid.
**yastık** *n.* cushion.
**yaşamak** *v.* live;.
**yaşasın!** *interj.* hurrah!
**yaşlı** *adj.* old.
**yatak** *n.* bed.
**yavaş** *adj.* slow.
**yaya geçidi** *n.* crosswalk, pedestrian crossing.
**yaz** *n.* summer.
**yazar** *n.* writer, author.
**yazık** *n.* pity; *interj.* alas!
**yazmak** *v.* write.
**yedek** *adj.* spare.
**yeğlemek** *v.* prefer.
**yemek** *n.* meal.
**yemek yemek** *v.* eat.
**yemin etmek** *v.* swear.
**yeni** *adj. / pref.* new.

**yenilmek** *v.* be beaten
 **yenmek, alt etmek** *v.* beat.
**yer** *n.* ground, flour; place, space; position, location.
**yeşil** *adj.* green.
**yetenek** *n.* talent, skill; capability.
**yetenekli** *n.* talent, *adj.* talented.
**yeterli** *adj.* enough, adequate.
**yetişkin** *adj.* grown up, adult.
**yıkamak** *v.* wash.
**yıkmak** *v.* destroy.
**yıl** *n.* year.
**yılan** *n.* snake.
**yıldırım** *n.* lightning.
**yıldız** *n.* star.
**yırtmak** *v.* tear.
**yine** *adv.* again.
**yiyecek** *n.* food.
**yorulmak** *v.* be tired.
**yönetici** *n.* administrator, director.
**yönetmek** *v.* manage, govern.
**yukarıya doğru** *adv.* upwards.
**yumurta** *n.* egg.
**yurtdışı(nda)** *adv.* abroad.
**yuva** *n.* home; nest.
**yuvarlak** *adj.* circular; spherical.
**yük** *n.* load, burden.
**yüklemek** *v.* load, burden.
**yüksek** *adj.* high, tall.
**yün** *n. / adj.* wool.

**yürümek** *v.* walk; march.
**yüz** *n.* face.
**yüzey** *n.* surface.
**yüzmek** *v.* swim; float.
**yüzük** *n.* ring.
**yüzyıl** *n.* century.

## Z - z

**zafer** *n.* triumph, victory.
**zalim** *adj.* cruel.
**zaman** *n.* time.
**zamk** *n.* gum, glue.
**zannetmek** *v.* guess.
**zarar** *n.* harm; damage; loss.
**zaten** *adv.* already; essentially.
**zayıf** *n. / adj.* thin; weak.
**zehirlenmek** *v.* be poisoned.
**zeki** *adj.* clever.
**zemin** *n.* floor.
**zemin kat** *n.* ground floor.
**zengin** *adj.* rich, wealthy.
**zıt** *adj.* contrary, opposite.
**zincir** *n.* chain.
**ziyaret etmek** *v.* visit.
**ziyaretçi** *n.* visitor.
**zor** *adj.* hard, difficult.
**zorunluluk** *n.* necessity.
**zulüm** *n.* cruelty.
**zücaciye** *n.* glassware.
**zürafa** *n.* giraffe.

# ENGLISH - TURKISH
# **DICTIONARY**

## İNGİLİZCE - TÜRKÇE
# **SÖZLÜK**

### Abbreviations  Kısaltmalar

| | | | | |
|---|---|---|---|---|
| *n.* | : noun | *pron.* | : pronoun |
| *adj.* | : adjective | *prep.* | : preposition |
| *v.* | : verb | *conj.* | : conjunction |
| *adv.* | : adverb | *interj.* | : interjection |
| *pref.* | : prefix | *suf.* | : suffix |

## A - a

**a, an** *indefinite article* bir, herhangi bir.

**a.m.** *adv.* öğleden önce

**abandon** *n.* serbestlik, kayıtsızlık, kendini bırakma. *v.* terk etmek, (yüzüstü) bırakmak, yarıda bırakmak

**ABC** *n.* alfabe.

**ability** *n.* kabiliyet, yetenek .

**able** *adj.* muktedir, güçlü.

**abnormal** anormal.

**about** *adv.* hakkında, dair, ilişkin, etrafında, hemen hemen, civarında, aşağı yukarı, şöyle böyle.

**above** *prep.* üstünde, yukarı, yukarıda, yukarısında. **above all** her şeyden üstün, özellikle.

**abroad** *adv.* yabancı ülkede, hariçte, dışarıda.

**absence** *n.* yokluk, eksiklik.

**absent** *adj.* yok, eksik, bulunmayan

**absurd** *adj.* anlamsız, saçma, gülünç.

**accelerator** *n.* gaz pedalı.

**accent** *n.* aksan, şive.

**accept** *v.* kabul etmek. **acceptance** *n.* kabul, onama.

**accident** *n.* tesadüf, rastlantı, kaza, arıza. **accidental** *adj.* tesadüfen, rastlantı sonucu.
**accommodate** *v.* uydurmak, yerleştirmek.
**accommodation** *n.* uyma, yerleşme, konaklama.
**accompany** *v.* eşlik etmek.
**account** *v.* hesap vermek, sorumlu olmak. **accountant** *n.* muhasebeci, sayman.
**accuse** *v.* suçlamak, itham etmek. **accusation** *n.* suçlama, itham.
**accusative** *n.* ismin 'i' hali.
**accustom** *v.* alıştırmak. **accustomed** *adj.* alışık, alışkın.
**ache** *n.* ağrı, sızı, *v.* ağrımak, sızlamak.
**achieve** *v.* elde etmek, meydana çıkarmak, başarmak.
**acknowledge** *v.* kabul etmek, doğrulamak, tanımak. **acknowledgement** *n.* doğrulama, kabul, alındı.
**acquire** *v.* elde etmek, ele geçirmek, kazanmak. **acquirement** *n.* kazanma, elde etme, başarı, hüner.
**across** *prep.* çapraz, çaprazlamasına, karşıdan karşıya, bir yandan bir yana.
**act** *n.* hareket, iş, yapılan şey *v.* rol yapmak, hareket etmek, davranmak. **action** *n.* faaliyet, etki, dava.
**active** *adj.* faal, enerjik, canlı. **activity** *n.* faaliyet, etkinlik.
**actor** *n.* aktör, rol yapan, oyuncu. **actress** *n.* kadın oyuncu.

**actual** *adj.* gerçek, asıl, güncel.
**add** *v.* katmak, eklemek, ulamak. **addition** *n.* ilâve, ek, zam, **additional** eklenilen, ek olarak.
**address** *n.* adres.
**adjective** *n.* sıfat.
**administer** *v.* yönetmek, idare etmek, tayin etmek. **administration** *n.* yönetim.
**admire** *v.* hayran olmak, takdir etmek.
**admit** *v.* itiraf etmek, kabul etmek. **admittance** *n.* kabul, giriş.
**adult** *adj.* yetişkin, buluğa ermiş, büyük.
**advance** *n.* ilerleme, gelişme. **advanced** *adj.* ilerlemiş, ileri.
**advantage** *n.* öncelik, avantaj, çıkar, fayda.
**adventure** *n.* macera, serüven. **adventurer** *n.* maceraperest.
**adverb** *n.* zarf.
**advertise** *v.* ilân etmek, reklâm vermek. **advertisement** *n.* ilân, reklâm.
**advice** *n.* nasihat, öğüt, tavsiye, öneri.
**advise** *v.* öğüt vermek.
**advocate** *n.* avukat, savunucu, *v.* savunmak.
**aero-** *pref.* hava- . **aerodrome** *n.* askeri havaalanı.
**aeroplane** *n.* uçak.
**affect** *v.* etkilemek, tesir etmek, dokunmak.
**affectionate** *adj.* sevecen, şefkatli.
**affix** *v.* eklemek, yapıştırmak.

afraid *adj.* korkmuş, korkan.
be afraid of *v.* korkmak.
after *adv.* sonra, bundan
sonra, -den sonra, itibaren.
afternoon *adv.* ikindi, öğleden
sonra.
afterwards *adv.* sonradan.
again *adv.* tekrar, yine, bir
daha, bundan başka.
against *prep.* -ye karşı, -ye
muhalif, rağmen, karşısında,
aykırı.
age *n.* yaş, çağ, devir. aged
*adj.* yaşlı.
agency *n.* ajans, aracı, daire,
vekillik, vasıta. agenda *n.*
ajanda, gündem, agent *n.*
acente, vekil, casus, ajan.
ago *adv.* evvel, önce.
agree *v.* aynı fikirde olmak,
razı olmak, uyuşmak, anlaşmak. agree with ile
anlaşmak, bir fikirde olmak.
agreement *n.* anlaşma,
sözleşme.
aid yardım, destek, imdat, *v.*
yardım etmek.
air *n.* hava, nefes, tavır,
nağme. air condition klima.
airline hava yolu. airmail
uçak postası. airplane uçak.
alike *adj.* eş, benzer, aynı.
alive *adj.* canlı, hayatta, diri.
all *adj.* hepsi, tamamen,
bütün. all right tamam,
haklısın, pekâlâ.
allow *v.* izin vermek, razı
olmak, hoş görmek.
almost *adv.* aşağı yukarı, az
kaldı, hemen hemen.
alone *adv.* yalnız, tek başına,
sade.

along *prep.* boyunca,
uzunlamasına, along side
yan yana.
already *adv.* şimdiye kadar,
daha şimdiden, kadar, zaten.
also *adv.* dahi, de, ayrıca, bir
de.
although *conj.* bununla
beraber, her ne kadar.
always *adv.* daima, her
zaman.
amaze *v.* şaşırtmak, hayret
ettirmek. amazing *adj.*
şaşırtıcı.
ambassador *n.* büyük elçi.
among *n.* arasında
an bir, herhangi bir.
Anatolia *n.* Anadolu.
ancestor *n.* cet, ata.
ancient *adj.* eski.
and *conj.* ve, ile, bir de, daha,
de.
angry *adj.* hiddetli, kızgın,
öfkeli, dargın. angrily *adv.*
hiddetle, öfke ile
animal *n.* hayvan.
anniversary *n.* yıldönümü.
annual *n.* senelik, yıllık.
another *adj.* başka, diğer.
one after another sırayla.
answer *n.* yanıt, cevap, *v.*
yanıtlamak.
ant *n.* karınca.
anti- *pref.* karşı, zıt.
any *adv.* bir, herhangi, bazı,
bir miktar. not any hiç. any
more başka, daha fazla.
anybody / anyone bir
kimse, biri(si), kim, herkes.
anyhow / anyway her
nasılsa, nasıl olsa, herhalde,
her neyse, anymore artık

**anything** (herhangi) bir şey, ne olsa, her şey.

**anywhere** nerede olursa olsun, her(hangi bir) yerde.

**apologize** *v.* özür dilemek.

**apparent** *adj.* aşikar, besbelli. **apparently** *adv.* görünüşe göre, anlaşılan, galiba.

**apple** *n.* elma.

**apply** *v.* müracaat etmek, üstüne koymak, başvurmak.

**appoint** *v.* kararlaştırmak, atamak, **appointee** atanmış.

**April** *n.* Nisan.

**area** *n.* saha, alan, avlu, yüz ölçüsü.

**argument** *n.* tartışma, münakaşa

**arise** *v.* kalkmak, çıkmak, doğmak.

**arm** *n.* kol, şube.

**army** *n.* ordu.

**around** *adv.* etrafında, çevre(sin)de, yaklaşık olarak, yakın(ın)da, orada burada.

**arrange** *v.* düzeltmek, sıraya koymak, ayarlamak, düzenlemek.

**arrest** *v.* tut(ukla)mak, yakalamak, tevkif etmek.

**arrive** *v.* varmak, gelmek, ulaşmak. **arrival** *n.* varış, gelme, ulaşma.

**art** *n.* sanat, zanaat, hüner.

**as** *adv.* kadar, iken, gibi, olarak, çünkü.

**ashtray** *n.* kül tablası

**Asia** *n.* Asya.

**ask** *v.* sormak, rica etmek, istemek, davet etmek. **ask for** sormak, istemek.

**asleep** *adj.* uykuda.

**assistant** *n.* yardımcı.

**at** *prep.* de, da, ye, halinde, yanında, üstünde. **at home** evde. **at all** hiç, **at last** sonunda, **at once** hemen, derhal.

**attach** *v.* bağlamak, birleştirmek, haczetmek.

**attack** *n.* akın, saldırı, *v.* saldırmak.

**attain** *v.* ermek, ulaşmak, elde etmek.

**attempt** *n.* girişim, deneme, yeltenme, *v.* girişmek, teşebbüs etmek, gayret etmek.

**attend** *v.* hazır bulunmak, beraberinde olmak, refakat etmek, katılmak, **attention** dikkat, hazır ol.

**attitude** *n.* davranış, tutum, vaziyet.

**attract** *v.* çekmek, cezp etmek. **attraction** *n.* cazibe, çekim, **attractive** *adj.* çekici, alımlı.

**August** *n.* Ağustos, *adj.* aziz, yüce.

**aunt** *n.* teyze, hala, yenge.

**autumn** *n.* sonbahar, hazan.

**auxiliary** *n.* yardımcı, yedek.

**available** *adj.* mevcut, emre hazır, elverişli.

**avalanche** *n.* çığ, heyelan.

**avenue** *n.* geniş cadde, iki tarafı ağaçlı yol.

**avoid** *v.* sakınmak, kaçınmak. **avoidance** *n.* sakınma.

**awake** *adj.* uyanık, *v.* uyanmak, uyandırmak.

**away** *adv.* ötede, uzakta, uzağa.

**awkward** *adj.* acemi, beceriksiz, sıkıntılı.

## B - b

**baby** *n.* bebek.

**bachelor** *n.* bekar, ergin erkek.

**back** *n.* arka, sırt, geri.

**bacon** *n.* tuzlanmış tütsülenmiş domuz eti, domuz pastırması.

**bad** *adj.* berbat, kötü, kusurlu, değersiz.

**bag** *n.* çanta, torba, çuval, kese.

**baggage** *n.* bagaj, taşınacak yolcu eşyası.

**bake** *v.* (fırında) pişirmek. **baked** pişmiş, sertleşmiş, **baker** *n.* fırıncı, ekmekçi. **bakery** *n.* fırın.

**balance** *n.* balans, terazi, kantar, denge, mizan.

**balcony** *n.* balkon.

**bandage** *n.* sargı, bandaj, *v.* sarmak.

**bank** *n.* kıyı, kenar; banka. *v.* bankaya yatırmak. **bank account** *n.* banka hesabı. **bank card** *n.* kredi kartı., **banknote** *n.* banknot.

**barber** *n.* berber.

**bare** *adj.* çıplak, açık, çorak, sade. **barely** hemen hemen, ancak.

**bargain** *n.* ticari anlaşma, iş, pazarlık, kelepir, elden düşme, indirimli. *v.* pazarlık etmek, ummak, beklemek.

**base** *n.* taban, temel, esas, kural.

**basement** *n.* bodrum katı.

**basic** *adj.* asıl, temel.

**basin** *n.* tas, küvet, leğen, havuz.

**basket** *n.* sepet, küfe.

**bath** *n.* banyo, yıkanma yeri, yunak. *v.* banyo yapmak, yıkamak.

**bathtub** *n.* küvet.

**battery** *n.* batarya, pil.

**bay** *n.* koy, körfez.

**bazaar** *n.* pazar, çarşı.

**be** *v.* olmak, bulunmak.

**beach** *n.* kumsal, plaj.

**bean** *n.* fasulye, bakla, baklagiller.

**bear** *n.* ayı.

**beard** *n.* sakal. **bearded** *adj.* sakallı.

**beat** *n.* vuruş, çalma, tempo, *v.* dövmek, vurmak.

**beautiful** *adj.* güzel, hoş. **beauty** *n.* güzellik.

**because** *conj.* çünkü, zira. **because of** nedeniyle, dolayı, yüzünden.

**become** *v.* olmak, dönüşmek, yakışmak. **becoming** *adj.* uygun, yakışık alır.

**bed** *n.* yatak, yatacak yer, karyola. **bedroom** *n.* yatak odası. **bedtime** yatma zamanı.

**bee** *n.* bal arısı.

**beef** *n.* sığır eti. **beefsteak** *n.* biftek.

**beer** *n.* bira.

**before** *adv.* (-den) önce. **the day before** bir gün önce. **beforehand** daha önce, evvelden.

**beggar** *n.* dilenci, çapkın.

**begin** *v.* başlamak, işe koyulmak. **beginning** başlangıç, kaynak.

**behalf** *n.* yan, taraf. **on behalf of** adına, namına, lehinde.

**behave** *v.* davranmak, hareket etmek. **behave yourself** uslu dur, terbiyeni takın, **behaviour** *n.* davranış.

**behind** *n.* kıç, arka. *prep.* arka(sın)da, gerisinde. *adv.* arkada, arkadan, geride.

**being** *n.* oluş, yaratık, varlık, insan.

**belief** *n.* inanç, iman, güven.

**believe** *v.* inanmak, güvenmek, iman etmek.

**bell** *n.* çan, zil, kampana. **bellboy / bellhop** *n.* komi.

**belly** *n.* karın, göbek.

**belong** *v.* ait olmak. **belongings** *n.* kişisel eşya, pılı pırtı.

**beloved** *adj.* sevilen, sevgili, aziz.

**below** *adv.* aşağı(sında), alt(ında), aşağıda.

**belt** *n.* kuşak, kemer, kayış.

**beneath** *adv.* altında, altta.

**benefit** *n.* yarar, fayda, hayır, kâr. *v.* faydalı olmak, iyiliği dokunmak.

**berry** *n.* böğürtlen, çilek.

**beside** *prep.* yanına, yanında.

**besides** *adv.* bundan başka, ayrıca, üstelik.

**best** *n.* en iyisi. *adj.* en iyi, en uygun. **at best** olsa olsa. **bestseller** satış rekoru kıran kitap.

**better** *adj.* daha iyi, daha güzel, daha çok. **better and better** gittikçe daha iyi.

**between** *prep.* arasında, arada, araya.

**beware** *v.* sakınmak, dikkat etmek.

**beyond** *prep.* ileri, öte, ötede, öteye, dışında, üstünde, çok fazla.

**bicycle** *n.* bisiklet.

**big** *adj.* iri, büyük, kocaman, önemli.

**billiards** *n.* bilârdo.

**binoculars** *n.* dürbün.

**bird** *n.* kuş. **bird's eye view** kuş bakışı.

**birth** *n.* doğma, doğum. **give birth to** doğurmak. **date of birth** doğum tarihi. **birthday** doğum günü

**bit** *n.* gem, parça, lokma, kırıntı.

**bite** *n.* ısırma, ısırık, lokma. *v.* ısırmak, sokmak, dişlemek.

**bitter** *adj.* acı, keskin, sert.

**black** *adj.* kara, siyah, zenci, kirli. **blackboard** kara tahta, yazı tahtası. **black smith** demirci, nalbant.

**blade** *n.* bıçak ağzı, jilet, kılıç.

**blame** *n.* ayıplama, kınama. *v.* ayıplamak, kınamak. **blame (something) on** (bir şey)in suçunu birisine yüklemek.

**blanket** *n.* battaniye.

**bleed** *v.* kan kaybetmek, kanamak.

**bless** *v.* kutsamak, hayır duası etmek.

**blind** *adj.* kör, anlayışsız, çıkmaz sokak. *n.* perde, kepenk.

**blond** *n.* / *adj.* sarı, sarışın (kimse)

**blonde** *n.* sarışın (kadın / kız.)

**blood** *n.* kan, soy, ırk.
 **bloody** kanayan, kanlı, belâlı.
**blouse** *n.* bluz
**blue** *adj.* mavi.
**board** *n.* tahta, yönetim kurulu. **boarding school** yatılı okul. **boarder** pansiyoner, yatılı öğrenci.
**boat** *n.* kayık, sandal, tekne, bot, gemi.
**body** *n.* vücut, gövde.
**boil** *n.* çıban. *v.* kaynamak, haşlamak.
**bone** *n.* kemik, kılçık.
**book** *n.* kitap, defter. *v.* yer ayırtmak, rezervasyon. **bookcase** kitap dolabı. **booking office** bilet gişesi. **bookshop** kitap evi, kitapçı.
**boot** *n.* ayakkabı, çizme.
**border** *n.* kenar, sınır. **border on** sınır komşusu olmak.
**bore** *v.* delmek, oymak, usandırmak, can sıkmak, **bored with** -den sıkılmış
**boring** *adj.* can sıkıcı.
**borrow** *v.* borç almak, ödünç almak.
**boss** *n.* işveren, amir, patron. *v.* yönetmek.
**both** her ikisi de. *adj.* her iki.
**bother** *n.* canını sıkma, sıkıntı. *v.* taciz etmek, canını sıkmak.
**bottle** *n.* şişe, biberon. *v.* şişelemek.
**bottom** *n.* dip, alt, temel, kıç.
**bowl** *n.* kase, tas, çanak. *v.* yuvarlanmak.
**box** *n.* kutu, sandık.
**boy** *n.* erkek çocuk, oğlan.
**bracelet** *n.* bilezik, kelepçe.

**brain** *n.* beyin.
**brake** *n.* fren. *v.* frenlemek, fren yapmak.
**branch** *n.* dal, kol, şube. *v.* kollara ayrılmak.
**brave** *adj.* cesur, yakışıklı. *v.* göğüs germek. **bravely** *adv.* cesurca.
**bread** *n.* ekmek.
**break** *n.* kırık, ara, mola, şans. *v.* kırmak, koparmak, bozmak. **break down** bozulmak.
**breakfast** *n.* kahvaltı.
**breast** *n.* göğüs, meme.
**breath** *n.* nefes, soluk, nefes alma.
**bride** *n.* gelin.
**bridge** *n.* köprü, briç. **bridge over** atlatmak.
**bright** *adj.* parlak, berrak, renkli, canlı, zeki.
**bring** *v.* getirmek. **bring up** yetiştirmek, büyütmek.
**broadcast** *n.* radyo yayını. *v.* radyo ile yayınlamak.
**broken** *adj.* kırık, kopuk, bozuk.
**brother** *n.* erkek kardeş.
**brown** *adj.* kahverengi.
**brush** *n.* fırça, çalılık. *v.* fırçalamak.
**bucket** *n.* kova.
**budget** *n.* bütçe.
**build** *v.* inşa etmek, yapmak, kurmak.
**building** yapı, bina.
**burn** *n.* yanık, yanık yeri. *v.* yanmak, yakmak.
**bus** *n.* otobüs.
**bush** *n.* çalı, fidan.
**business** *n.* iş, meslek, görev, ticaret.

**İNGİLİZCE – TÜRKÇE SÖZLÜK**

**ENGLISH – TURKISH DICTIONARY**

**busy** *adj.* meşgul, faal, işlek.
**but** *prep.* fakat, ama, lakin, den başka.
**butcher** *n.* kasap. *v.* kesmek.
**butter** *n.* tereyağı. *v.* tereyağı sürmek.
**butterfly** *n.* kelebek.
**button** *n.* düğme, elektrik düğmesi.
**buy** *v.* satın almak. **buyer** *n.* alıcı, müşteri.
**by** *prep.* ile, kadar, tarafından, yakınında, kenarında, -in yanında, vasıtasıyla, göre.

## C - c

**cake** *n.* pasta, kek, çörek. *v.* katılaşmak.
**calculate** *v.* hesaplamak. **calculation** hesap, **calculator** *n.* hesap makinesi.
**calendar** *n.* takvim.
**call** *v.* bağırmak, seslenmek, çağırmak, telefon etmek, isimlendirmek.
**calm** *adj.* sakin, durgun.
**camp** *n.* kamp, kışla, *v.* kamp yapmak.
**can {1}** *v.* gücü yetmek, -ebilmek.
**can {2}** *n.* maşrapa, teneke kutu, kap.
**cancel** *v.* iptal etmek, üstüne çizgi çekmek, silmek.
**candle** *n.* mum. **candlelight** mum ışığı.
**candy** *n.* şeker, bonbon.
**capacity** *n.* kapasite, hacim, yetenek, güç, iktidar.
**captain** *n.* kaptan, yüzbaşı, deniz albayı.

**car** *n.* otomobil, vagon.
**care** *n.* dikkat, bakım, merak, endişe. *v.* merak etmek, ilgilenmek, önemsemek.
**careful** *adj.* dikkatli.
**careless** *adj.* dikkatsiz.
**carpenter** *n.* marangoz, doğramacı.
**carpet** *n.* halı.
**carry** *v.* taşımak, nakletmek.
**cash** *n.* para, peşin para, nakit. *v.* tahsil etmek, paraya çevirmek.
**castle** *n.* kale, hisar, şato.
**cat** *n.* kedi.
**catch** *n.* tutma, yakalama. *v.* tutmak, yakalamak, (taşıta) yetişmek.
**cause** *n.* neden, sebep, amaç. *v.* neden olmak, doğurmak.
**ceiling** *n.* tavan.
**celebrate** *v.* kutlamak. **celebration** *n.* kutlama.
**cell** *n.* hücre, küçük oda, pil.
**center (centre)** *n.* merkez, orta. *v.* ortaya koymak, ortalamak.
**century** *n.* yüzyıl.
**certain** *adj.* kesin, belli, emin. **for certain** şüphesiz, kuşkusuz.
**chair** *n.* sandalye, kürsü. *v.* başkanlık etmek.
**chance** *n.* şans, talih, fırsat. *v.* rast gelmek. *adj.* şans eseri.
**change** *n.* değiştirme, para bozma. *v.* değiştirmek, değişmek, para bozdurmak.
**chapter** *n.* bölüm.
**character** *n.* karakter, tip, nitelik, kişilik.

**charge** *n.* fiyat, ücret, suçlama, şarj, görev. *v.* fiyatlandırmak, suçlamak, şarj etmek, görevlendirmek, **free of charge** parasız, karşılıksız.

**cheap** *adj.* ucuz, değersiz.

**check** *n.* kontrol, vestiyer fişi, lokantada hesap, çek. *v.* engellemek, kontrol etmek.

**check out** otelden ayrılmak.

**cheese** *n.* peynir.

**chemist** *n.* kimyager, eczacı.

**chemistry** kimya.

**cheque (check)** *n.* çek.

**cherry** *n.* kiraz.

**chess** *n.* satranç.

**chew** *v.* çiğnemek.

**chicken** *n.* piliç, tavuk, *adj.* korkak.

**chief** *n.* şef. *adj.* büyük, belli başlı. **chiefly** *adv.* başlıca.

**child** *n.* çocuk. **children** çocuklar.

**chocolate** *n.* çikolata.

**choice** *n.* seçme, tercih, seçenek. *adj.* seçkin.

**choose** *v.* seçmek, tercih etmek.

**Christ** *n.* İsa. **Christian** Hıristiyan.

**cinema** *n.* sinema.

**circle** *n.* daire, çember, halka. *v.* etrafını dönmek, çember içine almak.

**city** *n.* şehir, kent, site.

**civilization** *n.* uygarlık.

**claim** *n.* talep, iddia. *v.* hakkını istemek, iddia etmek.

**class** *n.* sınıf, zümre, çeşit, mevki. *v.* sınıflandırmak, **classroom** *n.* sınıf (odası).

**clause** *n.* madde, fıkra, cümlecik.

**clean** *adj.* temiz, pak. *v.* temizlemek.

**clear** *adj.* berrak, açık, net, temiz. *v.* temizlemek, temize çıkarmak. **clearly** *adv.* açık bir şekilde, net olarak.

**clever** *adj.* akıllı, zeki, becerikli.

**climate** *n.* iklim, hava.

**climb** *v.* tırmanmak, çıkmak.

**clock** *n.* saat, kronometre, taksimetre

**close** *n.* yakın, son, *v.* kapatmak, **closed** *adj.* kapalı.

**cloth** *n.* kumaş, bez, masa örtüsü. **clothing** *n.* giyim.

**cloud** *n.* bulut. **cloudy** bulutlu.

**club** *n.* kulüp, dernek, sopa.

**coat** *n.* palto, ceket. *v.* kaplamak.

**coffee** *n.* kahve. **coffeepot** *n.* kahve cezvesi.

**coiffeur** *n.* berber, kuaför.

**coin** *n.* metal para. *v.* para basmak.

**cold** *n.* soğuk algınlığı, nezle. *adj.* soğuk, üşümüş.

**colleague** *n.* meslektaş.

**collect** *v.* toplamak, biriktirmek, tahsil etmek. *adj.* ödemeli.

**colour** *n.* renk, boya, *v.* boyamak.

**comb** *n.* tarak, ibik, petek. *v.* taramak, taranmak.

**come** *v.* gelmek, sonuçlanmak. **come in** içeri girmek, **come across** rastlamak.

INGILIZCE – TÜRKÇE SÖZLÜK

ENGLISH – TURKISH DICTIONARY

**comfort** *n.* konfor, refah.
**comfortable** *adj.* rahat, konforlu.
**comment** *n.* yorum. *v.* fikrini söylemek.
**commerce** *n.* ticaret, iş,
**commission** *n.* görev, hizmet, kurul, komisyon.
**common** *adj.* genel, herkese ait, kamusal.
**compare** *v.* karşılaştırmak, kıyaslamak.
**complain** *v.* şikâyet etmek, içini dökmek. **complaint** *n.* şikâyet, dert, keyifsizlik.
**complete** *adj.* tamam, eksiksiz, bütün. *v.* tamamlamak.
**concept** *n.* fikir, kavram, görüş.
**concert** *n.* konser.
**condition** *n.* hal, durum, koşul, şart.
**confirm** *v.* onaylamak, doğrulamak.
**congratulate** *v.* tebrik etmek, kutlamak, **congratulation** *v.* tebrik, kutlama.
**connect** *v.* bağlamak, birleştirmek.
**conscience** *n.* vicdan.
**conscious** *adj.* bilinçli, haberdar, uyanık.
**consonant** *n.* sessiz harf.
**construct** *v.* kurmak, inşa etmek. **construction** *n.* inşaat, yapı, bina.
**consult** *v.* danışmak, müracaat etmek.
**contain** *v.* kapsamak, içermek, içine almak.
**content** *n.* öz, içerik, gerçek anlam, içindekiler.

**continent** *n.* anakara, kıta.
**continue** *v.* devam etmek, sür(dür)mek. **continuous** *adv.* sürekli, devamlı, kesintisiz.
**conversation** *n.* konuşma, sohbet
**cook** *n.* aşçı. *v.* pişmek, pişirmek.
**cool** *n.* serin, soğuk, sakin, kayıtsız.
**copper** *n.* bakır.
**copy** *n.* kopya, suret, yazı. *v.* kopyalamak.
**corner** *n.* köşe, köşe başı.
**correct** *v.* düzeltmek. *adj.* doğru, yanlışsız.
**cost** *n.* eder, bedel, fiyat, maliyet. *v.* mal olmak, değeri olmak, bedeli olmak.
**cotton** *n.* pamuk, pamuk bezi. *adj.* pamuklu.
**cough** *n.* öksürük. *v.* öksürmek.
**country** *n.* ülke, memleket, yurt, taşra.
**couple** *n.* çift, karı koca. *v.* birleştirmek, çiftleştirmek.
**courage** cesaret, mertlik.
**courageous** *adj.* cesur, yiğit, mert.
**course** *n.* ders, kurs, rota. **of course** tabii, elbette.
**craft** *n.* el sanatı, marifet, tekne, gemi.
**create** *v.* yaratmak, meydana getirmek. **creative** *adj.* yaratıcı.
**creature** *n.* yaratık.

**cross** *n.* çarpı işareti, haç. *v.* çarpı işareti koymak, karşıya geçmek, karşılaşmak. *adj.* dargın. **crossword** çapraz bilmece, **crossroads** *n.* kavşak.
**crowd** *n.* kalabalık, yığın, ahali. *v.* doldurmak, sıkıştırmak.
**cry** *v.* ağlamak, bağırmak, feryat etmek
**culture** *n.* kültür, terbiye, uygarlık, ekin, yetiştirme.
**cup** *n.* fincan, bardak, kupa.
**cupboard** *n.* dolap, büfe.
**cure** *n.* tedavi, çare, ilaç. *v.* tedavi etmek.
**currency** *n.* nakit para, geçerlilik, döviz.
**curtain** *n.* perde, pano, siper.
**custom** *n.* örf, gelenek, alışkanlık.
**customer** *n.* müşteri, gümrükçü.
**customs** *n.* gümrük.
**cut** *n.* kesik, yara, dilim, parça. *v.* kesmek, dilimlemek.

### D - d

**dad(dy)** *n.* baba(cığım).
**daily** *n.* günlük, gündelik.
**damage** *n.* zarar, ziyan, hasar. *v.* zarar vermek, hasar yapmak. **damages** tazminat.
**dance** *n.* dans. *v.* dans etmek.
**danger** *n.* tehlike.
**dark** *n.* karanlık. *adj.* karanlık, koyu, gizli.
**darling** *n.* sevgili.

**date** *n.* tarih, zaman, randevu. *v.* tarih atmak, randevulaşmak.
**daughter** *n.* kız evlât.
**day** *n.* gün, gündüz. **daylight** *n.* gün ışığı.
**deaf** *adj.* sağır.
**dear** *adj.* sevgili, aziz, samimi, değerli.
**death** *n.* ölüm.
**debt** *n.* borç. **debtor** *n.* borçlu.
**deceive** *v.* aldatmak, kandırmak.
**December** *n.* Aralık ayı.
**decide** *v.* karar vermek, kararlaştırmak, belirlemek
**decrease** *n.* azalma, eksilme. *v.* azalmak, azaltmak, eksiltmek.
**deep** *adj.* derin. **deepfreeze** *n.* derin dondurucu.
**degree** *n.* derece, aşama, diploma.
**delay** *n.* erteleme. *v.* ertelemek, geciktirmek.
**delicious** *adj.* lezzetli, nefis.
**delight** *n.* haz, zevk, sevinç. *v.* sevindirmek, zevk almak, sevinmek. **delightful** *adj.* hoş, nefis, zevkli.
**deliver** *v.* teslim etmek, vermek, dağıtmak, ulaştırmak.
**dentist** *n.* dişçi.
**deny** *v.* yalanlamak, inkar etmek.
**department** *n.* şube, kısım, bölüm, dal.
**departure** *n.* hareket, kalkış, gidiş.
**depend** *v.* asılmak, asılı olmak. **depend on** *v.* -e bağlı olmak, tabi olmak.

İNGİLİZCE – TÜRKÇE SÖZLÜK

ENGLISH – TURKISH DICTIONARY

**describe** *v.* tanımlamak, açıklamak, anlatmak.
**description** *n.* tanımlama, tarif etme, cins, çeşit.
**desert {1}** *n.* çöl, bozkır, ıssız yer.
**desert {2}** *v.* bırakmak, terk etmek, kaçmak, firar etmek
**despite** *prep.* -e rağmen, -e karşın.
**dessert** *n.* meyve, tatlı.
**destination** *n.* gidilecek yer, varış yeri, hedef.
**detail** *n.* detay, ayrıntı.
**develop** *v.* gelişmek, geliştirmek, büyütmek.
**dialogue** *n.* karşılıklı konuşma, tartışma, diyalog.
**die** *n.* zar, oyun zarı, şans. *v.* ölmek, vefat etmek.
**differ** *v.* farklı olmak, ayrılmak.
**difference** *n.* ayrılık, fark.
**different** *adj.* farklı, ayrı, başka.
**difficulty** *n.* zorluk, güçlük, sıkıntı.
**dinner** *n.* akşam yemeği.
**direction** *n.* yön, taraf, yönetim, idare.
**directly** *adv.* Doğrudan, doğrudan doğruya, dolaysız.
**dirt** *n.* kir, toz, leke. **dirty** *adj.* kirli, pis.
**discover** *v.* keşfetmek, meydana çıkarmak.
**discoverer** *n.* kâşif.
**discovery** *n.* keşif.
**discuss** *v.* tartışmak, görüşmek.
**dislike** *v.* hoşlanmamak, beğenmemek
**distance** *n.* mesafe, uzaklık.

**disturb** *v.* rahatsız etmek, düzenini bozmak.
**divide** *n.* bölme, pay etme. *v.* böl(üştür)mek, ayırmak, paylaştırmak, dağıtmak.
**do** *v.* yapmak, etmek.
**doctor** *n.* doktor.
**document** *n.* belge, senet. *v.* belgelemek.
**dog** *n.* köpek.
**doll** *n.* (oyuncak) bebek.
**dolly** *n.* bebek, kukla.
**dollar** *n.* dolar.
**donkey** *n.* eşek.
**door** *n.* kapı.
**double** *n.* / *adj.* çift, iki misli, ikilik. . *v.* iki misli yapmak, ikilemek, iki kat yapmak. *adv.* iki misli olarak.
**doubt** *n.* şüphe, kuşku. *v.* şüphelenmek, kuşkulanmak.
**in doubt** şüpheli. **no doubt** hiç şüphesiz.
**dozen** *n.* düzine.
**draw** *n.* kura çekilişi. *v.* çekmek, germek, çizmek.
**dream** *n.* rüya, hayal. *v.* rüya görmek, hayal kurmak.
**dress** *n.* elbise, giyim. *v.* giyinmek, giydirmek.
**drink** *n.* içki, içecek. *v.* içmek, şerefe kaldırmak.
**drive** *v.* sürmek, yürütmek, araba kullanmak.
**driver** *n.* şoför, sürücü.
**drugstore** *n.* eczane
**dry** *v.* kurutmak, kurumak. *adj.* kuru, susuz, kurak.
**during** *prep.* esnasında, sırasında, boyunca, süresince.
**duty** *n.* görev, vazife, vergi.

## E - e

**each** *adj.* her, her bir, **each one** her biri.

**ear** *n.* Kulak. **earring** *n.* küpe.

**early** *adv.* ilk, önce, erken, erkenden.

**earn** *v.* kazanmak, edinmek, hak etmek.

**earth** *n.* toprak, yeryüzü, dünya.

**earthquake** *n.* deprem, zelzele.

**east** *n.* doğu, **eastern** *adj.* doğuya ait.

**easy** *adj.* kolay, rahat, **easily** *adv.* kolayca, rahatça.

**eat** *v.* yemek, tüketmek, kemirmek.

**egg** *n.* yumurta.

**either** ikisinden biri, her iki, her biri.

**elbow** *n.* dirsek, *v.* dirsekle dürtmek.

**element** *n.* eleman, unsur, **elementary** *adj.* temel, başlangıç, **elementary school** *n.* ilkokul.

**elephant** *n.* fil.

**elevator** *n.* asansör.

**else** *adv.* başka, daha, diğer.

**embassy** *n.* elçilik.

**emergency** *n.* acil vaka, olağanüstü durum, ani tehlike.

**emotion** *n.* heyecan, duygu, **emotional** *adj.* duygulu, duygusal.

**employ** *v.* işe almak, iş vermek, **employee** *n.* işçi, memur, **employer** *n.* patron, işveren.

**empty** *adj.* boş, *v.* boşaltmak, dökmek. emsalsiz, eşsiz.

**encourage** *v.* teşvik etmek, cesaret vermek.

**end** *n.* son, uç, bitim, *v.* sona ermek, bit(ir)mek.

**engineer** *n.* mühendis.

**England** *n.* İngiltere, **English** *adj.* İngiliz, İngiltere'ye ait, İngilizce.

**enjoy** *v.* zevk almak, beğenmek, hoşlanmak.

**enough** *adj.* kafi, yeter, yeterli.

**enter** *n.* giriş, *v.* girmek, dahil olmak.

**envelop** *v.* sarmak, kuşatmak, **envelope** *n.* zarf.

**environment** *n.* çevre, civar, yöre.

**envy** *n.* gıpta, imrenme, haset, kıskanma *v.* kıskanmak, imrenmek.

**equal** *adj.* eşit, aynı, eş değerli.

**erase** *v.* silmek, çizmek, bozmak, **eraser** *n.* silgi.

**error** *n.* hata, yanlış.

**especial** *adj.* özel, seçkin, **especially** *adv.* bilhassa, özellikle.

**etc** (**et cetera**) vesaire, vs., vb.

**Europe** *n.* Avrupa.

**even** *adj.* düz, aynı hizada, *adv.* bile, hatta, *v.* düzeltmek, tesviye etmek, **even number** çift sayı.

**evening** *n.* akşam, **good evening** iyi akşamlar.

**event** *n.* olay, vaka.

**ever** *adv.* daima, her zaman, herhangi bir zamanda, **forever** sonsuza kadar.

**every** *adj.* her, her bir, her türlü, **everybody** herkes, **everyday** her günkü, **everything** her şey, **everywhere** her yer(e), her yerde.

**examination** *n.* sınav, yoklama, muayene.

**examine** *v.* incelemek, gözden geçirmek, sınav yapmak.

**example** *n.* örnek, **for example** örneğin, mesela.

**except** *v.* hariç tutmak, ayrı tutmak, saymamak, *prep.* -den başka, -nin dışında, **exception** *n.* istisna, ayrılık.

**exchange** *n.* değiş tokuş, takas, *v.* (para, döviz) bozmak, değiştirmek.

**excuse** *n.* özür, mazeret, *v.* affetmek, **excuse me** özür dilerim, affedersiniz.

**exercise** *n.* egzersiz, uygulama, alıştırma.

**exist** *v.* varolmak, yaşamak, bulunmak, **existence** varoluş, varlık, yaşayış.

**exit** *n.* çıkış.

**expect** *v.* beklemek, ummak, tahmin etmek, **expectation** *n.* bekleme, umut etme.

**expense** *n.* masraf, gider, **expensive** *adj.* masraflı, pahalı.

**experience** *n.* tecrübe, deney, *v.* başından geçmek, denemek.

**explain** *v.* açıklamak, **explanation** *n.* açıklama, izahat.

**explode** *v.* patlamak, patlatmak.

**export** *n.* ihraç, dış satım, ihraç malı, *v.* ihracat yapmak.

**extraordinary** *adj.* olağanüstü, fevkalade, sıra dışı.

**eye** *n.* göz, iğne deliği, bakış, **eyebrow** *n.* kaş, **eyelash** *n.* kirpik, **eyelid** *n.* göz kapağı.

## F - f

**fabric** *n.* yapı, bina, kumaş, bez.

**face** *n.* yüz, çehre, saygınlık, karşılaşmak.

**fact** *n.* gerçek, olay, **in fact** gerçekten.

**factory** *n.* fabrika.

**fail** *v.* başaramamak. **failure** *n.* başarısızlık.

**faith** *n.* inanç, itikat, güven, **faithful** *adj.* sadık, güvenilir.

**fall** *n.* düşme, dökülme, yıkılma, çökme, *v.* düşmek, dökülmek.

**fame** *n.* şan, şöhret, nam, ün.

**familiar** *adj.* aşina, bildik, tanıdık.

**family** *n.* aile, **family name** soyadı.

**famous** *adj.* ünlü, meşhur.

**far** *adj.* uzak, **far away** uzakta.

**farm** *n.* çiftlik, tarla, *v.* ekip biçmek, çiftçilik yapmak.

**farther** *adj.* daha uzak, daha öte, daha fazla.

**fashion** *n.* moda, tarz, biçim, *v.* şekil vermek.
**fast** *adv.* çabuk, hızlı, seri, **fast food** hazır yiyecek.
**fat** *n.* yağ, *adj.* şişman.
**father** *n.* baba, ata.
**favour** *n.* lütuf, iltifat, yardım *v.* lütuf göstermek, kayırmak.
**favourable** *adj.* uygun, elverişli, **favourate** favori, gözde, en beğenilen.
**fear** *n.* korku, endişe, kuruntu, *v.* korkmak, **fearful** *adj.* korkunç.
**February** *n.* Şubat.
**fee** *n.* vizite, ücret.
**feed** *n.* yem, besin, gıda, *v.* yedirmek, beslemek, otlamak.
**feel** *v.* hissetmek, duymak, elle yoklamak, **feeling** *n.* his, duygu, dokunma.
**feet çoğul** *n.* ayaklar.
**female** *n.* dişi, kadın.
**ferry** *n.* feribot, araba vapuru.
**fever** *n.* vucut ısısı, ateş, heyecan, telaş.
**few** *adj.* az, az miktar veya kişi.
**field** *n.* tarla, alan, kır.
**fifteen** *n.* on beş.
**fight** *n.* kavga, dövüş, savaş, *v.* kavga etmek, savaşmak
**figure** *n.* şekil, biçim, sayı, rakam, vücut, *v.* hesaplamak, şekil vermek.
**fill** *v.* dolmak, doldurmak.
**find** *v.* bulmak, keşfetmek.
**fine** *adj.* güzel, hoş, iyi, nazik.
**finger** *n.* parmak.
**finish** *n.* son, bitirme, *v.* bit(ir)mek, sona erdirmek, tüketmek.

**fire** *n.* ateş, alev, yangın, *v.* ateşlemek, ateş etmek, tutuşturmak, işten atmak.
**fireman** *n.* itfaiyeci.
**first** birinci, ilk, önce.
**fish** *n.* balık, *v.* balık avlamak, **fisher, fisherman** *n.* balıkçı.
**flat** *n.* apartman dairesi, *adj.* düz, yassı, harap, mat, doğrudan.
**flavour** *n.* tat, lezzet, *v.* tat vermek.
**flight** *n.* uçuş, seyir, göç, kaçış.
**floor** *n.* yer, zemin, döşeme, taban.
**florist** *n.* çiçekçi, çiçek yetiştiricisi.
**flour** *n.* un.
**flow** *v.* akmak, dolaşmak.
**flower** *n.* çiçek, *v.* çiçek açmak.
**fluid** *adj.* akıcı, sıvı.
**fly** *n.* sinek, olta iğnesi, uçuş, *v.* uçmak, uçurmak, uçakla gitmek.
**fog** *n.* sis, duman, **foggy** *adj.* sisli, bulutlu.
**follow** *v.* takip etmek, izlemek, riayet etmek, **following** *n.* taraftar, *adj.* takip eden, izleyen.
**fond** *adj.* meraklı, düşkün, seven, **to be fond of** -e düşkün olmak, bayılmak.
**food** *n.* yiyecek, yemek, besin, gıda.
**fool** *n.* aptal, ahmak, soytarı, *v.* aldatmak, kandırmak, **foolish** *adj.* akılsız, saçma.

**foot** *n.* ayak, adım, dip, etek (dağ), piyade, piyade birliği, uyak.

**for** *prep.* için, -den dolayı, -den beri, nedeniyle, çünkü, zira, **for sale** satılık, **for example** örneğin, mesela.

**forbid** *v.* yasaklamak.

**force** *n.* güç, kuvvet, erk, *v.* zorlamak, mecbur etmek.

**forecast** *n.* tahmin, *v.* tahmin etmek. **weather forecast** *n.* hava raporu

**forefinger** *n.* işaret parmağı.

**forehead** *n.* alın.

**foreign** *adj.* yabancı, harici, dış **foreigner** *n.* yabancı, ecnebi.

**forever** *adv.* daima, her zaman.

**forget** *v.* unutmak, ihmal etmek.

**forgive** *v.* affetmek, bağışlamak.

**formal** *adj.* resmi, **formality** *n.* formalite, usul, resmiyet.

**former** *adj.* önceki, evvelki, **formerly** *adv.* eskiden, daha önce.

**fortunate** *adj.* şanslı, talihli.

**fortune** *n.* talih, şans, kısmet, **fortune-teller** *n.* falcı.

**forward** *n.* ileri, akıncı, *adj.* / *adv.* ilerideki, öndeki, *v.* ilerletmek, göndermek.

**four** dört, **fourteen** on dört, **fourth** dördüncü.

**fox** *n.* tilki, tilki gibi kurnaz olan kişi.

**fragile** *adj.* kırılgan, kolay kırılır, ince, nazik.

**free** *adj.* / *adv.*. özgür, serbest, bedava, *v.* serbest bırakmak, **freedom** hürriyet, özgürlük, serbestlik.

**frequency** *n.* sıklık derecesi, frekans, **frequently** *adv.* sık sık.

**fresh** *adj.* taze, körpe, canlı, yeni, **freshly** *adv.* taze olarak, dipdiri.

**Friday** *n.* Cuma.

**fridge** *n.* buzdolabı.

**fried** *n.* (yağda) kızarmış, kızartılmış.

**friend** *n.* arkadaş, dost, ahbap, **friendly** *adj.* arkadaşça, dostça, **friendship** arkadaşlık, dostluk.

**from** *prep.* den, dan, dolayı, nedeniyle.

**front** *n.* ön, yüz, cephe, **frontier** *n.* sınır, boş bölge.

**fruit** *n.* meyve, yemiş, **fruitful** *adj.* verimli.

**fry** *v.* tavada kızarmak, kızartmak, **frying pan** *n.* tava.

**fuel** *n.* akaryakıt.

**full** *adj.* dolu, meşgul, **full-time** tam gün.

**fun** *n.* eğlence, zevk, şaka.

**funny** *adj.* komik, gülünç, tuhaf, acayip.

**fur** *n.* kürk, post.

**furnish** *v.* döşemek, donatmak, tedarik etmek.

**furniture** *n.* mobilya, mefruşat.

**further** *adv.* daha ileri, ayrıca.

**future** *n.* gelecek, istikbal.

## G - g

**gain** *n.* kazanç, kâr, fayda. *v.* kazanmak, elde etmek.

**game** *n.* oyun, spor.

**garden** *n.* bahçe, bostan, **gardener** *n.* bahçıvan.

**garlic** *n.* sarımsak.

**gas** *n.* gaz, havagazı, benzin, **gasoline** *n.* benzin.

**gate** *n.* bahçe kapısı, büyük kapı.

**gather** *v.* toplamak, toplanmak, biriktirmek.

**general** *n.* general, *adj.* genel, umumi, **generally** *adv.* çoğunlukla, genel olarak.

**generation** *n.* kuşak, nesil.

**gentle** *adj.* nazik, kibar, soylu, **gentleman** *n.* kibar adam, centilmen.

**gerund** *n.* fiile ' ing ' eklenerek yapılan isim.

**get** *v.* elde etmek, almak, kazanmak, erişmek, ulaşmak, tutmak, olmak, yakalamak.

**gift** *n.* hediye, armağan, yetenek, kabiliyet.

**girl** *n.* kız, sevgili, **girl friend** kız arkadaş.

**give** *v.* vermek, ödemek, devretmek, **give up** vazgeçmek, bırakmak.

**glad** *adj.* memnun, hoşnut, neşeli.

**glass** *n.* cam, cam bardak, kadeh, **glasses** *n.* gözlük.

**glorious** *adj.* şanlı, şerefli, muhteşem, parlak.

**glory** *n.* şan, şeref, debdebe, parlaklık.

**glove** *n.* eldiven.

**glue** *n.* zamk, tutkal, *v.* tutkallamak.

**go** *v.* gitmek, uzaklaşmak.

**goal** *n.* amaç, hedef, gol.

**God** *n.* Tanrı, İlâh, Allah.

**gold** *n.* altın, altın para.

**golden** *adj.* altın renkli, altından, **Golden Horn** *n.* Haliç, Altın Boynuz.

**good** *adj.* iyi, güzel, hoş, **goodbye** Allahaısmarladık, güle güle, hoşça kal, **goodness** *n.* iyilik, erdem, **goods** *n.* eşya, mal, **good morning** günaydın, **good afternoon** tünaydın.

**gossip** *n.* dedikodu, gevezelik, *v.* gevezelik etmek.

**government** *n.* hükümet.

**governor** *n.* vali, müdür, yönetici.

**grade** *n.* derece, basamak, sınıf, *v.* sınıflandırmak, derecelere ayırmak.

**graduate** *n.* mezun, diplomalı, *v.* mezun olmak, diploma almak.

**gram(me)** *n.* gram.

**grammar** *n.* dilbilgisi.

**grand** *adj.* büyük, muhteşem, görkemli, **grandchild** *n.* torun, **grandfather** *n.* büyükbaba, dede, **grandmother** *n.* büyükanne, nine, **grandparents** *n.* büyükanne ve büyükbaba.

**grass** *n.* ot, çimen, çayır.

**grateful** *adj.* minnettar, müteşekkir.

**grave** *n.* mezar, kabir, **gravestone** *n.* mezar taşı, **graveyard** *n.* mezarlık.

İNGİLİZCE – TÜRKÇE SÖZLÜK

**great** *adj.* büyük, ulu, iri, kocaman, muazzam.
**Greece** *n.* Yunanistan.
**Greek** *n.* / *adj.* Yunan(lı), (eski) Yunanca, Yunanistan'a ait.
**green** *adj.* yeşil, **greengrocer** *n.* manav.
**grey** *adj.* gri.
**grill** *n.* ızgara, *v.* ızgarada pişirmek.
**grocer** *n.* bakkal, **grocery** *n.* bakkal dükkânı.
**gross** *n.* düzine, on iki, hantal, toptan, brüt, *s.* kaba, şişman, hantal.
**ground** *n.* yer, zemin, toprak, arazi.
**group** *n.* grup, küme, takım, *v.* grup halinde toplanmak.
**grow** *v.* büyümek, gelişmek, yetiş(tir)mek, çoğalmak, artmak, **growth** *n.* kalkınma, gelişme, büyüme.
**guarantee** *n.* kefil, teminat, garanti, *v.* kefil olmak, garanti etmek.
**guess** *n.* tahmin, *v.* tahmin etmek, sanmak.
**guest** *n.* konuk, misafir, davetli.
**guide** *n.* rehber, kılavuz, *v.* yol göstermek, kılavuzluk etmek.
**guilty** *adj.* suçlu, günahkâr.
**gum** *n.* dişeti, zamk, *v.* yapıştırmak.
**gun** *n.* silâh, top, tüfek, tabanca.
**gym** *n.* beden eğitimi, **gymnastics** *n.* idman, beden eğitimi.

## H - h

**habit** *n.* adet, alışkanlık, huy. *v.* giydirmek.
**hair** *n.* saç, kıl, tüy, **hairdresser** *n.* berber, kuaför
**half** *adj.* yarım, yarı, *adv.* yarı yarıya.
**hallo** *interj.* alo, merhaba, baksan(ız)a, yahu.
**hammer** *n.* çekiç, *v.* çekiçle çakmak, yumruklamak.
**hand** *n.* el, ibre, saatin akrebi, *f.* el ile vermek, uzatmak, **handmade** *n.* el yapımı.
**handkerchief** *n.* mendil.
**handle** *n.* sap, kulp, *v.* el sürmek, ele almak, yönetmek, kullanmak.
**handsome** *adj.* yakışıklı.
**happen** *v.* olmak, meydana gelmek.
**happy** *adj.* mutlu, sevinçli, **happiness** *n.* mutluluk.
**hard** *adj.* zor, güç; sert, katı, **hardly** *adv.* hemen hemen hiç, güçlükle, **hardworking** *adj.* çalışkan.
**harm** *n.* zarar, kötülük, *v.* zarar vermek.
**harmony** *n.* ahenk, uyum.
**hat** *n.* şapka.
**hate** *n.* nefret, kin, *v.* nefret etmek, kin beslemek.
**have** *v.* sahip olmak, malik olmak.
**he** *pron.* o.
**head** *n.* baş, kafa, kelle, reis, **headache** *n.* baş ağrısı.
**health** *n.* sıhhat, sağlık, afiyet, **healthy** *adj.* sıhhatli, sağlıklı.

ENGLISH – TURKISH DICTIONARY

**hear** *v.* işitmek, duymak, haber almak.

**heart** *n.* kalp, yürek.

**heat** *n.* ısı, sıcaklık, *v.* ısınmak, ısıtmak

**heaven** *n.* gök, sema, cennet.

**heavy** *adj.* ağır, şiddetli, güçlü, **heavily** *adv.* şiddetli, ağır şekilde.

**height** *n.* yükseklik, yükselti, rakım.

**hell** *n.* cehennem.

**hello** *interj.* merhaba, alo.

**help** *n.* yardım, çare, yardımcı, *v.* yardım etmek, faydalı olmak, *interj.* imdat, yardım edin.

**her** *pron.* ona, onu, *adj.* onun.

**here** *adv.* burada, buraya, burası, işte.

**hero** *n.* kahraman, yiğit.

**hesitate** *v.* tereddüt etmek, duraksamak.

**hi** *interj.* merhaba.

**hide** *n.* hayvan derisi, post, *v.* saklamak, saklanmak, gizlemek.

**high** *adj.* yüksek, yukarı, **highly** *adv.* epey, pek çok, hayli, **highway** *n.* anayol, karayolu, otoyol.

**him** *pron.* onu, ona

**hire** *n.* kira, kiralama, *v.* kiralamak.

**his** *adj.* onun, *adv.* onunki.

**history** *n.* tarih.

**hit** *v.* vurmak, çarpmak, isabet etmek.

**hobby** *n.* zevk için uğraşma, ilgi, merak, hobi.

**hold** *v.* tutmak, kavramak, içine almak.

**holiday** *n.* tatil, tatil günü, bayram günü.

**holy** *adj.* kutsal.

**home** *n.* ev, yuva, vatan, yurt, **homework** *n.* ev ödevi.

**honest** *adj.* dürüst, namuslu, hilesiz.

**honey** *n.* bal, **honeymoon** *n.* balayı.

**honour** *n.* onur, şeref, namus.

**hope** *n.* umut, *v.* umut etmek, **hopeful** *adj.* umutlu, **hopeless** *adj.* umutsuz.

**horror** *n.* korku, dehşet.

**horse** *n.* at, beygir.

**hospital** *n.* hastane.

**host** *n.* (erkek) ev sahibi, otel sahibi, konuk eden kişi.

**hostel** *n.* öğrenci yurdu.

**hostess** *n.* ev sahibesi, hostes.

**hot** *adj.* sıcak, kızgın, acı.

**hotel** *n.* otel.

**hour** *n.* saat.

**house** *n.* ev, mesken, *v.* barındırmak, **household** *n.* ev halkı, aile, **housewife** *n.* ev kadını.

**how** *adv.* nasıl, ne şekilde, **however** *adv.* bununla birlikte, her ne kadar.

**huge** *adj.* çok iri, kocaman.

**human** *n.* insan, *adj.* insani, insanca, insana ait, **humanity** *n.* insanlık, beşeriyet.

**humour** *n.* huy, mizaç, mizah, şaka, ruh hali, geçici istek.

**hundred** *adj.* yüz.

**hunt** *v.* avlamak, avlanmak, peşine düşmek, **hunter** *n.* avcı.

**INGILIZCE – TÜRKÇE SÖZLÜK**

**ENGLISH – TURKISH DICTIONARY**

hurry *v.* acele etmek, telaşlanmak, **hurry up** çabuk ol, acele et.

hurt *n.* yara, bere, acı, *v.* yaralamak, zarar vermek, incitmek.

husband *n.* koca (eş).

## I - i

I *pron.* ben.

ice *n.* buz, **ice cream** *n.* dondurma.

idea *n.* fikir, düşünce.

ideal *n.* ilke, ülkü, ideal, *adj.* ülküsel, ideal.

identity *n.* kimlik, hüviyet, benzerlik.

idiom *n.* deyim, şive, dil.

if *conj.* eğer, ise, şayet.

ignorant *adj.* cahil, haberi olmayan.

ignore *v.* aldırmamak, önemsememek, görmezden gelmek.

ill *adj.* hasta, rahatsız, kötü, **illness** *n.* hastalık.

illegal *adj.* yasal olmayan, kanunsuz.

immediate *adj.* acil, **immediately** *adv.* derhal, hemen.

imperative *adj.* zorunlu, emir.

import *n.* ithalat, dış alım, *v.* ithal etmek.

importance *n.* önem, **important** *adj.* önemli.

impossible *adj.* imkânsız, olanaksız.

in *prep.* içinde, içeriye, içine, de / da, **in front of** önünde, **in spite of** ...ye rağmen, karşın.

incident *n.* olay, hadise.

include *v.* kapsamak, içermek, içine almak.

income *n.* gelir, kazanç.

indeed *adv.* gerçekten, hakikaten, *interj.* öyle mi.

indefinite *adj.* belirsiz.

independence *n.* bağımsızlık, **independent** *adj.* bağımsız.

individual *adj.* birey, kişi, fert, tek, yalnız, **individually** *adv.* kişisel olarak, ayrı ayrı, şahsen.

indoor *adj.* ev içine ait, ev içinde yapılan.

inevitable *adj.* kaçınılmaz, zorunlu.

infant *n.* küçük çocuk, bebek.

infinite *adj.* sonsuz, sınırsız, **infinity** *n.* sonsuzluk.

influence *n.* etki, etkileme, *v.* etkilemek.

inform *v.* bilgi vermek, haber vermek, **information** haber, bilgi, danışma.

informal *adj.* teklifsiz, resmi olmayan,

inhabitant *n.* oturan, ikamet eden kimse.

inherit *v.* miras almak, mirasa konmak.

ink *n.* mürekkep, **inkpot** *n.* mürekkep hokkası.

innocent *adj.* masum, suçsuz, günahsız.

inquire *v.* sormak, soruşturmak, araştırmak, **inquiry** *n.* sorgu, soruşturma, araştırma.

insect *n.* böcek, haşere.

insert *v.* araya sıkıştırmak, sokmak, eklemek.

**inside** *n.* iç, iç taraf, dahil, *adj.* içteki, dahili, *prep.* İçinde.

**insist** *v.* ısrar etmek, üstelemek.

**install** *v.* yerine koymak, kurmak, tesis etmek, **installment** *n.* taksit, kısım.

**instead** *adv.* yerine, karşılık olarak.

**instruct** *v.* öğretmek, talimat vermek, **instructions** *n.* talimat, tanıtım.

**instrument** *n.* alet, enstrüman, çalgı, araç, vasıta.

**intellect** *n.* akıl, zihin, **intellectual** *adj.* aydın, kültürlü, akıllı, entelektüel.

**intelligence** *n.* akıl, zeka, **intelligent** *adj.* zeki, akıllı.

**intend** *v.* niyet etmek, kastetmek, tasarlamak.

**inter-** *pref.* -arası(nda)

**interest** *n.* ilgi, merak, kazanç, faiz, *v.* ilgilendirmek, meraklandırmak, **interesting** *adj.* ilginç, enteresan, **interested in** ile ilgili.

**intermediate** *adj.* orta, ortadaki, aradaki.

**interrupt** *v.* sözünü kesmek, araya girmek, yarıda kesmek.

**interval** *n.* fasıla, aralık, süre.

**interview** *n.* röportaj yapmak, görüşmek.

**into** *prep.* -e/a, içine, içeriye, -in içerisine, içeri doğru.

**introduce** *v.* tanıştırmak, takdim etmek, başlatmak.

**introduction** *n.* takdim, tanıtma, başlangıç.

**invalid** *adj.* geçersiz, hükümsüz.

**invent** *v.* icat etmek, yaratmak, **invention** *n.* icat, buluş.

**invest** *v.* yatırım yapmak, para yatırmak.

**investigate** *v.* araştırmak, incelemek, **investigation** *n.* araştırma, soruşturma.

**invite** *v.* davet etmek, çağırmak, **invitation** *n.* davet, çağrı, davetiye.

**invoice** *n.* fatura.

**iron** *n.* demir, ütü, *v.* ütülemek, *adj.* demir gibi.

**irregular** *adj.* düzensiz, kuralsız.

**Islam** *n.* İslâm, İslâmiyet, Müslümanlık.

**island** *n.* ada.

**issue** *n.* yayın, yayımlama, basım, mesele, *v.* basmak, yayımlamak.

**it** *pron.* o, onu, ona.

**ivory** *n.* fil dişi.

## J - j

**jacket** *n.* ceket.

**jail** *n.* cezaevi, hapishane, *v.* hapsetmek.

**jam** *n.* reçel, marmelat, *v.* sıkışmak.

**January** *n.* Ocak ayı.

**jar** *n.* kavanoz.

**jaw** *n.* çene.

**jealous** *adj.* kıskanç, **jealousy** *n.* kıskançlık, haset.

**jelly** *n.* pelte, jöle.

**Jew** *n.* Yahudi.

**jewellery** *n.* mücevherat, kuyumculuk.

**job** *n.* görev, meslek, iş, hizmet.

**join** *v.* katılmak, birleşmek, bir araya getirmek.
**joint** *n.* eklem, ek yeri, ortak, *adj.* birleşik, bitişik.
**joke** *n.* şaka, fıkra, *v.* şaka yapmak.
**journal** *n.* gazete, dergi, gündem, **journalist** *n.* gazeteci.
**journey** *n.* seyahat, gezi, yolculuk, *v.* seyahat etmek.
**joy** *n.* sevinç, neşe, zevk.
**judge** *n.* yargıç, hakem, bilirkişi, *v.* hüküm vermek, **judgement** *n.* yargı, hüküm, karar.
**juice** *n.* meyve suyu.
**July** *n.* Temmuz.
**jump** *n.* atlama, sıçrama, zıplama, *v.* atlamak, sıçramak, zıplamak, fırlamak.
**junction** *n.* kavşak.
**June** *n.* Haziran.
**jungle** *n.* vahşi ve balta girmemiş orman.
**just** *adj.* doğru, dürüst, adaletli, hak bilir, *adv.* tam, az önce, ancak, yalnızca, sadece.
**justice** *n.* adalet, hak, doğruluk.
**justify** *v.* doğrulamak, haklı çıkarmak, kanıtlamak.

## K - k

**keep** *v.* tutmak, saklamak, korumak.
**kettle** *n.* tencere, çaydanlık.
**key** *n.* anahtar.
**kid** *n.* çocuk, oğlak.
**kidnap** *v.* fidye için birini kaçırmak.

**kill** *v.* öldürmek, **killer** *n.* katil.
**kind** çeşit, tür, cins, nevi, nazik.
**kindergarten** *n.* ana okulu, yuva.
**king** *n.* kral.
**kiss** *n.* öpücük, buse, *v.* öpüşmek.
**kitchen** *n.* mutfak.
**kite** *n.* uçurtma, çaylak.
**knee** *n.* diz, pantolonun diz kısmı.
**kneel** *v.* diz çökmek.
**knife** *n.* bıçak, çakı, *v.* bıçaklamak.
**knit** *n.* örgü, *v.* örgü örmek, sıkı bağlamak.
**knock** *v.* vurmak, çarpmak, kapı vurmak, kapı çalmak.
**know** *n.* bilgi, *v.* bilmek, tanımak, **known** *adj.* tanınmış, bilinen, **knowledge** *n.* bilgi, ilim.

## L - l

**lack** *n.* olmayış, eksiklik, yok(sun)luk, *v.* eksiği olmak, yoksun kalmak.
**lady** *n.* bayan, hanımefendi.
**lake** *n.* göl.
**lamb** *n.* kuzu, kuzu eti.
**lamp** *n.* lâmba.
**language** *n.* lisan, dil.
**large** *n.* büyük, iri
**last** *adj.* son, sonuncu, geçen, önceki, *v.* sürmek, devam etmek.
**late** *adj.* geç, geç kalmış, gecikmiş, **later** daha geç, daha sonra, **lately** *adv.* son günlerde, yakınlarda.

**laugh** *n.* gülme, gülüş, *v.* gülmek, **laughter** *n.* kahkaha.

**laundry** *n.* çamaşırhane, kirli çamaşır.

**lavatory** *n.* tuvalet, yıkanma yeri.

**law** *n.* kanun, yasa, adalet, **lawyer** *n.* avukat.

**lay** *v.* yatırmak, koymak, sermek, kurmak.

**leaf** *n.* yaprak.

**learn** *v.* öğrenmek, duymak, haber almak.

**least** *adj.* / *adv.* en küçük, en ufak, en az, asgari, **at least** hiç olmazsa, en azından, bari.

**leather** *n.* deri, kösele.

**leave** *n.* izin, veda, ruhsat, *v.* bırakmak, terk etmek, ayrıl-mak.

**left** *n.* sol, *adj.* kalan, artan.

**leg** *n.* bacak.

**legal** *adj.* kanuni, yasal, meşru.

**legend** *n.* efsane, masal, hikâye.

**lemon** *n.* limon, **lemonade** *n.* limonata.

**lend** *v.* ödünç vermek, borç vermek.

**length** *n.* uzunluk, boy, süre.

**less** daha az, eksik, noksan.

**lesson** *n.* ders.

**let** *v.* izin vermek, bırakmak, kiralamak, **let's go** gidelim.

**letter** *n.* mektup, harf, **letterbox** *n.* posta kutusu.

**liar** *n.* yalancı.

**library** *n.* kütüphane, kitaplık.

**license** *n.* ruhsat, izin, lisans.

**lid** *n.* kapak.

**lie** *n.* yalan(lama), yalan söyleme, *v.* yalan söylemek; yatmak, uzanmak, bulunmak, durmak, kalmak, yayılmak.

**life** *n.* hayat, yaşam, canlılık, can, **life jacket** *n.* can kurtaran yeleği, **lifeboat** *n.* can kurtaran sandalı.

**light {1}** *n.* ışık, aydınlık, lamba, *v.* yakmak, yanmak, **lighter** *n.* çakmak.

**light {2}** *adj.* hafif, önemsiz, kolay, açık

**like** *prep.* gibi, benzer, *adj.* eş, *v.* hoşlanmak, beğenmek.

**likely** *adj.* olası, muhtemel.

**lion** *n.* aslan.

**liquid** *n.* sıvı, *adj.* akıcı, paraya kolay çevrilebilir.

**liquor** *n.* içki, çözelti.

**list** *n.* liste, fihrist.

**listen** *v.* dinlemek, kulak vermek, dikkat etmek.

**litre** *n.* litre.

**literature** *n.* edebiyat, yazın, literatür.

**little** *n.* az miktar, ufak şey, *adj.* küçük, ufak, kısa, **a little** biraz.

**live {1}** *adj.* canlı, diri, hayatta, neşeli.

**live {2}** *v.* yaşamak, oturmak, hayat sürmek.

**loaf** *n.* somun (ekmek).

**local** *adj.* yerel, mahalli, yöresel.

**lock** *n.* kilit, emniyet, *v.* kilitle(n)mek, kenetle(n)mek.

**locksmith** *n.* çilingir.

**lonely** *adj.* yalnız, kimsesiz, ıssız.

**long** *adj.* uzun, uzun süren, yorucu, *adv.* uzun zamandır, çoktan.

**look** *v.* bakmak, görünmek, gözükmek, **look after** birisinin / bir şeyin bakımını üstlenmek, **look at** birisine / bir şeye bakmak, **look for** birisini/bir şeyi aramak.

**loose** *adj.* bol, gevşek, bağlanmamış, **loosen** *v.* gevşetmek, çözmek.

**lose** *v.* kaybetmek, yitirmek, tutamamak.

**loss** *n.* kayıp, zarar, ziyan, hasar, **lost** *adj.* kayıp

**lotion** *n.* losyon.

**lottery** *n.* piyango, lotarya, çekiliş.

**loud** *adj.* gürültü(lü), patırtı(lı), yüksek ses(li).

**love** *n.* aşk, sevgi, sevgili, *v.* aşık olmak, sevmek, **lovely** *adj.* sevimli, cana yakın, hoş, **lover** *n.* aşık, sevgili.

**luck** *n.* şans, baht, talih, uğur, **lucky** şanslı, talihli, uğurlu.

**luggage** *n.* bagaj, yolcu eşyası, bavul.

**lunch** *n.* öğle yemeği.

## M - m

**macaroni** *n.* makarna.

**machine** *n.* makine, motorlu araç.

**magazine** *n.* dergi.

**magic** *n.* sihir, büyü, **magician** *n.* sihirbaz, büyücü.

**mail** *n.* posta, posta arabası, *v.* postalamak, **mailbox** *n.* posta kutusu.

**main** *adj.* ana, esas, temel, **mainland** *n.* anakara, **mainly** *adv.* başlıca, asıl.

**major** *adj.* esas, çok önemli, başlıca, **majority** *n.* oy çokluğu, çoğunluk, ekseriyet.

**make** *v.* yapmak, yaratmak, imal etmek, meydana getirmek.

**male** *adj.* erkek.

**man** *n.* erkek, adam, insan, **manly** *adj.* erkekçe.

**manage** *v.* idare etmek, yönetmek, **management** *n.* idare, yönetim, **manager** *n.* yönetici, müdür.

**manufacture** *n.* imalât, *v.* imal etmek.

**many** *adj.* çok, bir çok, bir hayli, **so many** o kadar çok.

**map** *n.* harita, plân, *v.* haritasını yapmak, plânlamak.

**March** *n.* Mart ayı.

**marry** *v.* evlenmek, evlendirmek, **married** *adj.* evli, **married to** ile evli, **marriage** *n.* evlilik, evlenme.

**massage** *n.* ovma, masaj, *v.* ovmak, masaj yapmak.

**match** *n.* kibrit, fitil, maç.

**matter** *n.* madde, mesele, sorun, konu, iş, *v.* sorun, önemi olmak.

**May** *n.* Mayıs ayı.

**may** *v.* -ebilmek, mümkün olmak, olasılığı olmak.

**me** *adv.* beni, bana.

**meal** *n.* yemek, öğün, yulaf ezmesi, elenmemiş kaba un.

mean *v.* demek istemek, kastetmek, anlamına gelmek.

meantime, meanwhile *n.* ara, aradaki zaman, süre, *adv.* arada, aynı zamanda, bu sırada.

measure *n.* ölçü, ölçü birimi, önlem, *v.* ölçmek.

meat *n.* et, **meaty** *adj.* etli, özlü.

medicine *n.* ilaç, deva, tıp.

meet *v.* karşılaşmak, görüşmek, rastlamak, tanışmak, buluşmak, toplanmak, **meeting** *n.* toplantı, miting.

member *n.* üye, organ, aza.

memory *n.* hafıza, bellek, hatıra, anı.

men çoğul *n.* erkekler, adamlar.

mend *v.* tamir etmek, onarmak, iyileştirmek.

mention *n.* söyleme, anma, *v.* sözünü etmek, anmak.

menu *n.* yemek listesi, mönü.

message *n.* haber, mesaj.

middle *adj.* orta, ara, vasat.

midnight *n.* gece yarısı.

might {1} *n.* kuvvet, kudret, güç.

might {2} 'may' yardımcı fiilinin geçmiş zamanı.

migrate *v.* göç etmek.

milk *n.* süt, *v.* süt sağmak, **milkman** *n.* sütçü.

million *n.* milyon, **millionaire** *n.* milyoner.

mince *n.* kıyma, *v.* kıymak.

mind *n.* akıl, zihin, fikir, *v.* aldırış etmek, önemsemek, bakmak.

minister *n.* bakan, **ministry** *n.* bakanlık.

minus *adj.* eksi.

minute *n.* dakika, kısa süre, an.

mirror *n.* ayna.

mis- *pref.* yanlış-, kötü-.

miss {1} *n.* genç kız, bekâr bayan.

miss {2} *v.* isabet ettirememek, boşa gitmek, (otobüs vb.) kaçırmak, yakalayamamak, özlemek, **missing** *adj.* eksik, kayıp, olmayan.

mistake *n.* hata, yanlışlık, *v.* hata etmek, yanlış anlamak, yanılmak.

mister *n.* bay.

mix *v.* karıştırmak, katmak, birleştirmek, **mixture** *n.* karışım.

mobile *adj.* hareket eden, gezici, oynak.

moment *n.* (çok kısa) an, önem, güç, fırsat, uygun zaman.

Monday *n.* Pazartesi.

money *n.* para, **money order** para havalesi.

monkey *n.* maymun.

month *n.* ay, **monthly** *adv.* ayda bir, aylık.

monument *n.* anıt, abide.

moon *n.* ay, kamer, uydu, **moonlight** *n.* mehtap, ay ışığı.

more *n.* daha çok miktar, *adj.* daha çok, daha fazla, *adv.* daha, **moreover** bundan başka, üstelik, zaten, ayrıca, bir de.

İNGİLİZCE – TÜRKÇE SÖZLÜK

**morning** *n.* sabah, **good morning** günaydın.
**Moslem** *adj.* Müslüman, İslâm.
**mosque** *n.* cami.
**mosquito** *n.* sivrisinek.
**most** *adj.* en çok, çok fazla, *adv.* son derece, çok, en, pek.
**motel** *n.* motel.
**mother** *n.* anne, ana.
**mountain** *n.* dağ, tepe.
**mouse** *n.* fare, sıçan.
**mouth** *n.* ağız.
**move** *v.* harekete geçmek, kımıldatmak, kımıldamak, taşınmak, **movement** *n.* hareket.
**movie** *n.* sinema filmi. **the movies** *n.* sinema.
**Mr.** *n.* bay.
**Mrs.** *n.* (evli) bayan.
**Miss** *n.* (evlenmemiş) bayan.
**much** *adj.* çok, çok fazla, çokça, epeyce.
**museum** *n.* müze.
**music** *n.* müzik, nağme, makam, nota, **musical** *n.* müzikal, **musician** *n.* müzisyen, çalgıcı.
**Muslim** *n.* Müslüman, *adj.* İslam.
**must** *n.* zorunluluk, *v.* -meli, -malı.
**mustache** *n.* bıyık.
**my** benim.
**myself** *adv.* kendim, ben.
**mystery** *n.* sır, esrar, gizem, **mysterious** *adj.* esrarengiz, gizemli, sır dolu.
**myth** *n.* efsane, mit.

ENGLISH – TURKISH DICTIONARY

**N - n**

**nail** *n.* çivi, tırnak, *v.* çivilemek, kavramak, meydana çıkarmak, yakalamak.
**naked** *adj.* çıplak, yalın.
**name** *n.* ad, isim, ün, *v.* isimlendirmek, atamak.
**napkin** *n.* peçete.
**nation** *n.* ulus, millet, **national** *adj.* ulusal, milli, **nationality** milliyet, uyruk.
**native** *n.* yerli, doğuştan.
**natural** *adj.* doğal.
**nature** *n.* doğa, tabiat, yaradılış, dünya.
**navy** *n.* deniz kuvvetleri, donanma.
**near** *adv.* yakın, yakında, hemen hemen, neredeyse, **nearby** *adj.* yakınında, yanında.
**necessary** *adj.* gerekli, zorunlu.
**neck** *n.* boyun, boğaz, **necklace** *n.* gerdanlık, kolye.
**need** *n.* ihtiyaç, gereksinme, *v.* ihtiyacı olmak.
**needle** *n.* iğne, örgü şişi, ibre.
**neglect** *v.* ihmal etmek, boşlamak, aldırmamak.
**neighbour** *n.* komşu, *v.* bitişik olmak.
**neither** *adj. adv.* hiçbiri, ne bu, ne öteki.
**nephew** *n.* erkek yeğen.
**nervous** *adj.* sinirli, asabi.
**net** *n.* ağ, tuzak, **network** *n.* şebeke, *adj.* saf, net, kesintisiz.
**never** *adv.* asla, hiçbir zaman, hiç, katiyen.
**new** *adj.* yeni, taze, acemi.

**news** *n.* haber, havadis,
**newspaper** *n.* gazete.
**next** *adj.* sonraki, gelecek,
ertesi, öbür, *adv.* hemen
sonra.
**nice** *adj.* hoş, güzel, iyi, zarif,
nefis, tatlı.
**night** *n.* gece, akşam.
**ninth** *adj.* dokuzuncu.
**no** *adv.* hayır, yok, hiç, öyle
değil.
**nobody** *adv.* hiç kimse.
**noise** *n.* ses, gürültü, şamata,
**noiseless** *adj.* sessiz,
gürültüsüz, **noisy** *adj.*
gürültülü, gürültücü,
yaygaracı.
**none** *adv.* hiçbiri, hiç kimse.
**nonsense** *n.* saçma,
anlamsız, boş.
**noon** *n.* öğle.
**nor** *conj.* ne, ne de.
**normal** *adj.* normal,
**normalization** *n.*
normalleşme.
**north** *n.* kuzey, **northern** *adj.*
kuzeye ait, kuzeyli.
**nose** *n.* burun, *v.* koklamak.
**note** *n.* not, işaret, nota, *v.*
not etmek, **notebook** defter.
**nothing** *n.* hiçbir şey, hiç.
**notice** *n.* ilan, ihbar, özen,
dikkat, farkına varma, *v.*
dikkat etmek, farkında olmak,
önem vermek.
**noun** *n.* isim, ad.
**novel** *n.* roman, *adj.* yeni,
yeni çıkmış, **novelist** *n.*
romancı.
**November** *n.* Kasım ayı.
**now** *adv.* şimdi, şu anda, *conj.*
madem ki, işte.
**nowadays** *adv.* bu günlerde.

**nowhere** *adv.* hiçbir yerde.
**number** *n.* sayı, numara,
adet, rakam, *v.* numarala-
mak.
**nurse** *n.* hemşire,
hastabakıcı, **nursery** *n.*
çocuk odası, kreş, fidanlık,
**nursery school** *n.* ana
okulu.
**nut** *n.* fındık, ceviz, cıvata
somunu.

## O - o

**o'clock** *n.* saat, **it's five
o'clock** saat beş.
**oat** *n.* yulaf.
**obey** *v.* itaat etmek, boyun
eğmek.
**object {1}** *n.* madde, nesne,
hedef, amaç.
**object {2}** *v.* itiraz etmek,
protesto etmek, karşı koymak,
razı gelmemek.
**objective** *adj.* duygularına
kapılmadan, nesnel, objektif.
**obligation** *n.* zorunluluk,
senet, borç.
**observation** *n.* gözlem,
inceleme.
**obvious** *adj.* aşikar, besbelli,
açık, net, **obviously** *adv.*
açıkça.
**occasionally** *adv.* ara sıra,
arada sırada, bazen.
**occupy** *v.* işgal etmek,
meşgul etmek, uğraşmak,
**occupation** *n.* meşguliyet,
iş, meslek, sanat, işgal.
**occur** *v.* olmak, meydana
gelmek, vuku bulmak.
**ocean** *n.* okyanus.
**October** *n.* Ekim ayı.

**octopus** *n.* ahtapot.

**of** *prep.* -in, -nin, -li, -den, -nin hakkında.

**off** *adj.* bozuk, yorgun, kötü, çalışmayan, *prep.* -den, -dan, -den uzak, sapa, *adv.* uzağa, dışarıya, öteye, ötede.

**offer** *n.* teklif, öneri, *v.* teklif etmek, sunmak, önermek.

**office** *n.* yazıhane, işyeri, büro, ofis, **officer** *n.* memur, subay, **official** *adj.* resmi, memur.

**often** *adv.* sık sık, çoğu kez.

**oil** *n.* yağ, sıvı yağ, petrol, *v.* yağlamak.

**okay (OK)** *interj.* peki, tamam, olur, doğru, uygun.

**old** *adj.* yaşlı, ihtiyar, eski.

**olive** *n.* zeytin, **olive oil** *n.* zeytin yağı.

**on** *prep.* üzerinde, üstünde, üstüne, -de, -da, **and so on** v.b., vs.

**once** *adv.* bir kez, bir defa, vaktiyle, eskiden.

**one** *adj.* bir (tane), tek.

**onion** *n.* soğan.

**only** *adj.* biricik, tek, *adv.* yalnızca, ancak, sadece.

**open** *adj.* açık, serbest, meydanda, aleni, *v.* açmak, açılmak, başlamak, **opening** *n.* açılış, başlangıç, delik, açıklık.

**opinion** *n.* fikir, düşünce, tahmin.

**opportune** *adj.* uygun, tam yerinde, **opportunity** *n.* fırsat, elverişli durum, olanak.

**oppose** *v.* karşı gelmek, engel olmak, direnmek, **opposite** *adj.* karşı, karşıda, karşı karşıya, zıt, ters.

**or** *conj.* yahut, veya, yoksa, ya da.

**orange** *n.* portakal.

**order** *n.* düzen, tertip, emir, sipariş, rütbe, sınıf, biçem, *v.* düzenlemek, emretmek, sipariş etmek, ısmarlamak, atamak, tayin etmek.

**ordinary** olağan, her zamanki, adi, sıradan.

**organ** *n.* organ, uzuv, araç.

**organize** *v.* kurmak, örgütlemek, düzenlemek, **organization** *n.* örgüt, kurum, organizasyon.

**orient** *n.* doğu, doğu ülkeleri, **oriental** *adj.* doğulu, Asyalı, doğuya ait, oryantal.

**origin** i. köken, başlangıç, kaynak, **original** *adj.* ilk, asıl, ilk şekli, kökeni, başlangıcı, orijinal.

**ornament** *n.* süs, ziynet, *v.* süslemek.

**other** *adj.* diğer, öteki, öbür, başka, *adv.* başka türlü, **otherwise** *adv.* başka türlü, aksi takdirde.

**ought** *n.* yükümlülük, zorunluluk, *v.* -meli, -malı, gerek, -sa iyi olur.

**our** *adj.* bizim, **ours** *adv.* bizimki, bize ait.

**out** *adv.* dışarı, dışarıya, dışarıda, uzakta, **outcome** *n.* sonuç, **outdoor** dışarıda olan, açık havada yapılan.

**outside** *n.* dış, dış taraf, dışında, *adv.* dışarıda.

**oven** *n.* fırın.
**over** *prep.* üzerinden, üzerinde, üstünde, normalden fazla, aşırı, *adj.* bitmiş, *adv.* yukarıda, tekrar, baştan, **overall** *adj.* bir uçtan bir uca, etraflı.
**oversea** *adj.* deniz aşırı.
**overwork** *v.* aşırı çalışmak.
**owe** *v.* borçlu olmak, borcu olmak.
**own** *adj.* kendisine ait, kendi kendine, has, kendi *v.* malik olmak, sahip olmak, **owner** *n.* mal sahibi, **ownership** *n.* mülkiyet.
**ox** *n.* öküz, sığır.
**oxygen** *n.* oksijen.
**oyster** *n.* istiridye.

## P - p

**package** *n.* paket, ambalaj.
**page** *n.* sayfa.
**pain** *n.* acı, ağrı, sızı, elem, keder.
**paint** *n.* (yağlı) boya, allık, makyaj, boyama *v.* boyamak, resim yapmak, **painter** *n.* ressam, boyacı.
**pair** *n.* eş, çift, *v.* eşleştirmek.
**pan** *n.* tava, çanak, kefe.
**pants** *n.* pantolon.
**paper** *n.* kâğıt, evrak, gazete, *v.* kâğıt kaplamak.
**pardon** *n.* af, bağışlama, *v.* affetmek.
**parent** *n.* ebeveyn, anne-baba.
**park** *n.* park, otopark, *v.* park etmek.
**part** *n.* parça, kısım, pay, hisse, *v.* ayırmak, ayrılmak.

**participate** *v.* katılmak, iştirak etmek.
**participle** *n.* ortaç, sıfat, eylem.
**party** *n.* parti, ziyafet, eğlence, siyasi parti.
**passenger** *n.* yolcu.
**passport** *n.* pasaport.
**past** *n.* geçmiş zaman, *adj.* geçmiş, geçmişe ait, *prep.* -den sonra, -ın ötesinde, ilerisinde, öbür tarafın(d)a.
**pastry** *n.* hamur işi, pasta.
**patient** *n.* hasta, *adj.* sabırlı, dayanıklı.
**pay** *n.* maaş, ücret, bedel, *v.* ödemek, karşılığını vermek.
**payment** *n.* ödeme.
**peach** *n.* şeftali.
**pearl** *n.* inci.
**pen** *n.* dolmakalem.
**pencil** *n.* kurşun kalem, **pencil sharpener** *n.* kalemtıraş.
**people** *n.* halk, ahali, insanlar, ulus, kişiler.
**pepper** *n.* biber.
**per** *prep.* aracılığıyla, tarafından, her bir, -in başına.
**percent** *n.* yüzde, **percentage** *n.* yüzdesi, oran, komisyon, kâr payı.
**perfect** *v.* tamamlamak, bitirmek, *adj.* tam, mükemmel, kusursuz, **perfectly** *adv.* tümüyle, mükemmel olarak.
**perhaps** *adv.* belki.
**permission** *n.* izin, ruhsat.
**permit** *n.* izin, permi, ruhsat, paso, *v.* izin vermek, ruhsat vermek, permi.

INGILIZCE – TÜRKÇE SÖZLÜK

ENGLISH – TURKISH DICTIONARY

**person** *n.* şahıs, kişi, insan, **personal** *adj.* kişisel, şahsi, **personally** *adv.* şahsen, bizzat, fikrimce, kişisel olarak.
**personnel** *n.* personel, kadro.
**pharmacy** *n.* eczacılık, eczane.
**phone** *n.* telefon, *v.* telefon etmek.
**photo** *n.* fotoğraf, **photograph** *n.* fotoğraf, **photographer** *n.* fotoğrafçı.
**picnic** *n.* kır gezisi, piknik.
**picture** *n.* resim, tablo, **picturesque** *adj.* resim gibi, resme uygun, hoş.
**piece** *n.* parça, kısım, dama taşı.
**pill** *n.* hap.
**pillow** *n.* yastık.
**pilot** *n.* pilot, kılavuz, rehber, *v.* kılavuzluk yapmak, uçak kullanmak.
**pink** *adj.* pembe.
**pity** *n.* merhamet, acıma, *v.* acımak, merhamet etmek, **what a pity** ne yazık.
**place** *n.* yer, mahal, alan, *v.* yerleştirmek, koymak.
**planet** *n.* gezegen.
**plant** *n.* bitki, fabrika, *v.* fidan vs. ekmek, dikmek.
**plate** *n.* tabak, madeni levha, plaka.
**play** *n.* oyun, piyes, *v.* oynamak, eğlenmek, çalgı (aleti) çalmak, **player** *n.* oyuncu, **playground** *n.* oyun alanı.
**please** *v.* hoşnut etmek, sevindirmek, hoşuna gitmek, *interj.* lütfen, **pleasing** *adj.* hoş, sevimli.

**plenty** *n.* bolluk, çokluk, *adj.* bereketli.
**plural** *adj.* / *n.* çoğul, çoklu.
**plus** *adj.* artı, pozitif, *prep.* ayrıca, ve, ve de.
**p.m.** öğleden sonra
**poem** *n.* şiir.
**point** *n.* nokta, puan, uç, özellik, amaç, *v.* işaret etmek, göstermek.
**poison** *n.* zehir, *v.* zehirlemek, **poisonous** *adj.* zehirli.
**police** *n.* polis, zabıta, **policeman** *n.* polis memuru, **police station** *n.* karakol.
**polite** *adj.* nazik, kibar, **politely** *adv.* nezaketle, kibarca, **politeness** *n.* terbiye, nezaket, kibarlık, incelik.
**pool** *n.* havuz, su birikintisi, gölcük.
**poor** *n.* yoksul, zavallı, aciz.
**popular** *adj.* halka ait, halk için, halkın hoşuna giden, popüler.
**population** *n.* nüfus.
**pork** *n.* domuz eti.
**porter** *n.* hamal, kapıcı.
**possibility** *n.* olanak, imkan, ihtimal, olabilirlik, **possible** *adj.* mümkün, olanaklı, olası.
**post** *n.* posta, görev, *v.* yapıştırmak, ilan etmek, postalamak, **postage** *n.* posta ücreti, **poster** *n.* afiş, **postman** *n.* postacı, **post office** *n.* postane.
**postpone** *v.* ertelemek.
**potato** *n.* patates.
**pound** *n.* İngiliz lirası, sterlin, libre (454 gram).

**pour** *v.* akmak, akıtmak, dökülmek.

**practice** *n.* uygulama, tatbikat, egzersiz, idman, prova, *v.* uygulamak, yapmak, **practise** *v.* yapmak, uygulamak, çalışmak.

**pray** *v.* dua etmek, , yalvarmak, **prayer** *n.* dua, yakarış

**prefer** *v.* tercih etmek, yeğlemek.

**prefix** *n.* önek.

**pregnant** *adj.* gebe, hamile.

**prepare** *v.* hazırlamak, hazırlanmak.

**preposition** *n.* edat, ilgeç, öntakı.

**prescription** *n.* reçete.

**present {1}** *adj.* şimdiki, hazır, halihazır, *n.* şimdiki (zaman), hediye, armağan.

**present {2}** *v.* sunmak, arz etmek, **presenter** *n.* sunucu.

**president** *n.* başkan.

**pretty** *adj.* hoş, sevimli, güzel, *adv.* oldukça, hayli.

**price** *n.* fiyat, bedel, değer. iğnelemek.

**primary** *n.* asıl, ana, en önemli, başlıca, **primary school** *n.* ilkokul.

**prime** *adj.* birinci, ilk, esas, başlıca, baş.

**prison** *n.* cezaevi, hapishane, **prisoner** *n.* mahkum, esir.

**private** *n.* er, asker, *adj.* özel, kişisel, gizli, mahrem.

**prize** *n.* ödül, mükafat, *v.* değer vermek.

**problem** *n.* sorun, mesele, problem.

**produce** *v.* meydana getirmek, üretmek, çıkarmak.

**product** *n.* ürün, sonuç, **production** *n.* imal, üretim.

**proficiency** *n.* yeterlilik, beceriklilik.

**profit** *n.* kâr, kazanç, fayda, *v.* kâr etmek, yararlanmak.

**prohibit** *v.* yasaklamak, engel olmak.

**promise** *n.* vaat, söz, umut, *v.* vaat etmek, söz vermek, **promising** *adj.* umut verici.

**pronoun** *n.* zamir.

**pronunciation** *n.* telâffuz, söyleniş.

**proof** *n.* delil, kanıt.

**property** *n.* mal, mülk, emlak.

**propose** *v.* önermek, teklif etmek, evlenme teklifinde bulunmak.

**prove** *v.* kanıtlamak, ispat etmek, doğruluğunu saptamak.

**proverb** *n.* atasözü, deyiş.

**public** *adj.* umumi, halk için, halka ait, aleni, ulusal, **publication** *n.* yayın, ilân, duyuru, **publicity** *n.* propaganda.

**pull** *n.* çekme, çekiş, dayanıklılık, *v.* çekmek, koparmak.

**purchase** *n.* satın alınan şey, *v.* satın almak.

**pure** *adj.* saf, halis, arı, temiz.

**purpose** *n.* maksat, amaç, niyet, *v.* niyet etmek.

**purse** *n.* para kesesi, hazine.

**push** *n.* itme, dürtme, çaba, *v.* itmek, dürtmek.

**put** *v.* koymak, yerleştirmek.

**pyramid** *n.* piramit.

## Q - q

**quake** *n.* titreme, deprem, zelzele, *v.* titremek, sallanmak, sarsılmak.

**qualification** *n.* nitelik, özellik, **qualified** *adj.* kaliteli, vasıflı, ehliyetli, **quality** kalite, nitelik.

**quantity** *n.* nicelik, miktar, sayı.

**quarrel** *n.* kavga, çekişme, *v.* kavga etmek.

**quarter** *n.* dörtte bir, çeyrek.

**queen** *n.* kraliçe.

**question** *n.* soru, söz konusu, mesele, *v.* sormak, sorguya çekmek, şüphe etmek, karşı gelmek.

**queue** *n.* kuyruk (bekleyen kişiler), sıra, dizi, saç örgüsü.

**quick** *adj.* çabuk, hızlı, çevik, tez elden, **quickly** *adv.* çabuk, acele.

**quiet** *adj.* sessiz, sakin, durgun, hareketsiz, **quietly** *adv.* sakin bir şekilde, sessizce, hareketsizce.

**quit** *v.* bırakmak, terk etmek, vazgeçmek, ayrılmak.

**quite** *adv.* tamamen, epey, bütün bütün, oldukça.

**quiz** *n.* küçük sınav, test, şaka, *v.* şaka yapmak, sorgulamak.

**quote** *v.* aktarmak, bir sözden veya yazıdan parça almak, piyasa fiyatını bildirmek, tırnak içine almak.

## R - r

**radio** *n.* radyo, telsiz telefon, telgraf.

**railroad**, **railway** *n.* demiryolu.

**rain** *n.* yağmur, *v.* yağmur yağmak, **rainbow** *n.* gökkuşağı, **rainy** yağmurlu.

**rapid** *adj.* çabuk, hızlı, **rapidly** *adv.* hızlı şekilde.

**rare** *adj.* nadir, az bulunur, seyrek, **rarely** *adv.* nadiren, seyrek olarak.

**rather** *adv.* oldukça, epeyce, az çok.

**raw** *adj.* pişmemiş, çiğ, ham, tecrübesiz.

**razor** *n.* ustura, tıraş makinesi.

**read** *v.* okumak, yorumlamak, **reader** *n.* okuyucu.

**ready** *adj.* hazır.

**real** *adj.* gerçek, asıl, hakikat, **real estate** gayrimenkul, mülk, taşınmaz mal, **reality** *n.* gerçek, sahi, hakikat, **really** *adv.* gerçekten, hakikaten.

**reason** *n.* sebep, neden, gerekçe, akıl, mantık, **reasonable** *adj.* makul, mantıklı, akla uygun.

**receipt** *n.* makbuz, alındı.

**recipe** *n.* yemek tarifesi, reçete.

**recognize** *v.* tanımak, onaylamak, seçmek, ayırt etmek, itiraf etmek, kabul etmek, doğrulamak.

**recommend** *v.* tavsiye etmek, öğütlemek, önermek.

**red** *adj.* kırmızı.

**reduce** *v.* azalmak, küçülmek, **reduction** *n.* indirim, tenzilât.

**refrigerator** *n.* buzdolabı, soğutucu.

refund *n.* iade edilen para *.v.* ödemek, parayı geri vermek.
refuse *v.* reddetmek, kabul etmemek, çekinmek.
register *n.* sicil, kütük, *v.* kaydetmek, deftere yazmak, **registered** *adj.* kayıtlı, taahhütlü.
reject *v.* reddetmek, geri çevirmek.
relate *v.* anlatmak, bağlantısı olmak, ilgili olmak, **relation** *n.* ilişki, akraba, ilgi, anlatış.
relative *adj.* bağlantılı, göreli, ilişkin, akraba.
reliable *adj.* güvenilir.
religion *n.* din, inanç, **religious** *adj.* dindar, dinsel.
remain *v.* (elde) kalmak, artmak, durmak.
remedy *n.* çare, ilâç, deva, *v.* gereğine bakmak, bakmak, düzeltmek, iyileştirmek.
remember *v.* hatırlamak, anımsamak, anmak.
remind *v.* hatırlatmak, anımsatmak.
rent *n.* kira, *v.* kiralamak.
repair *n.* tamir, onarım, *v.* tamir etmek, onarmak.
repeat *n.* tekrar, *v.* tekrarlamak, ezbere söylemek.
reply *n.* cevap, yanıt *v.* yanıtlamak, karşılık vermek.
represent *v.* göstermek, temsil etmek, sunmak, anlatmak, vekili olmak, **representative** *n.* vekil, temsilci, delege, milletvekili.
republic *n.* Cumhuriyet.
request *n.* dilek, istek, rica, talep, *v.* rica etmek, istemek.

require *v.* gerek(sin)mek, istemek, **requirement** *n.* gereksinim, ihtiyaç.
research *n.* araştırma, tetkik, *v.* araştırmak.
resemble *v.* benzemek, **resemblance** *n.* benzeyiş.
reserve *n.* yedek, stok, kayıt, koşul, *v.* yedek olarak saklamak, saklamak, ayırmak, kenara koymak, **reservation** *n.* yer ayırtma, rezervasyon, *adj.* ayrılmış, saklı.
resort *n.* dinlenme yeri, sayfiye, barınak.
respect *n.* saygı, itibar, bakım, yön, ilişki, *v.* saygı göstermek, **respectable** *adj.* saygıdeğer, saygın.
respond *v.* yanıtlamak, cevap vermek, **response** *n.* cevap, yanıt.
responsible *adj.* sorumlu, güvenilir.
rest {1} *n.* kalan, ötesi, diğerleri, artan.
rest {2} *v.* dinlenmek, yatmak, oturmak, kalmak.
restaurant *n.* lokanta.
result *n.* sonuç.
return *n.* geri dönüş, iade, kazanç, *v.* geri dönmek, geri gelmek, geri vermek.
reward *n.* ödül, mükâfat, *v.* ödüllendirmek.
rich *adj.* zengin, verimli, bol, bereketli, **riches** *n.* servet, zenginlik, varlık.
right *n.* sağ taraf, *adj.* sağ (taraf), doğru, haklı, uygun, tam, *adv.* doğru, dosdoğru.
ring *n.* zil sesi, yüzük, *v.* (zil, çan) çalmak, çınlamak.

İNGİLİZCE – TÜRKÇE SÖZLÜK

**rinse** *v.* çalkalamak, durulamak.

**ripe** *adj.* olgun, olgunlaşmış.

**rise** *n.* doğuş, yükseliş, artış, *v.* yükselmek, artmak, ayağa kalkmak, (güneş) doğmak.

**river** *n.* nehir, ırmak.

**road** *n.* yol.

**rock** *n.* kaya(lık), sallanma, *v.* sallamak, sallanmak, sarsılmak, **rocky** *n.* kayalık.

**roof** *n.* çatı, dam.

**room** *n.* oda, yer.

**rose** *n.* gül.

**rubber** *n.* kauçuk, lâstik, silgi.

**rug** *n.* kilim, halı.

**ruin** *n.* harabe, yıkıntı, yıkılma, *v.* tahrip etmek, yıkmak.

**rule** *n.* kural, usul, idare, *v.* idare etmek, yönetmek, hükmetmek, **ruler** *n.* yönetici, hükümdar, cetvel.

**run** *n.* koşu, rağbet, süre, *v.* koşmak, kaçmak, akmak, işlemek, **runner** *n.* koşucu.

# S - s

**sad** *adj.* kederli, acıklı, üzgün.

**safe** *adj.* emin, sağlam, güvenceli, tehlikesiz, **safety** *adv.* emniyet, güvenlik.

**saint** *n.* aziz, evliya.

**salary** *n.* maaş, aylık, ücret.

**sale** *n.* satış, **salesman** *n.* satıcı.

**salt** *n.* tuz, *v.* tuzlamak, **salty** *adj.* tuzlu.

**same** *adj.* aynı, tıpkı.

**Saturday** *n.* Cumartesi.

**save** *v.* kurtarmak, korumak, biriktirmek, **savings** *n.* birikim.

**say** *v.* söylemek, demek, *adv.* aşağı yukarı.

**school** *n.* okul, **schoolroom** *n.* sınıf, dershane.

**scissors** *n.* makas.

**screw** *n.* vida, uskur, *v.* vidalamak, **screw-driver** *n.* tornavida.

**seaside** *n.* kıyı, deniz kenarı, sahil.

**season** *n.* mevsim.

**seat** *n.* oturacak yer, koltuk, *v.* oturtmak, yerleştirmek.

**second** *n.* ikinci, yardımcı; saniye, **secondary** *adj.* ikinci derecede, **second-hand** kullanılmış, elden düşme.

**section** *n.* kısım, bölüm, parça, şube, kesit, manga.

**security** *n.* güvenlik, emniyet, rehin, güvence.

**see** *v.* görmek, bakmak, anlamak.

**seem** *v.* (gibi) görünmek, gibi gelmek.

**seldom** *adv.* nadiren, seyrek olarak, pek az.

**select** *v.* seçmek, *adj.* seçme, seçkin, **selection** *n.* seçme, seçmeler.

**self** *n.* kendi, kişi, öz, **selfish** *adj.* bencil.

**sell** *v.* satmak, **seller** *n.* satıcı.

**send** *v.* göndermek, yollamak.

**sense** *n.* duyu, his, zeka, duygu, akıl. *v.* hissetmek, farkında olmak.

**sentence** *n.* cümle, karar, hüküm, *v.* mahkum etmek.

ENGLISH – TURKISH DICTIONARY

separable *adj.* ayrılabilir, ayrılabilen.

separate *n.* ayrı, bağımsız, bireysel, tek, *v.* ayırmak, ayrılmak, bölmek.

September *n.* Eylül ayı.

serious *adj.* ciddi, ağırbaşlı, önemli, seriously *adv.* ciddi olarak.

servant *n.* hizmetçi, uşak.

serve *v.* hizmet etmek, iş görmek.

set *n.* takım, grup, seri, koleksiyon, *adj.* belirli, düzenli, ayarlı, *v.* kurmak, yerleştirmek, saptamak.

several *adj.* bir miktar, birkaç, çeşitli, ayrı, başka.

sew *v.* (dikiş) dikmek.

shall *v.* -ecek / acak.

shampoo *n.* şampuan.

shape *n.* şekil, biçim, *v.* şekil vermek, biçimlendirmek.

shave *n.* (sakal) tıraş, *v.* tıraş olmak, tıraş etmek.

she *pron.* o, *n.* kadın, *adj.* dişi.

sheep *n.* koyun(lar).

sheet *n.* yatak çarşafı, kâğıt yaprağı, levha, tabaka.

shell *n.* kabuk, midye kabuğu, mermi kovanı.

shine *n.* parıltı, parlaklık, *v.* parlamak, parlatmak.

ship *n.* gemi, vapur, *v.* gemi ile nakletmek.

shirt *n.* gömlek.

shoe *n.* ayakkabı.

shop *n.* dükkân, shopkeeper *n.* dükkâncı, shopping *n.* alışveriş.

shore *n.* kıyı, sahil, destek, dayanak.

short *adj.* kısa, kısa boylu, shortage kıtlık, yokluk, shorten *v.* kısalmak, kısaltmak.

shorts *n.* kısa pantolon/don, şort.

should tavsiye, öneri, hafif zorunluluk belirten yardımcı fiil, -meli / malı.

show *n.* gösteri, sergi, *v.* göstermek, sergilemek.

shower *n.* duş, sağanak, *v.* sağanak halinde yağmak.

shut *v.* kapamak, kapatmak, kapanmak, *adj.* kapalı, kapanmış, shut up sus, çeneni kapa.

shy *adj.* utangaç, sıkılgan, çekingen.

sick *adj.* hasta, sickness *n.* hastalık.

sight *n.* görme, manzara, nişangah, görüş, sightseeing *n.* turistik gezi.

sign *n.* işaret, iz, belirti, *v.* işaret etmek, imzalamak, signal *n.* işaret.

signature *n.* imza.

silk *n.* ipek, *adj.* ipekli.

silly *adj.* aptal, sersem, budala.

silver *n.* gümüş, gümüş para, gümüş eşya.

similar *adj.* benzer, gibi, similar to bir şeyle benzer.

simple *adj.* basit, kolay, yalın, sade, simplify *v.* basitleştirmek, sadeleştirmek, simply *adv.* sadece, sade bir şekilde.

since *prep.* -den beri, *conj.* -den dolayı, madem ki, *adv.* o zamandan beri, önce.

**sincere** *adj.* candan, samimi, **sincerely** *adv.* içtenlikle.

**sing** *v.* şarkı söylemek, ötmek, şakımak, **singer** *n.* şarkıcı.

**single** *n.* tek kişilik oda, *adj.* tek, yalnız, bekâr, tek kişilik.

**singular** *adj.* tekil, yalnız, tek, eşsiz.

**sir** *n.* efendim, beyefendi.

**sister** *n.* kız kardeş, abla, hemşire.

**sit** *v.* oturmak, tünemek, **sitting room** oturma odası.

**size** *n.* hacim, büyüklük, boy, boyut, ölçü.

**skill** *n.* hüner, marifet, beceri, ustalık.

**skin** *n.* deri post, kabuk, *v.* derisini yüzmek, kabuğunu soymak.

**skirt** *n.* etek, eteklik, kenar, *v.* kenarından geçmek.

**sky** *n.* gökyüzü, gök, hava, **skyline** *n.* ufuk çizgisi, **skyscraper** *n.* gökdelen.

**slang** *n.* argo.

**sleep** *n.* uyku, *v.* uyumak, **sleepy** *adj.* uykulu, uykusu gelmiş.

**slice** *n.* dilim, parça, *v.* dilimlemek.

**slight** *adj.* önemsiz, hafif, az, *v.* küçümsemek, **slightly** *adv.* az, biraz, hafifçe.

**slipper** *n.* terlik.

**slow** *adj.* yavaş, ağır, gecikmiş, *v.* yavaşlamak, **slowly** *adv.* yavaş yavaş, ağır ağır.

**small** *adj.* ufak, küçük, az, önemsiz.

**smell** *n.* koku, *v.* koklamak, kokmak.

**smile** *n.* gülümseme, *v.* gülümsemek.

**smoke** *n.* duman, *v.* sigara içmek, tütmek, **no smoking** sigara içilmez.

**snack** *n.* hafif yemek, çerez.

**snake** *n.* yılan.

**snow** *n.* kar, *v.* kar yağmak.

**so** *adv.* öyle, öyleyse, böyle, böylece, şöyle, o kadar, bundan dolayı.

**soap** *n.* sabun, *v.* sabunlamak.

**sock** *n.* kısa çorap.

**soft** *adj.* yumuşak, tatlı, hafif, uysal, **soften** *v.* yumuşatmak, yumuşamak.

**solve** *v.* halletmek, çözmek.

**some** *adj.* bazı, kimi, biraz, birkaç, bir takım, **somebody** *adv.* birisi, bir kimse, **somehow** *adv.* her nasılsa, **someone** *adv.* birisi, **something** *n.* bir şey, **sometimes** *adv.* bazen, ara sıra, arada sırada, **somewhere** *adv.* bir yere, bir yerde.

**son** *n.* oğul, erkek evlât.

**song** *n.* şarkı, türkü, nağme.

**soon** *adv.* hemen, şimdi, yakında, çok geçmeden.

**sore** *adj.* ağrılı, yaralı, acıyan, küskün.

**sorry** *adj.* üzgün, kederli, müteessir, pişman, üzücü.

**sound** *n.* ses, gürültü, *v.* ses çıkarmak, ses vermek, gibi gelmek.

**soup** *n.* çorba.

**south** *n.* güney, **southeast** *n.* güneydoğu.

**souvenir** *n.* hatıra.

spare *adj.* yedek, fazla, serbest, *v.* bir kenara koymak, tutumlu olmak

speak *v.* konuşmak, ifade etmek, söylemek, **speak to** birisiyle konuşmak, **speaker** *n.* konuşmacı, spiker.

special *adj.* özel, müstesna, **specialist** *n.* uzman, **specially** *adv.* bilhassa, özel olarak, özellikle.

speed *n.* hız, sürat, çabukluk.

spell *n.* büyü, *v.* hecelemek, büyülemek.

spend *v.* harcamak, (zaman) geçirmek, **spend (money) on** bir şey için (para) harcamak.

spice *n.* baharat, *v.* baharat koymak.

spoon *n.* kaşık.

sport *n.* spor, oyun, eğlence, *v.* eğlenmek, oynamak.

spot *n.* benek, nokta, yer, mahal, projektör ışığı.

spring *n.* ilkbahar, kaynak, pınar, *v.* sıçramak, fırlamak.

square *n.* kare, alan, meydan.

staff *n.* değnek, sopa, kadro, personel.

stair *n.* merdiven basamağı, **stairs** merdiven.

stale *adj.* bayat, eski, yıpranmış, *v.* bayatlamak.

stand *n.* duruş, yer, tezgâh, sergi, *v.* ayakta durmak, dayanmak, katlanmak, **standard** *n.* ölçü birimi, düzey, standart.

start *n.* başlangıç, başlama, kalkış, çıkış, *v.* başlamak, harekete geçmek, kalkmak, hareket etmek.

state *n.* durum, vaziyet, devlet, *v.* bildirmek, söylemek, *adj.* resmi, devlete ait, **statesman** *n.* devlet adamı.

station *n.* istasyon, durak yeri.

stationer *n.* kırtasiyeci, **stationery** *n.* kırtasiye.

statue *n.* heykel.

steal *v.* çalmak, aşırmak, hırsızlık yapmak.

still *adj.* hareketsiz, durgun, *v.* sakinleştirmek, yatıştırmak, *adv.* hâlâ, yine de, daima, bununla beraber.

stocking *n.* uzun çorap.

stomach *n.* mide, karın, *v.* hazmetmek, sindirmek.

stone *n.* taş, değerli taş, meyve çekirdeği.

stop *n.* durma, durak, *v.* durmak, durdurmak, engellemek.

store *n.* mağaza, dükkân, depo, *v.* saklamak, depo etmek, biriktirmek.

storm *n.* fırtına, bora, **stormy** *adj.* fırtınalı.

story *n.* hikâye, öykü, masal, palavra, makale.

stove *n.* soba, ocak, fırın.

strange *adj.* tuhaf, acayip, yabancı.

street *n.* cadde, sokak, yol.

strong *adj.* sağlam, güçlü, dayanıklı, şiddetli, keskin.

student *n.* öğrenci, talebe.

study *n.* tahsil, öğrenim, tetkik, inceleme, çalışma, okuma, çalışma odası, *v.* okumak, çalışmak, araştırmak, öğrenim yapmak.

**stuff** *n.* madde, malzeme, eşya, *v.* tıka basa doldurmak.
**subject** {1} *n.* konu, ders, söz konusu, özne, uyruk, fail, gerekçe.
**subject** {2} *v.* boyun eğdirmek, maruz bırakmak.
**subjunctive** *n.* şart kipi, dilek kipi.
**subordinate** *adj.* tabi, bağlı, ikincil.
**subscribe** *v.* abone olmak, kayıt olmak, yazılmak, **subscription** *n.* abonelik, imza, bağış, üye aidatı.
**subtract** *v.* çıkarmak, çıkarma yapmak.
**subway** *n.* metro, yeraltı geçidi.
**successful** *adj.* başarılı, **successfully** *adv.* başarılı şekilde.
**such** *adj.* öyle, böyle, şöyle, bunun gibi, bu derece.
**sudden** *adj.* ani, **suddenly** *adv.* ansızın.
**suffix** *n.* sonek, *v.* sonuna eklemek.
**sugar** *n.* şeker.
**suit** *n.* takım elbise, kostüm, *v.* yakışmak, uygun gelmek.
**suitable** *adj.* uygun.
**suitcase** *n.* valiz, bavul.
**suite** *n.* maiyet, takım, suit, suit oda.
**sum** *n.* toplam, tutar, *v.* toplamak.
**summer** *n.* yaz.
**sun** *n.* güneş, **sunflower** *n.* ay çiçeği, **sunlight** *n.* güneş ışığı, **sunrise** *n.* şafak vakti, gün doğuşu, **sunset** *n.* gün batımı, akşam.

**Sunday** *n.* Pazar.
**superlative** *adj.* en yüksek, en üstün.
**supper** *n.* akşam yemeği, yemekli gece toplantısı, akşama doğru yenen hafif yemek.
**supply** *n.* arz, sunu, tedarik, sağlama, stok, mevcut, *v.* ihtiyacı karşılamak, tedarik etmek, arz etmek, sunmak.
**sure** *adj.* emin, kesin, güvenilir, sağlam, *interj.* tabii, elbette, **surely** *adv.* elbette, muhakkak.
**surname** *n.* soyadı.
**surprise** *n.* sürpriz, hayret, şaşkınlık, *v.* şaşır(t)mak.
**survive** *v.* sağ kalmak, yaşamak, **survivor** *n.* sağ kalan kimse.
**suspicion** *n.* şüphe, kuşku.
**swear** *v.* yemin etmek, küfretmek.
**sweater** *n.* kazak, süveter.

**sweet** *adj.* tatlı, şekerli, hoş, **sweetheart** *n.* sevgili.
**swim** *v.* yüzmek, **swimmer** *n.* yüzücü.
**symptom** *n.* belirti.

## T - t

**table** *n.* masa, sofra, cetvel, liste, tablo.
**tail** *n.* kuyruk; yazı (paranın resimli yanı).
**tailor** *n.* terzi.
**take** *v.* almak, götürmek, yakalamak, anlamak, **take care of** birisine / bir şeye bakıp kollamak, ilgilenmek.

**talk** *v.* konuşmak, söylemek, görüşmek.

**tall** *adj.* uzun (boylu).

**taste** *n.* tat, lezzet, zevk, *v.* tatmak, tat vermek, tadı olmak, **tasty** *adj.* lezzetli, tatlı.

**tax** *n.* vergi, *v.* vergilendirmek.

**tea** *n.* çay, **teacup** *n.* çay bardağı, **teapot** *n.* çaydanlık.

**teach** *v.* öğretmek, okutmak, eğitmek, **teacher** *n.* öğretmen.

**team** *n.* takım, ekip, *v.* takım kurmak.

**tear** {1} *n.* gözyaşı.

**tear** {2} *v.* yırtmak, yırtılmak, yaralamak, kesmek, parçalamak, çok üzmek, bölmek.

**telephone** *n.* telefon, *v.* telefon etmek.

**television** *n.* televizyon.

**tell** *v.* anlatmak, söylemek, bildirmek.

**tense** *n.* fiil zamanı, *v.* ger(il)mek, gerginleşmek, *adj.* gergin, sinirli.

**tent** *n.* çadır.

**terminal** *n.* son, nihayet, uçta olan, dönem sonu, gar, terminal.

**than** *conj.* -dan, -den, daha.

**thank** *v.* teşekkür etmek, **thank God** Allaha şükür, **thanks** *n.* teşekkür, teşekkürler.

**that** *adv.* şu, o, ki, ki o, öyle, o kadar.

**theatre** *n.* tiyatro.

**theft** *n.* hırsızlık.

**then** *adv.* o zaman, ondan sonra, şu halde, sonra.

**there** *adv.* orada, oraya, orası, **therefore** *adv.* onun için, bu yüzden.

**these** *adv.* bunlar.

**they** *pron.* onlar.

**thief** *n.* hırsız.

**thing** *n.* şey, nesne, madde.

**think** *v.* düşünmek, sanmak, tasarlamak.

**thirst** *n.* susuzluk, *v.* susamak.

**this** *adv. adj.* bu, şu.

**those** *adv.* onlar, şunlar.

**though** *conj.* her ne kadar, gerçi, -diği halde, ise de, olsa da.

**thousand** *adj.* bin.

**thrice** *adv.* üç kere, üç misli.

**throat** *n.* boğaz, gırtlak.

**Thursday** *n.* Perşembe.

**thus** *adv.* böylece, bu nedenle.

**ticket** *n.* bilet.

**tidy** *adj.* temiz, düzenli, muntazam, toplu.

**tie** *n.* bağ, boyunbağı, kravat, *v.* bağlamak.

**till** *prep.* -e kadar, -e gelinceye kadar, -e değin, o kadar.

**time** *n.* zaman, vakit, süre, mühlet, vade, kere, defa, saat.

**tiny** *adj.* minicik, ufacık.

**tired** *adj.* yorgun, bitkin, usanmış.

**to** *prep.* -a, -e, -ya, -ye, -e doğru, için, -mak, -mek, ile.

**tobacco** *n.* tütün.

**today** *adv.* bugün.

**together** *adv.* beraber, birlikte, bir arada.

**toilet** *n.* tuvalet.

**tomorrow** *adv. n.* yarın.

İNGİLİZCE – TÜRKÇE SÖZLÜK

ENGLISH – TURKISH DICTIONARY

**tongue** *n.* dil, lisan, konuşma tarzı.

**tonight** *adv.* bu gece, bu akşam.

**too** *adv.* da, de, dahi, çok, fazla, aşırı, ilaveten, keza.

**tool** *n.* alet, **tools** *n.* takım.

**tooth** *n.* diş, **toothbrush** *n.* diş fırçası, **toothpaste** *n.* diş macunu, **toothpick** *n.* kürdan.

**touch** *n.* temas, dokunuş, *v.* dokunmak, ellemek, değmek.

**tour** *n.* gezi, seyahat, tur, turne, **tourist** *n.* turist.

**toward(s)** *prep.* -e doğru, tarafına doğru, -e karşı, -e yakın.

**tower** *n.* kule, burç, hisar.

**town** *n.* kasaba, şehir.

**toy** *n.* oyuncak, süs eşyası.

**trade** *n.* iş, meslek, zanaat, alışveriş, takas, *v.* ticaret yapmak, iş yapmak, alışveriş yapmak.

**tradition** *n.* gelenek, görenek, örf, adet, anane.

**traffic** *n.* trafik.

**train** *n.* tren, katar, sıra, dizi, silsile, takım, *v.* alıştırmak, idman yaptırmak, **trainer** *n.* antrenör, **trained** *adj.* eğitilmiş, yetiştirilmiş.

**transfer** *n.* nakil, devir, *v.* nakletmek, devretmek, aktarmak, değiştirmek, havale etmek.

**translate** *v.* tercüme etmek, çevirmek, dönüştürmek, **translation** *n.* tercüme, çeviri.

**transport** *v.* taşımak, nakletmek, sürgün etmek.

**travel** *n.* yolculuk, seyahat, *v.* seyahat etmek, hareket etmek.

**treasure** *n.* hazine, define, servet.

**tree** *n.* ağaç.

**trip** *n.* kısa yolculuk, gezinti, hata, yanlış.

**trouble** *n.* dert, üzüntü, sıkıntı, *v.* rahatsız etmek, canını sıkmak.

**trousers** *n.* pantolon.

**true** *adj.* doğru, gerçek, sadık, vefalı, **truly** *adv.* gerçekten, içtenlikle, doğru olarak.

**truth** *n.* gerçek, doğru.

**try** *n.* tecrübe, deney, deneme, uğraşma, *v.* uğraşmak, gayret etmek, denemek, araştırmak,

**Tuesday** *n.* Salı.

**Turk** *n.* Türk, **Turkey** *n.* Türkiye, **Turkish** *adj.* Türklere/Türkiye'ye ait, Türkçe.

**turkey** *n.* hindi,

**turn** *n.* dönüş, devir, viraj, sıra, köşe, *v.* dönmek, çevirmek, dönüşmek.

**tyre** *n.* otomobil lâstiği.

## U  -  u

**ugly** *adj.* çirkin, nahoş, kötü, iğrenç.

**ultra-** *pref.* son derece, **ultraviolet** *adj.* mor ötesi, ültraviyole.

**umbrella** *n.* şemsiye.

**unable** *adj.* güçsüz, elinden gelmez, beceriksiz.

**unaware** *adj.* habersiz.

**uncle** *n.* amca, dayı, enişte.

**unconscious** *adj.* baygın, bilinçsiz, bihaber.

**under** *prep.* altında, altına, -den aşağı, aşağısına.

**undergraduate** *n.* üniversite öğrencisi.

**understand** *v.* anlamak, kavramak, bilmek.

**underwear** *n.* iç çamaşırı.

**unexpected** *adj.* beklenilmedik, umulmadık.

**unforgettable** *adj.* unutulmaz.

**unfortunate** *adj.* şanssız, başarısız, **unfortunately** *adv.* maalesef, ne yazık ki.

**uniform** *adj.* üniforma, muntazam, bir kararda.

**union** *n.* birleşme, birlik, sendika.

**unique** *adj.* tek, eşsiz, yegâne, biricik.

**unit** *n.* birim, unite.

**unite** *v.* birleştirmek, bağlamak, birleşmek.

**unity** *n.* birlik.

**universe** *n.* evren, kâinat.

**university** *n.* üniversite.

**unjust** *adj.* haksız, adaletsiz.

**unknown** *n.* bilinmeyen kişi/nesne, *adj.* bilinmeyen, tanınmayan, yabancı.

**unless** *conj.* meğer ki, -medikçe.

**unlike** *adj.* farklı, benzemez, **unlikely** *adj.* muhtemel olma-yan, ihtimal dışı.

**unpack** *v.* bavuldan çıkarmak, bohça açmak.

**until** *prep. conj.* -e kadar, -e değin, -e dek.

**unto** *prep.* -e kadar.

**unusual** *adj.* nadir, görülmemiş, seyrek.

**unwilling** *adj.* isteksiz, gönülsüz.

**up** *adv.* yukarı(ya), yukarıda, **up to** ...ye kadar, -e ait, -e bağlı.

**upon** *prep.* üstüne, üzerine, üstünde, üzerinde.

**upper** *adj.* üst, daha üst, yukarıdaki, rütbece daha büyük.

**upset** *adj.* huzursuz, keyifsiz, bozulmuş, *v.* keyfini bozmak, altüst etmek, bozmak.

**upstairs** *n.* üst kat, *adj.* yukarıdaki, *adv.* yukarıya, yukarıda.

**upward(s)** *adv.* yukarı, yukarıya doğru.

**urban** *adj.* şehirle ilgili, kentsel, şehirde bulunan.

**urgent** *adj.* acil, zorunlu, kaçınılmaz.

**urine** *n.* idrar.

**us** *adv.* bizi, bize.

**usage** *n.* kullanım, örf, adet, usul.

**use** *n.* fayda, kullanım, *v.* kullanmak, yararlanmak, **used** *adj.* kullanılmış, **useful** *adj.* yararlı, faydalı, **useless** *adj.* faydasız, işe yaramaz.

**usual** *adj.* olağan, alışılmış, her zamanki, **usually** genel-likle.

**utility** *n.* yarar, fayda.

**utmost** *adj.* azami, en uzak, en büyük, son derece.

## V - v

**vacancy** *n.* boşluk, boş yer, aralık, **vacant** *adj.* boş.

**İNGİLİZCE – TÜRKÇE SÖZLÜK**

**vacate** *v.* boşaltmak, terk etmek, bırakmak, **vacation** *n.* tatil.

**vaccinate** *v.* aşılamak, aşı yapmak.

**vacuum** *n.* boşluk, **vacuum cleaner** *n.* elektrik süpürgesi.

**value** *n.* değer, *v.* değer biçmek, **valuable** *n.* değerli şey, *adj.* değerli.

**various** *adj.* çeşitli, farklı, türlü, değişik.

**vase** *n.* vazo.

**vegetable** *n.* sebze, yeşillik, bitki, *adj.* bitkisel, **vegetarian** *n.* et yemeyen kişi.

**vehicle** *n.* taşıt, araç, vasıta.

**verb** *n.* fiil, eylem.

**verify** *v.* doğrulamak, soruşturmak, gerçekleşmek.

**vermin** *n.* haşarat, böcek.

**version** *n.* çeviri, tercüme, yorum.

**very** *adj.* pek, çok, tıpkı, aynısı.

**vessel** *n.* gemi, tekne, kap, tas, kanal.

**veterinary** *n.* veteriner.

**via** *prep.* yolu ile, -den geçerek.

**vice versa** *adv.* karşılık olarak, ve tersine.

**victim** *n.* kurban, mağdur.

**victory** *n.* zafer, galibiyet.

**view** *n.* bakış, görüş, manzara, fikir, düşünce.

**village** *n.* köy, **villager** *n.* köylü.

**vinegar** *n.* sirke.

**violate** *v.* bozmak, ihlâl etmek, tecavüz etmek.

**visa** *n.* vize, *v.* vize etmek.

**visible** *adj.* görülebilir, görünür, belli.

**vision** *n.* görüş, görme gücü, hayal, rüya.

**visit** *n.* ziyaret, teftiş, misafirlik, *v.* ziyaret etmek, **visitor** *n.* ziyaretçi.

**vital** *adj.* yaşamsal, yaşayan, hayat dolu.

**vocabulary** *n.* kısa sözlük, kelime bilgisi.

**vocation** *n.* meslek, iş, sanat, çağrı.

**voice** *n.* insan sesi, ses, ifade, söz söyleme hakkı.

**void** *n.* boşluk, eksiklik, *adj.* boş, ıssız, anlamsız, etkisiz, hükümsüz.

**voltage** *n.* gerilim, voltaj.

**voluntary** *adj.* isteyerek, gönüllü, **volunteer** *n.* gönüllü.

**vomit** *n.* kusma, *v.* kusmak.

**vowel** *n.* ünlü, sesli harf.

**voyage** *n.* yolculuk, deniz yolculuğu, seyahat, *v.* yolculuk etmek.

**vulgar** *adj.* kaba, terbiyesiz, bayağı, aşağılık.

## W - w

**wage** *n.* ücret, haftalık, maaş.

**wait** *v.* beklemek, hazır olmak.

**wake** *v.* uyanmak, uyandırmak, farkında olmak.

**walk** *v.* yürümek, dolaşmak, gezinmek, **walker** *n.* yaya, **walking** *n.* yürüyüş.

**wall** *n.* duvar, sur, *v.* duvar çekmek.

**want** *v.* istemek, arzu etmek, **wanted** *adj.* aranan, istenen.

**ENGLISH – TURKISH DICTIONARY**

**wardrobe** *n.* elbise dolabı, gardırop.

**warm** *adj.* ılık, sıcak, hararetli, canlı, heyecanlı, **warm-blooded** *adj.* sıcak kanlı.

**wash** *v.* yıkamak, yıkanmak.

**watch** *n.* cep veya kol saati, gözetleme, nöbetçilik, *f.* izle-mek, gözlemek, seyretmek.

**water** *n.* su, deniz, göl, gölet, maden suyu, **watery** *adj.* sulu.

**wave** *n.* dalga, el sallama, *v.* sallamak, dalgalanmak.

**way** *n.* yol, taraf, geçilen yer, gidiş, tarz, yöntem, biçim, gitme, **by the way** bu arada, unutmadan söyleyeyim ki.

**we** *pron.* biz.

**weak** *adj.* zayıf, güçsüz, halsiz, bitkin.

**wealth** *n.* zenginlik, servet, varlık, **wealthy** *adj.* zengin, varlıklı.

**wear** *v.* giymek, takmak, taşımak, kullanmak, eskitmek.

**weather** *n.* hava, **weather forecast** *n.* hava raporu.

**web** *n.* dokuma, örgü, ağ, örümcek ağı.

**wed** *v.* evlenmek, evlendirmek, **wedding** *n.* nikâh, düğün.

**Wednesday** *n.* Çarşamba.

**week** *n.* hafta, **weekday** *n.* iş günü, **weekend** *n.* hafta sonu, **weekly** *adj.* haftalık.

**weight** *n.* ağırlık, yük, sıklet.

**welcome** *v.* hoş karşılamak, nezaket göstermek, *interj.* hoş geldiniz, buyurun.

**well** *adj.* sağlıklı, sıhhatli, iyi, *adv.* iyi, hoş, güzel, *interj.* pekâlâ, ya.

**west** *n.* batı, **western** *n.* kovboy romanı veya filmi, *adj.* batıya ait.

**wet** *adj.* ıslak, rutubetli, *v.* ıslatmak.

**what** *adv.* ne, ne kadar, nasıl, hangi.

**whatever** her ne, herhangi.

**whatsoever** *adj.* / *adv.* ne, hangi, bütünü, hepsi, herhangi biri.

**wheat** *n.* buğday.

**wheel** *n.* tekerlek, çark, dolap.

**when** *adv.* ne zaman, *conj.* ne zaman ki, ta ki, -e kadar, olur olmaz, olduğu zaman, olduğunda, -iken, **whenever** *conj.* her ne zaman.

**where** *adv.* nerede, nereye, **wherever** *conj.* her nereye, her neresi, nerede olursa.

**whether** *conj.* olup olmadığını, -mediğini, -ise de, -mi acaba.

**which** *adv.* / *adj.* hangi, hangisi, *conj.* olan, bulunan, ki o(nlar).

**while** *n.* müddet, süre, *conj.* iken, sırasında, müddetçe, sürece, olduğu halde, **for a while** bir süre, bir süre için.

**whistle** *n.* ıslık, düdük, *v.* ıslık çalmak.

**white** *adj.* beyaz, **whiteness** *adj.* beyazlık.

**who** *adv.* kim, *conj.* o(nlar) ki, **whoever** *adv.* kim olursa olsun, her kim, **whose** kimin.

**whole** *adj.* tam, bütün, toptan, hepsi, bütünü.

**why** *adv.* niçin, neden, niye.

**wide** *adj.* geniş, açık, engin, **widely** *adv.* genellikle, geniş ölçüde, **widespread** *adj.* yaygın.

**width** *n.* en, genişlik.

**wife** *n.* eş, zevce, hanım, karı.

**will {1}** *v.* -ecek/acak.

**will {2}** *n.* istek, dilek, amaç, *v.* dilemek, istemek, **willing** *adj.* istekli.

**win** *v.* kazanmak, yenmek, galip gelmek, elde etmek.

**wind** *n.* rüzgâr, yel, *v.* dönmek, dolaşmak, dolaştırmak, **windy** *adj.* rüzgârlı.

**window** *n.* pencere, pencere çerçevesi, vitrin.

**wine** *n.* şarap, **winery** *n.* şaraphane.

**wing** *n.* kanat, kol; çamurluk.

**winner** *n.* kazanan kimse, yenen.

**winter** *n.* kış, *v.* kışlamak.

**wire** *n.* tel, kablo, telgraf teli, **wireless** *n.* radyo, *adj.* telsiz.

**wise** *n.* usul, tarz, yöntem, *adj.* akıllı, tedbirli, bilge.

**wish** *n.* arzu, istek, dilek, *v.* istemek, arzu etmek, dilemek, **wishful** *adj.* arzulu, istekli, **wishbone** *n.* lades kemiği.

**with** *prep.* ile, birlikte, -den, -e, -e rağmen, -e karşı, -in yanında.

**within** *adv.* içeride, *prep.* zarfında, süresinde, -in içinde.

**without** *prep.* -sız, -meden, hariç, dışında, olmaksızın.

**witness** *n.* tanık, şahit, kanıt, *v.* şahit olmak.

**woman** *n.* kadın.

**wonder** *n.* harika, mucize, şaşılacak şey, *v.* hayret etmek, şaşmak, hayran olmak, **I wonder** acaba, **wonderful** *adj.* harikulade, olağanüstü.

**wood** *n.* tahta, odun, orman, koru, **wooden** *adj.* tahtadan yapılmış, ahşap işi, **woodpecker** *n.* ağaçkakan.

**wool** *n.* yün, yapağı, **woolen** *adj.* yünlü.

**word** *n.* söz, sözcük, kelime.

**work** *n.* iş, görev, çalışma, eser, *v.* çalışmak, iş yapmak, işletmek, çalıştırmak, **worker** *n.* işçi, **workman** *n.* işçi, **workshop** *n.* atölye.

**world** *n.* dünya, evren, **world war** *n.* dünya savaşı, **worldwide** *adj.* dünya çapında, evrensel.

**worry** *n.* üzüntü, endişe, *v.* üzülmek, **worried** *adj.* endişeli, üzgün.

**worse** *adj.* daha kötü, beter.

**worship** *n.* ibadet, tapınma, *v.* ibadet etmek, tapınmak.

**worst** *adj.* en kötü, *adv.* en kötü şekilde.

**would** *v.* -ecek(ti), -irdi.

**wound** *n.* yara, bere, gönül yarası, *v.* yaralamak, incitmek.

**wrist** *n.* bilek, **wristwatch** *n.* kol saati

**write** *v.* yazmak, **writer** *n.* yazar, **writing** *n.* yazı, el yazısı, yazarlık.

**wrong** *adj.* yanlış, haksız, ters, uygunsuz.

## X - x

**xenon** *n.* ksenon, ağır bir gaz türü.

**xenophobia** *n.* yabancı düşmanlığı.

**Xmas (Christmas)** *n.* Noel, Hıristiyan yortusu.

**X-ray** *n.* röntgen ışını.

**xylonite** *n.* selüloit.

## Y - y

**yacht** *n.* yat, *v.* yatla dolaşmak, **yachting** *n.* yatçılık.

**yawn** *v.* esnemek.

**year** *n.* sene, yıl, yaş, **yearly** *adj.* yıllık, *adv.* her yıl.

**yellow** *adj.* sarı, **yellowness** *n.* sarılık.

**yes** *adv.* evet, olur.

**yesterday** *n. / adv.* dün.

**yet** *adv.* henüz, daha, şimdiye kadar, hâlâ, *conj.* ama, ancak, ve yine, gerçi, bununla beraber.

**you** *pron.* sen, siz, seni, sizi, sana, size.

**young** *n.* genç, *adj.* genç, küçük, yeni, tecrübesiz, **youngster** *n.* çocuk, delikanlı.

**your** *adv.* senin, sizin, **yours** seninki, sizinki, **yourself** kendin(iz).

**yummy** *adj.* lezzetli, tatlı, nefis.

## Z - z

**zeal** *n.* gayret, heves, istek, **zealous** *adj.* gayretli, istekli.

**zebra** *n.* yaban eşeği, zebra.

**zenith** *n.* zirve, doruk, başucu.

**zero** *n.* sıfır.

**zigzag** *n.* dolambaçlı yol, *v.* zikzak çizerek gitmek, *adj.* zikzak, dolambaçlı, eğri büğrü.

**zinc** *n.* çinko.

**zip** *n.* vız sesi, çaba, gayret, *v.* fermuarı kapatmak / açmak, hızlı gitmek, **zipper** *n.* fermuar.

**zone** *n.* mıntıka, bölge, yöre, kuşak, daire.

**zoo** *n.* hayvanat bahçesi, **zoology** *n.* hayvanbilim.

# INDEX DİZİN